Illustrated Battles of the
Napoleonic Age
Volume 4—1813-1815

San Sebastian, Vittoria, the Pyrenees,
Bergen op Zoom, the Gurkha War,
Lundy's Lane, Toulouse, Ligny,
New Orleans and Waterloo

Arthur Griffiths, D. H. Parry,
Archibald Forbes
and Others

Illustrated Battles of the Napoleonic Age: Volume 4—1813-1815
San Sebastian, Vittoria, the Pyrenees, Bergen op Zoom, the Gurkha War,
Lundy's Lane, Toulouse, Ligny, New Orleans and Waterloo
by Arthur Griffiths, D. H. Parry, Archibald Forbes and Others

Leonaur is an imprint of Oakpast Ltd

Material original to this edition and presentation of the
text in this form copyright © 2014 Oakpast Ltd

ISBN: 978-1-78282-247-9 (hardcover)
ISBN: 978-1-78282-248-6 (softcover)

http://www.leonaur.com

Publisher's Notes

The views expressed in this book are not necessarily those of the publisher.

Contents

The Siege of San Sebastian by Major Arthur Griffiths	7
Vittoria by Charles Lowe	29
The Battles in the Pyrenees by Major Arthur Griffiths	47
Bergen-op-Zoom by Colonel Percy Groves	73
The Gurkha War by Lieutenant-Colonel Newnham-Davies	97
Lundy's Lane by Angus Evan Abbott	123
Toulouse by D. H. Parry	145
The Battle of Ligny by Archibald Forbes	159
Campaign of New Orleans by C. Stein	187
Waterloo by D. H. Parry	215

August, 1813

The Siege of San Sebastian

Major Arthur Griffiths

This was the last and not the most creditable of the many great sieges of the Peninsular War: it was long protracted: the first serious assault failed; if the second proved successful, it was more through good luck than good management—a happy accident, the chance ignition of a quantity of explosives behind the French line of defence, which turned the scale just when the British stormers were on the verge of a second defeat. Finally, capture was followed by pillage and plunder and a series of atrocities, of "villainy which would have shamed the most ferocious barbarians of antiquity." The horrors of Ciudad Rodrigo and Badajoz were outdone; murder, rapine, the most revolting cruelty signalised the taking of San Sebastian; cruelty which, as Napier puts it, " staggers the mind with its enormous, incredible, indescribable barbarity." Discipline disappeared in universal drunkenness. The men when checked chased their officers away with volleys of small arms. A Portuguese adjutant who dared to interfere was deliberately put to death by a party of English soldiers. The sack did not cease until a general conflagration, following in the footsteps of the brutal and abandoned soldiery, completely destroyed the town.

The possession of San Sebastian, or of some good seaport upon the Bay of Biscay, became absolutely necessary to Lord Wellington in the closing campaign of the Peninsular War. When he left Portugal to march across Spain, driving the French before him, he abandoned his only base of supply at Lisbon. A new and nearer port was now needed; a good harbour at which food, stores, and reinforcements coming from England could be landed, and by which he could keep up his direct communication with home. The small port of Pasages he held already, but it was inconveniently near his active and enterprising enemy, Soult, who, after the crushing defeat of Vittoria, had replaced King Joseph as the French commander-in-chief. There were Bilbao, Santander, and further off Corunna, all very remote; Santoña was in the hands of the French. San Sebastian was the most suited to Wellington's purpose, and sooner or later, cost what it might, San Sebastian he meant to have. He made no secret of this determination, and his anxiety no doubt stimulated those entrusted with the siege—for Wellington was not constantly present in personal command—to premature efforts and an unwise departure from the instructions he gave. Had the plan of which he approved been followed exactly, history would not have to record the delays, disappointments, and disasters which have made San Sebastian memorable among the sieges in Spain. Wellington wished to lose no time in gaining the fortress, but he still wished it to be besieged according to rule. Sir Thomas Graham, who was in chief command, although one of his ablest lieutenants, was sometimes over-persuaded into errors that caused an undue and costly expenditure of men and material.

And first as to San Sebastian itself—nowadays the most fashionable of Spanish watering-places, the favourite resort of the queen and her youthful son, and occupying the whole frontage of its spacious bay. In 1813 it was limited to the low peninsula running north and south, on which stood the small town sur-

A. Great Breach
B. Small Breach.
C. English Mine.
D. French Do.
E. Burnt Bridge.
F. Retrenchment.

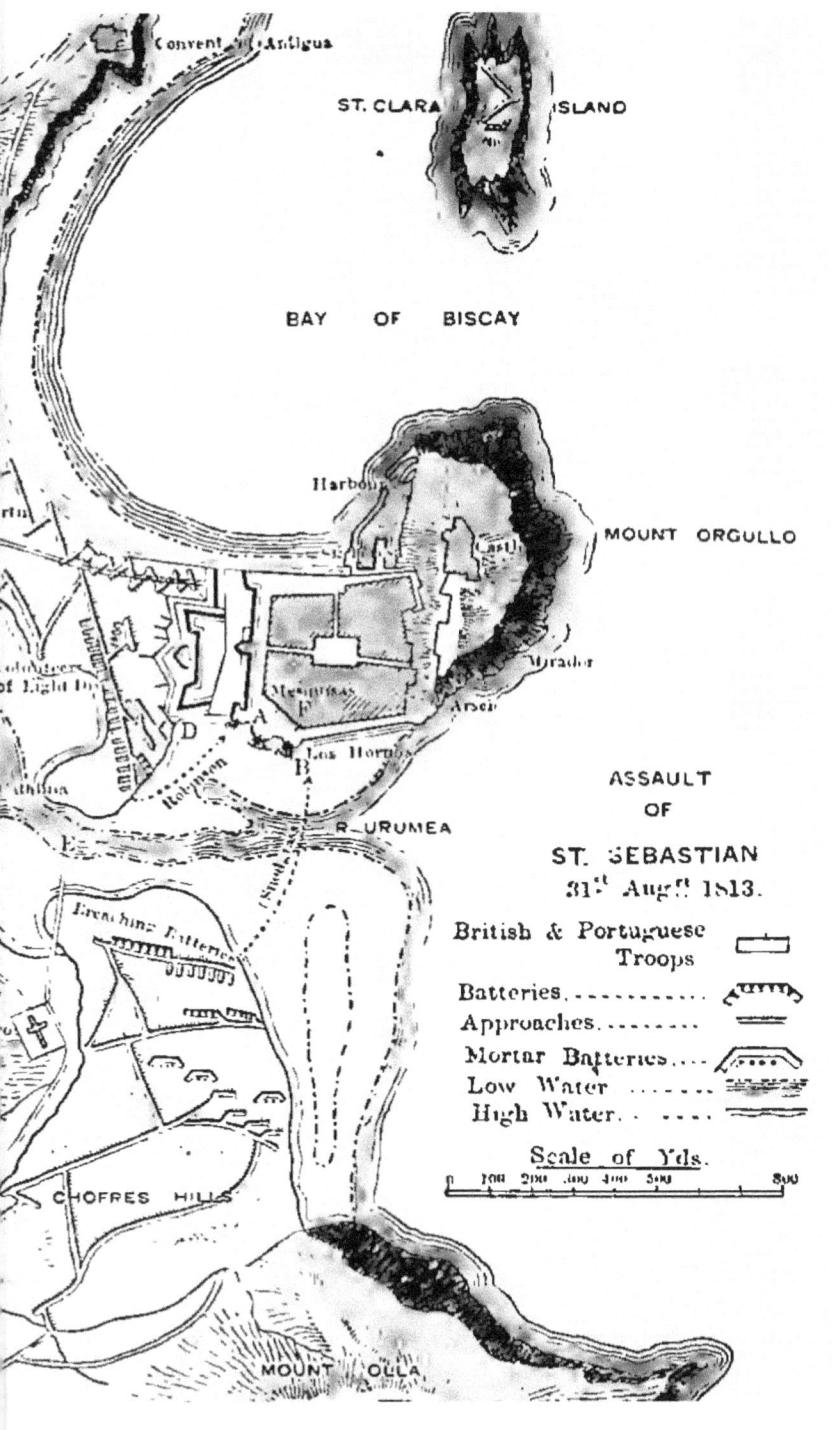

rounded by its fortifications. These defences to the landward or southern side of the isthmus were the most important, and consisted of a high rampart, or "curtain," 350 yards in length, at each end of which were half-bastions giving flanking or side fire along the ditch. In the centre of the curtain a complete bastion was pushed out to the front, and in front of that again was a more salient, more advanced work, called a horn work, which was covered by a ditch and glacis in the regular way. East and west of the town the only defence was a simple wall, indifferently flanked and unprotected by obstacles in front of it, while the waters washed its base—to the westward those of the sea, to the eastward of the River Urumea, a tidal shallow stream that ran out twice a day, and left a long firm strand exposed. The latter undoubtedly constituted the weakest part of the fortress, and it was within full view and easy reach of high land and commanding sand-hills, the Chofres, on the far side of the river.

San Sebastian had a second and a third—an outer and an inner line of defence. The first was the high ridge called San Bartolomeo, which crossed the isthmus at its throat; the other was the rock, height of the Monte Orgullo, or "Mountain of Pride," that rose steeply behind the town at the end of the peninsula. San Bartolomeo had been fortified directly the siege became imminent. A redoubt was constructed on the plateau connected with the convent buildings, and this redoubt was supported by a second made of casks nearer the town, and by strengthening the houses in the suburb just under and on the inner side of the ridge. The Monte Orgullo was crowned by the castle of La Mota, a small enclosed fort with batteries on each flank, the whole raised on such an elevation as to command the town and the length of the isthmus beyond. This La Mota formed the last refuge, the innermost kernel and key of the whole defence. It will be seen, then, that there were practically three lines of fortification to be overcome and taken, one after the other—the San Bartolomeo ridge with its supporting works, the main body of the place, and lastly the Monte Orgullo with its citadel.

San Sebastian sprang into sudden and great importance directly after Vittoria. When the fortunes of the French were at their lowest, any chance was seized of restoring them, and General Emanuel Rey, returning from the battlefield with the escort of a convoy he had taken to King Joseph, entered San Sebastian, determined to hold it at all hazards against the victorious English. Rey was a man of strong, soldierlike character. Although of a stout habit of body, fat and unwieldy in figure, there was nothing indolent in his nature, and his somewhat harsh, overbearing demeanour had a backbone of indomitable energy well suited to the present crisis. He was, like Phillipon of Badajoz and many other French governors of fortresses, the product of Napoleon's famous ordinance that a place of arms must never be surrendered until it has endured at least one open assault. Stirred and sustained by this doctrine, and knowing full well the value of San Sebastian to both sides, Rey strained every effort to reconstitute the fortress and develop its resources. The war commissary was sent off to Bayonne in an open boat, braving the English cruisers, to beg for substantial help. San Sebastian itself had been nearly dismantled. Many of its guns had been removed to arm other smaller places along the coast. It was very short of ammunition, food was scanty, the wells were mostly foul, brackish, and thick with mud, the only fit drinking-water was supplied by an aqueduct which was very soon cut off by the besiegers. Fortunately for the French, the British blockade in the Bay of Biscay was very ineffective, and sea communication was maintained between the fortress and Bayonne almost to the very end of the siege. In this way munitions of war, reinforcements, food, and all other necessaries were constantly received.

At the same time Rey set his garrison, which was now continually being strengthened by the arrival of fresh detachments, to labour on the fortifications. It was now that the redoubt was built on San Bartolomeo; the bridge across the Urumea was burnt down; and as guns began to arrive the batteries were armed and strengthened. When the siege actually began Rey could dispose of 76 pieces of artillery: 45 were in the main works, 13 on Monte Orgullo, 18 were held in reserve. Gunners were short; so drafts from the infantry were instructed in artillery drill. Still the garrison was without bomb-proof cover and very much exposed; so were the magazines. Another drawback which Rey dealt with in a very peremptory fashion was the non-combatant population. San Sebastian had been filled with a crowd of refugees from Madrid, the fugitive grandees of King Joseph's Court, and these helpless people—so many useless mouths encumbering the town and adding nothing but trouble to the defence—were promptly expelled.

Rey was pursued within a few days by small parties of Spaniards, but just a fortnight elapsed before the besiegers appeared in force before San Sebastian. Wellington, accompanied by his senior engineer officer. Major Smith, visited and reconnoitred the place upon the 12th of July, and with him concerted the plan of operations; but the ac-

tual conduct of the siege was given to Sir Thomas Graham, who had under his orders the 5th Division of British troops, two brigades of Portuguese, some bluejackets from H.M.S. *Surveillante*, and a party of sappers and miners—the first occasion on which these valuable soldiers were employed in a siege in Spain. The total force amounted to 10,000 men, being about three times the strength of the garrison. Forty pieces of artillery were available, part of them belonging to the battering-train prepared for Burgos, the whole being under the command of Colonel Dickson, a favourite artillery officer of Wellington.

The plan of attack was to be the same as that adopted by Marshal Berwick nearly a hundred years before. The weakest part of the de-

fences was to be breached—namely, a point in the eastern wall of the town, which was, moreover, within easy range of the Chofres, or sandhills, beyond the river. When the breach was formed, the assault was to be delivered, the assailants advancing at low water between the walls and the river. It was soon afterwards seen that the San Bartolomeo ridge must be wrested from the enemy: its works would have greatly harassed the attacking columns; moreover, its possession was an indispensable preliminary to the opening of trenches and forming a left attack on the isthmus or landward side. The capture of San Bartolomeo was accordingly the first enterprise undertaken. It was duly bombarded, then attacked on the morning of the 17th July by two columns—one of British, the other of Portuguese troops. The latter moved so slowly that Colonel Cameron, leading the 9th and Royals, raced forward and charged with such impetuosity that the French were driven straight out of the redoubt. Down below in San Martin they rallied, but, Cameron being reinforced, the suburb was presently won. Not so the cask redoubt beyond, which was next stormed by all the troops in hand, but without success. It was, however, taken a couple of nights later. The net result of the first affair was the capture of the ridge and room to work on the isthmus. The fire from the breaching batteries was continued without intermission, and effected great damage; the stone embrasures were destroyed, the guns dismounted, the walls shaken severely. Meanwhile the garrison met the bombardment bravely, and laboured hard to repair damages or neutralise them. On the 22nd a breach which appeared to be practicable was formed, although to foil the besiegers inner cuttings or retrenchments had been formed. Moreover, General Rey had posted guns to bear upon the open points and impede movement along the breach. On the 23rd a second breach was commenced beyond the first. Sir Thomas Graham had heard that the wall here was weaker (as it was), and he hoped by this second opening to "turn," or get round the inner entrenchment. About this time our shells ignited certain houses in the town, and a general conflagration was imminent, but it came to nothing, beyond delaying the British attack, which had been fixed for the 24th.

Everything seemed ready for this the last act in the siege. It was, of course, to be made by the breaches in the eastern flank wall. The storming party, 2,000 strong, was composed of General Hay's brigade of the 5th Division, for the first breach, while another battalion went at the second beyond. The whole of the stormers were to assemble in the foremost trench on the inner or right side of the isthmus. The signal for the advance was to be the explosion of a mine or "globe of compression" on the far left flank, a device due to the intrepid conduct

of a young officer of engineers, Lieutenant Reid. On the 21st, while digging at a parallel across the isthmus, he had come upon a pipe or drain four feet by three wide, which was actually the aqueduct conveying the water into the town. Reid had entered the mouth of this narrow opening and followed the passage right up to the counterscarp of the hornwork, where he was stopped by a closed door. Returning to report, it was decided to form a mine at the end of the drain: the explosion in this confined space of thirty barrels of powder lodged amongst sand-bags would, it was thought, force the dirt and rubbish into the ditch and so help the upward climb of the attacking column (Portuguese) on this side.

Mistake and misadventure waited on this first attack from the very outset. Its postponement alone did great mischief, for it unsettled the minds of the stormers and gave them an impression that the delay was due to the dangerous and desperate nature of the business before them. Again, the tide would have served well at daylight on the 24th: it was then, according to the local fishermen, to be at the lowest ebb, and the wide strand would have given ample space for the advancing columns. By moving to the attack too early on the 25th in the night, practically all such advantage was lost; the tide at that hour was only falling. Moreover, Wellington had expressly ordered that "fair daylight should be taken for the assault," owing to the intricacies of the fortifications. Nevertheless midnight found the whole body assembled in the advanced parallel. The troops employed were the Royal Scots, under Major Frazer, intended to assail the great breach, supported by the 9th Regiment, and the 38th, whose goal was the lesser breach beyond; in front of the Royals was a forlorn hope under Lieutenant Campbell, and a ladder party under Lieutenant Machel, of the Engineers. About 5 a.m. the column filed out of the trench on the signal given by the exploding mine. There were three hundred yards of the open to cover, and so great was the confusion caused by the mine that the assailants suffered little from the enemy's fire; but the signal had not been heard by our batteries on the sand-hills, and all the way our own batteries continued to play upon our own men. The advance was very arduous, the ground most difficult, much narrowed between the wall and the waters, very slippery from the receding tide, which left the rocks covered with sea-weed and here and there deep pools; besides, the fortifications on the flanks were still entire and were now lined by sharpshooters, who kept up an incessant and most telling fire. The first to reach the breach were Major Frazer of the Royal Scots and

Lieutenant (afterwards Sir Harry) Jones of the Engineers; a few men closely followed, but only a few, and they came up in disorder, straggling and out of breath. On the far side, down below was the yawning breach, filled with smoke and flames of the burning houses beyond. By this time a small handful of the most intrepid had gathered round their leaders, but quite two-thirds of the main column had turned aside on their road to the breach, and were engaged in a musketry battle with the enemy on the rampart. The rear was thus already in confusion, and the van would not advance. Frazer now was killed, so was Machel with the ladders; Jones was wounded and taken prisoner; the rest of the leading assailants were either slain or dispersed. The Colonels of the 38th and 9th, Greville and Cameron, and Captain Archimbeau of the Royals, strove hard to encourage and urge on their men; but all were dispirited and in inextricable confusion, and now a perfect hail of shot and shell fell upon them from the whole of the enemy's artillery, while continuous musketry fire with showers of grape and hand-grenades smote the struggling pent-up mass, which could neither advance nor retire, causing the most frightful slaughter. Some of the English wounded were stabbed where they lay by the infuriated French. Jones was only saved by the intervention of a humane sergeant, and soon afterwards another generous enemy, a captain of the grenadiers, lifted him from the ground, kissed him, and had him carried off to hospital. Such are the stern contrasts, the barbarities and the amenities of war.

According to the French account, at this last supreme moment, when defeat was unmistakable:

"The bravest English rushed upon the French bayonets to find an honourable death; the rest sought safety in flight, still decimated by the furious fire, so that few escaped alive."

The attack had proved a most signal failure, costly in valuable lives, of officers out of all proportion to men. Many reasons and some excuses were offered for the disaster; the most plausible were that the attack had been badly planned and feebly executed. Jones in his *Sieges of Spain*, says: "the efforts in the breach were certainly neither very obstinate nor very persevering." and his is the verdict of an eyewitness; but Sir Thomas Graham, in reporting to Wellington, declared the troops behaved "with their usual gallantry, and only retired when I thought a further perseverance in the attack would have occasioned a useless sacrifice of brave men." Napier, the great historian, is, however, of opinion that:

"A second and more vigorous assault on the great breach might have been effected by a recognised leader; but no general or staff officer went out of the trenches, and the isolated exertions of regimental officers failed."

Lord Wellington, although full of other pressing anxieties, repaired at once to San Sebastian and was inclined to immediately renew the attack. But the besiegers were short of ammunition, which was daily expected from England, and he thought it better to await its arrival. Then momentous events followed elsewhere. Soult advanced and began the serious movements that produced the first set of the battles of the Pyrenees, and Wellington was peremptorily called away from San Sebastian. The siege was suspended for several weeks and converted into a blockade. Now the French, elated at their respite, were constantly alert and made many mischievous sallies; moreover, while the siege operations languished, the garrison was actively engaged in preparing for the next attack. Reinforcements and supplies came in continually from France. At the same time under Rey's energetic impulse the damaged defences were repaired and strengthened, the magazines were refilled, guns were got up on the batteries, and sound fresh troops made up a garrison of 2,600 good soldiers, all animated with the sturdy, defiant spirit of their stout-hearted commander.

Their unabated confidence was shown on the occasion of the emperor's birthday-, when a great trophy, with the words "*Vive Napoleon le Grand*," was exhibited in fiery letters in front of the fortress and was plainly legible to the besiegers.

At last, however, Soult was beaten. On the 24th of August the trenches were reoccupied and the siege was resumed on much the same lines as before. The new battering train had arrived from England, although very scanty supplies of ammunition had been sent with it, and the batteries were enlarged to take more guns. Such diligence was employed that on the 26th, 57 pieces of ordnance of all kinds opened fire from the two attacks. The points selected for breaching were much the same as in the previous bombardment, and the results were soon and satisfactorily apparent. Rey reported to Soult that great damage had been effected both on the fortifications and town, and this went on steadily increasing as the hot and incessant firing was kept up. Yet the blockade was so ineffective that help constantly came in from France, and to check this the island of Santa Clara, lying to the westward of the peninsula, was attacked and captured. A battery

placed on this island caused very great annoyance to the castle, which it enfiladed, and with additional batteries on the isthmus contributed greatly to prepare the attack. On the 30th August it was found that the eastern flanking wall and the left or eastern half-bastion of the main rampart were in ruins, and that the breaches were practicable. That afternoon about 3 p.m. Lord Wellington arrived, and having made a close examination of the condition of the fortress, he ordered that the second assault should be made at 11 a.m. next day.

Yet the way even now was by no means open and easy for the assailants. Throughout the terrible bombardment, in the teeth of a murderous fire, the garrison had laboured indefatigably. The courage of the troops had been stimulated by ample rewards of the kind that Frenchmen love—crosses of the Legion of Honour were freely distributed, and many were promoted to the *Corps d'Élite*. Moreover, their spirits were kept up by the feeling that they were not cut off from France, with which a daily communication was now maintained. Yet they endured many terrible hardships—the want of hospitals, and the constant exposure of the sick and wounded to the enemy's fire, the scarcity of good rations, and especially of water.

The second assault of San Sebastian, like the first, was of the kind called *brusqnée*, or abruptly made, as distinguished from the attack *en règle*, which is deliberate, and according to rule. There was the risk of a second failure, of course, but Wellington was prepared to take it, while sparing no effort to succeed. His eagerness in this respect led him to do a grave injustice to the brave but unfortunate men who had been beaten back in the first attack. He would not again trust to the 5th Division alone, but he called for volunteers from the 1st, 4th, and Light, asking for "men who could show others how to mount a breach;" and 750 under intrepid officers at once responded to the appeal. But the commander of the 5th Division, Sir James Leith, who had general charge of the assault, would not suffer his own men to be put aside by the volunteers, and gave the main attack to one of his own brigades. Some of the volunteers he distributed along the line of the trenches to keep down the enemy's fire; the rest were in reserve with Leith's second brigade, held to support the attacking columns. A diversion from the main attack was to be made by a body of Portuguese, who would ford the Urumea at low water, and go up against the further and most distant breach in the eastern wall. At the same time the rear of the castle was to be threatened by a battalion embarked in the boats of the squadron.

In this second attack there was to be no doubt about daylight. The hour fixed was 11 a.m., when the tide was low, and there was room for the troops to move between the walls and the water. The British batteries were to have harassed the garrison from early dawn, but a thick fog hung like a screen till 8 a.m., and only from that time until the columns started was all possible mischief done. The first to move out was a brave sergeant, who, with a dozen men, had volunteered to run forward and cut off the slow match of a mine the French had ready to fire. These heroes failed; the train was exploded prematurely, and a mass of wall fell upon the advancing column, killing many. The forlorn hope had, however, got past before this catastrophe, and made for the breach, headed by Lieutenant Macguire, who, "conspicuous from his long white plume, his fine figure, and his swiftness," soon, alas! met his death, and the stormers swept onward over his corpse. The main column now followed and ascended the breach, but their foremost ranks were at once annihilated by the destructive musketry from the inner retrenchment. Those behind pressed forward undaunted, to suffer terribly, for there was no clear road, no descent possible, into the body of the place. Inner defences had been thrown up to bar progress beyond the breach, and the stormers when thus detained were exposed to a fierce fire from the ramparts, and from the far-off guns on the castle heights. The most favourable inlet was found at the breach in the left half-bastion; but here the dense masses of the assailants offered a fine mark, and hundreds were shot down. At the breach in the wall the sappers vainly strove to throw up some cover, and the loss was appalling.

Fresh troops were, however, sent constantly forward to keep the attack alive, and ere long more than half the 5th Division and all the volunteers were either actively engaged in the breaches or were already stricken down. About 1 p.m. the Portuguese made their attack: they crossed the sands in beautiful order and gallantly assaulted the third breach. This successful passage was speedily followed by that of a second column, who reinforced the assailants at the main breach.

And yet no substantial impression was made. All these heroic efforts proved fruitless. Napier says:

"The French musketry still rolled with deadly effect; the heaps of slain increased, and once more the great mass of stormers sank to the foot of the ruins unable to win. Success seemed more than doubtful. Nothing but a happy accident could give us the victory, and every moment failure loomed nearer, for the tide was rising, the reserves

were all engaged, and no greater effort could be expected from men whose courage had already been pushed to the verge of madness."

In this desperate situation Sir Thomas Graham, having consulted with the chief of the artillery determined to concentrate the fire of all our available guns upon the high curtain or rampart above the breached bastion. Forty-seven guns thus brought to bear spread dire havoc, and cleared away the defenders: they did far more, for being now well practised, the gunners knew the exact range, and pitched their shot and shell plump into the magazines and stores of combustibles—live shells, fire-barrels and hand-grenades—which speedily took light, explosion followed explosion, and a general conflagration ensued.

"Hundreds of the French defenders were destroyed, and the rest were thrown into confusion, and while the ramparts were still enveloped with suffocating eddies of smoke, the British soldiers broke in."

But the garrison, although at a disadvantage, were not yet conquered: a fierce hand-to-hand conflict ensued; the French held their ground inch by inch, and only yielded to the overwhelming numbers of their assailants. About the same time the Portuguese made good their entrance at the lesser breach. Then the stormers swept forward irresistibly; although the streets and squares were barricaded, the French, being instantaneously attacked in every direction, made no further resistance in the town. Several hundreds were taken prisoners; the rest were withdrawn by the still indomitable Rey into his citadel on the Monte Orgullo.

The last phases of this stubborn struggle had been fought amid the most terrific war of the elements; the thunder-clouds that had lowered all the day, producing pitch darkness at 3 p.m., broke at last in a fury of thunder and lightning and blinding drenching rain. Still worse was the unchaining of the ungovernable passions of humanity which now disgraced the conquerors, and soon made San Sebastian a shambles, the scene of the most hideous debauchery. If the valour that won the fortress was a proud record, the wild excesses that followed capture were an everlasting disgrace to the British arms. Plunder and rapine stalked rampant; drunkenness was universal, and it was said that had the French come down from the castle above, they might have retaken the town. Next morning the wreck was terrible to behold: houses in ruin, the furniture smashed, rich hangings torn down, clothes, rags, refuse thrown here and there amid corpses and starved cats, and drunken soldiers decked out in any tawdry finery they had picked up in their pillage. The town was in flames, even the churches, now converted into hospitals, were on fire. The wretched inhabitants—friends and non-combatants—steeped in misery, went about pale and squalid with a look of glazed horror on their faces, or stood undisturbed with lack-lustre eves, when a house crashed down close to them and others fled away. To show how all were enveloped in the recklessness of the marauders the story may be quoted of some master of a transport ship, who came on shore and fell among the thieving captors. He complained that the soldiers had robbed him of his coat, shoes, money, everything but his shirt.

"What shall I do?" he asked piteously.

"Hurry back to your ship, or you will lose your shirt too," was the answer.

The siege was not ended, however, with the capture of the town. Rey, with the remnant of his brave garrison, held out for many days in the citadel, and he would neither surrender nor could he be dislodged. He might have resisted longer, but his strength was shattered; his engineers had been slain, the troops had no cover or protection, and water was scarce. A murderous vertical fire was vigorously maintained, and did terrible execution, not only among the French, but amongst the English prisoners, of whom there were many in the castle. Wellington was now at San Sebastian in person, and he resolved to assault the castle by escalade, after concentrating on it the fire of all his guns. Fifty-nine heavy pieces opened simultaneously from all parts, and within a couple of hours nearly destroyed the works on the Orgullo hill; the batteries were broken down, magazines exploded, the ground around was torn and furrowed with shot and shell; the castle itself was untenable.

Then, at the eleventh hour, Rey surrendered and was granted the most generous terms. The next day he and his brave garrison marched out of their last stronghold with drums beating and flags flying, and all the honours of war.

June 21, 1813

Vittoria

Charles Lowe

It was a happy coincidence that the greatest of all Lord Wellington's victories in the Peninsula should have been won at a place near the foot of the Pyrenees called Vittoria—a name which is now proudly blazoned on the colours of no fewer than forty-four British regiments.

Begun in 1808, the Peninsular War, undertaken by England for the deliverance of Spain and Portugal from the insufferable yoke of the French, had already been dragging on its chequered course for a period of nearly five years. The glorious career of British victory had been diversified by defeats, disappointments, retreats—by everything but surrender and despair. Portugal had been twice purged of its French invaders; and Wellington's masterly retreat behind the famous lines of Torres Vedras, running from the Tagus to the sea, had been followed by the heroic storming of Ciudad Rodrigo and Badajoz, which secured the Spanish gates of Portugal; while the victory of Salamanca opened up the road to Madrid, and with it the prospect of a speedy and successful termination of the war.

But, again, the failure at Burgos, and the consequent retirement of Wellington into Portugal, gave the French a further respite from the certain doom that awaited them and their upstart emperor's brother, Joseph Bonaparte, whom the Corsican despot had foisted upon the people of Spain as their king. For with Wellington, to retreat was only to return after brief space as the repairer of his own reverses. His motto was, "*Réculer pour mieux santer.*" And, after all, it is only soldiers of the highest genius who can do this. Marshal Moltke was once in a company where someone ventured to say that his name would rank

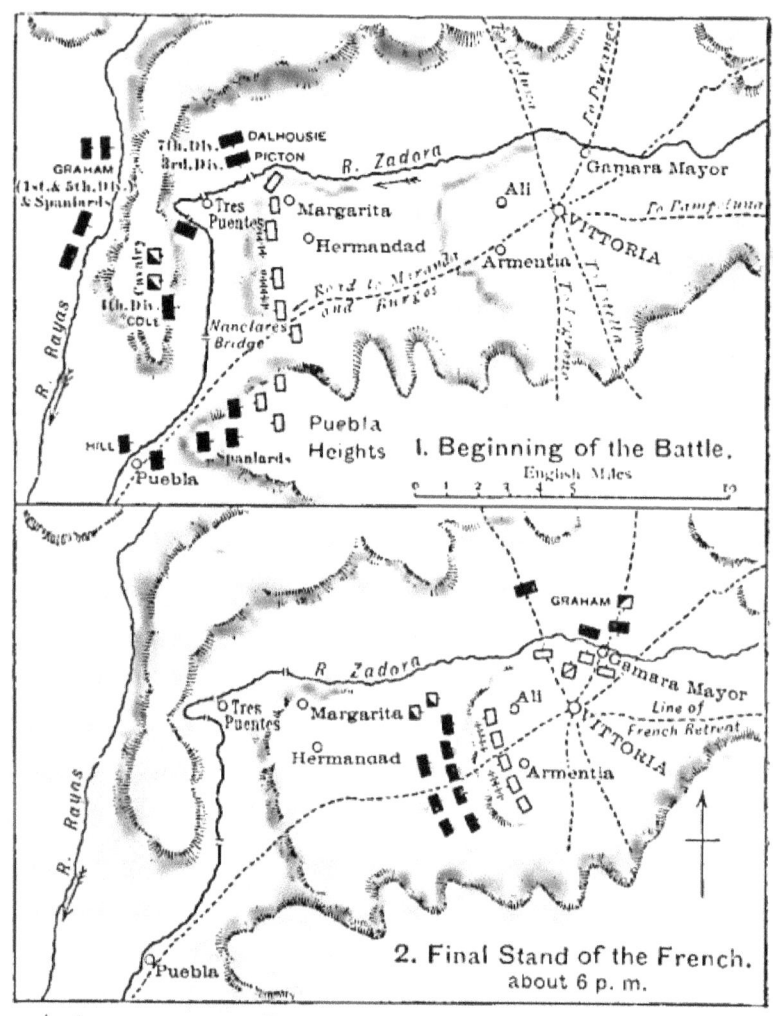

Battle of VITTORIA.

in history with those of Marlborough, Turenne, the Great Frederick, Napoleon, and Wellington. "No," said the immortal German strategist, "I have no right to be named with those great commanders, for I have never in my life conducted a retreat."

Hitherto the French had vastly outnumbered Lord Wellington's troops (British and Portuguese) in the Peninsula, but the winter of 1812-13, after his third retirement from Spain to Portugal, turned the scale in his favour. For this winter had all but destroyed Napoleon's "Grand Army" on its frozen flight from flaming Moscow; and on returning to Europe—as one may be said to do who comes from

Russia—the emperor had to weaken his armies in the Peninsula by the drafts required for enabling him to meet his allied foes at Leipzig. Thus, in the spring of 1813, the relative strength of the contending armies in the Peninsula was no longer in favour of the French, who had now only about 160,000 effective men with the Eagles; while Wellington had the command of a motley host of nearly 200,000, of which 44,000 only were British, 31,000 Portuguese, the rest being Spaniards and Sicilians. In May his Anglo-Portuguese army, numbering 75,000 men, lay cantoned from Lamego to the Baños Pass, and it is only this portion of his force that now concerns us.

Wellington had spent the winter in reorganising his army. He had received reinforcements from England, including the Life and Horse Guards; he had re-established with a stern hand the discipline which had been tending to become loose; tents and pontoon trains had been provided; and by the time the buds were on the tree, and the fields again green with the forage necessary for his cavalry, he found himself at the head of an army ready to go anywhere with him and do anything.

English leader on the move, the French knew full well. But what they did not know exactly was in what direction this movement would be taken. Hitherto Wellington had always operated from Portugal by the valley of the Douro—his audacious passage of this river in The face of Marshal Soult's army in 1809 had been one of his very finest feats; and the French concluded that this would again be the line of his advance.

In this expectation King Joseph Bonaparte—who commanded the French forces in Spain, though he had nothing of his brother's transcendent genius for the art of war—had posted the bulk of these forces between the Tagus and the Douro on a line extending from Toledo (once so famous for its sword-blades) through Madrid to beyond Salamanca. In this position he was fond enough to hope that he would be able to repel any frontal attack which might be made by Wellington on any part of his line; and Wellington, on his part, did all he could, by the circulation of false reports and other *ruses de guerre*, to encourage the French in their belief that he meant to re-invade Spain through the central provinces between the Tagus and the Douro.

But for various reasons Wellington resolved to make a flank march by the north, so as, if possible, to turn the French right and fall upon their rear. Dividing his forces into three armies—the left one under Sir Thomas Graham, the centre one commanded by himself, and that

on the right led by Sir Rowland Hill—Wellington, by a series of masterly movements which completely deceived the French and took them by surprise, crossed the Ebro and fought his difficult way across the successive affluents of its right bank, pushing the out-manoeuvred Frenchmen ever before him through Burgos, which they blew up in their retreat, and compelling them to transfer their main position from the line of the Douro to that of the Ebro. Napier, the eloquent historian of the Peninsular War wrote:

"A grand design, and grandly it was executed. For high in heart and strong of hand Wellington's veterans marched to the encoun-

ter, the glories of twelve victories played about their bayonets, and he the leader so proud and confident that, in passing the stream which marks the frontier of Spain, he rose in his stirrups, and, waving his hand, cried out: 'Farewell, Portugal!'"

Wellington, so to speak, had now burned his ships, or at least his bridges, behind him. For, having executed his splendid flank movement, which compelled his enemies to fall back on their lines of communication with France through the Pyrenees, he transferred his own base of supplies, formed by his ships, from the Tagus to the Biscayan ports. It was like a transformation scene in a theatre; and the curtain of war now rose on the pleasant little town and valley of Vittoria, whither Joseph Bonaparte had hastened to concentrate about 60,000 of his men, together with all his stores and baggage, the pillage of five years, the artillery depots of Madrid, Valladolid, and Burgos, and a convoy of treasure from Bayonne—the birthplace of bayonets. "*Was für Plünder!*"—"What a city to sack!" old Marshal Blücher once exclaimed on looking down on London from the dome of St. Paul's. But the sight of all the treasure which was now amassed in the valley of Vittoria would have almost made the fingers of "Marshal Vorwärts" itch still more.

While Wellington expected, and expected not in vain, of his redcoated soldiery that they should prove second to none in battle, he did not exact of them a familiar acquaintance with the historical associations of the scenes which they immortalised anew by their bravery. But had they been aware of the incidents which, in times long past, had been enacted on the scene of their present battle array, they would doubtless have felt doubly resolved to sustain the martial glory of their country. For here it was that, in the year 1367, Edward the Black Prince had routed some of the finest troops, of France under their famous leader Bertrand du Guesclin; and a prominent height in the region was still known as the "Englishmen's Hill" (*Altura de los Ingleses*), from the gallant stand which had been made by some English knights and their fol-

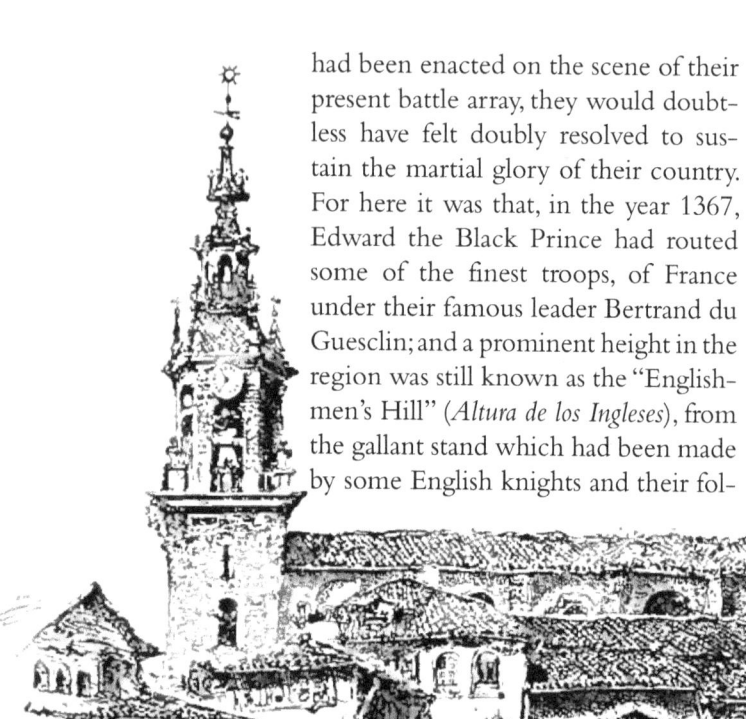

lowers against a large body of Spaniards under Don Telo. Vittoria had previously to this derived its name from some ancient and forgotten victory, but now it was to receive a fresh coating; of scarlet paint that would last to the end of time.

The position of the French could not well have been stronger by nature. Their left, under Maransin, rested on an elevated chain of craggy mountains; their right, under Reille, on a rapid river (the Zadora); while Gazan held the commanding heights in the centre, and a succession of undulating grounds afforded excellent situations for artillery. The French line extended for about eight miles, and this was guarded by. about 60,000 men with 152 guns. King Joseph himself was in nominal command of this army—a splendidly equipped one in every respect—though he allowed himself to be guided in all things by Marshal Jourdan, who, on this 21st of June, was suffering so acutely from fever that he was unable to mount his horse. The French army could not have consisted of better fighting material, but it was badly commanded. In respect of position, cavalry and artillery, King Joseph was decidedly superior to Wellington; but, on the other hand, Wellington had the advantage of being numerically stronger than his opponent by about 20,000 men.

After an early morning of mist the day broke in glorious sunshine, and then the British army began to move forward over very hilly and irregular ground from its bivouacs on the Bayas River, running almost parallel with the Zadora. The scene was one of the most splendid and animated that could be imagined, being a perfect picture of all "the pomp and circumstance of glorious war," all the panoramic sights of battle, and all the sounds:

"The neighing of the cavalry horses, the roll of tumbrils and gun-

carriages, the distant yet distinct words of command, the mingling music of many bands, the trumpets of the Horse, the bugles of the Rifles, and the hoarsely-wailing war-pipes of the Highland regiments, ever and anon swelling upon the breeze, pealing among the heights of Puebla, and dying away among the windings of the vale of Zadora."

The attack on the French position was begun by Sir Rowland Hill on the British right, where he advanced a Spanish brigade under Morillo to gain possession of the Puebla heights. With great difficulty, though unopposed, the Spaniards gallantly scrambled to the top of those heights. But presently they were sharply opposed by the French, who, perceiving the danger which thus threatened their left, detached a portion of their centre force, and began to make immense exertions to hurl the overweening Spaniards down the hill again. And it would now have gone extremely hard with the valiant *dons* had not Hill been quick to perceive the peril they were in, and tell off the 71st Highland Light Infantry with another light battalion, under Colonel Cadogan, to rush to their assistance. Then the pipers of the Highlanders struck up "Johnnie Cope," the regimental march, which had been written to celebrate the finest of all Highland victories—that of Prestonpans.

As though inspired by all the memories associated with these stirring strains, the 71st rushed to the succour of the hard-pressed Spaniards, and soon reached the summit of the heights, though at a great sacrifice of life. Scorning the use of bullets, the Highlanders, with levelled bayonets, swept up and upon the foe through clouds of smoke and tearing volleys of grape and musketry; and their fighting rage was further intensified by the sight of their idolised commander (Cadogan) falling mortally wounded from his horse. A few minutes later he died in the arms of Colonel Seaton, of the 92nd Highlanders. Nothing could now withstand their headlong charge, which was like that of the clans at Prestonpans; and after a desperate hand-to-hand conflict, Maransin's Frenchmen were hurled back and down the reverse side of the hill, which now began to resound with the victory *paeans* of the Highland war-pipe. A soldier of the 71st wrote:

"We lay on the heights for some time. Our drought was excessive. There was no water there, save a small spring, which was rendered useless. One of our men stooped to drink. A ball pierced his head. He fell in the well, which was discoloured by brains and blood. Thirsty as we were, we could not drink of it. There were only three hundred of us on the height able to do duty out of one thousand who drew rations that morning. The cries of the wounded were most heartrending."

The spirit which animated the British troops on this day of victorious battle was well described by Sergeant Donaldson, of the Scots Brigade, in his *Eventful Life of a Soldier*:—

"Those who have not known it from experience can form no idea of the indifference with which our soldiers entered a battle after being sometime in the Peninsula. As an instance of this, when we were lying in front of the enemy in expectation of being engaged, one of our men, a Highlander, having lost a small piece of ornamented leather which is worn in front of the uniform cap, on taking it off the deficiency caught his eye, and looking at it for a few moments, he said very seriously, 'I wish there may be an engagement today, that I may get a rosette for my cap!'"

While as yet the battle on the Puebla heights seemed doubtful, Wellington, with his eagle glance, had discerned the advance of the tartans, and then, turning to his staff, he announced that the hill had been won; and notwithstanding repeated efforts on the part of the French to dislodge them from this important position, the allies retained possession of them throughout the day.

Meanwhile, in the centre, where Wellington himself swayed the battle. General Picton, who commanded the famous "Fighting Third" Division, was fretting his heart away under his enforced inaction. His soldiers were straining to advance like greyhounds in leash, and their equally fiery leader had some difficulty in restraining them. As the day wore on, and the fight waxed ever warmer on his right, Picton became furious and observed to an officer, "D—n it! Lord Wellington must have forgotten us." His stick fell in rapid strokes upon the mane of his horse. At length a staff-officer galloped up from Lord Wellington.

Picton's face began to glow with animation at the prospect of his being ordered into action; but it suddenly grew black again on the officer simply asking whether he had seen Lord Dalhousie. "No, sir," answered Picton sharply; "but have you any orders for *me*?"

"None," replied the *aide-de-camp*.

"Then pray, sir," continued the irritated general, "what are the orders you *do* bring?"

"Why," answered the officer, "that as soon as Lord Dalhousie, with the 7th Division, shall commence an attack on the bridge (pointing to one on the left), the 4th and 6th are to support him."

Picton could not understand the idea of any other division fighting in *his* front, so, drawing himself up to his full height, he said to the astonished *aide-de-camp*, with some heat, "You may tell Lord Wellington from me. sir, that the 3rd Division under my command shall, in less than ten minutes, attack the bridge and carry it, and the 4th and 6th Divisions may support me if they choose."

Saying which, he turned from the *aide-de-camp* and put himself at the head of his eager men with a wave of his hand towards the bridge and the cry of "Come on, ye rascals! Come on, ye fighting villains!"

He well fulfilled his promise. Under a heavy fire of artillery his "fighting" division moved steadily on, his leading companies rushing over the bridge, where they formed up in open columns. Then they moved by their left, so as to attack the enemy's centre. Still advancing in the same order, they pressed up the heights, where they quickly deployed into line. The foe hardly awaited the attack, for so ably and rapidly were these bold manoeuvres carried out that the French for the moment were as if panic-stricken. Picton had gained the heights in front of him, but the divisions on his right had not yet made sufficient progress to come into line with and support him. Halting his impatient "rascals," he waited for the advance of the 7th Division (Lord Dalhousie's) and part of the "Lights," while the 4th (under General Cole) passed the Zadora a little further to the right by the Nanclares bridge.

During the tardier advance of these divisions, the French made desperate attempts to roll back Picton, opening upon him with fifty guns and hurling serried masses of infantry at his line. But the incessant fire which his "fighting villains" poured into the teeth of their assailants made terrible havoc in their ranks, and what they could not do with their bullets they did with their bayonets. When these were crossed with the enemy, the issue of the struggle in this part of the field was certain. As an eye-witness wrote:

"All this time Picton's Division acted in a manner which excited at once the surprise and admiration of the whole army. For nearly four hours did it alone sustain the unequal conflict, opposed to a vast superiority of force. From the nature of the ground, the rest of the army became witnesses of this animating scene; they beheld, with feelings more easily conceived than expressed, the truly heroic efforts of this gallant band. They saw the general—calm, collected, and determined—leading them on in the face of danger, amidst a shower of cannon and musket balls. Nothing could appal, nothing could resist, men so resolute and so led. They subdued every obstacle, bore down all opposition, and spread death, consternation, and dismay in the enemy's ranks."

The uneven and broken ground made Picton's advance difficult and his line irregular, but there was no confusion in his ranks. A sec-

ond time did the "fighting villains" charge down with the bayonet on the rearward position to which they had forced the enemy to retire, and so hasty was the French flight that they left twenty-eight of their guns in the hands of Picton's men.

Thus the fight went on for several miles, prominent incidents in its course being the storming of the village of Margarita by the Oxfordshire Light Infantry at the point of the bayonet, and a similar carrying of Hermandad by the Royal Irish Fusiliers with a rousing yell of victory. Thus, for a distance of six miles, the tide of battle rolled backwards towards Vittoria. The whole basin was a scene of sanguinary strife. Every valley and height and woodland was covered with sheets of flame, and every vineyard wall and hedgerow served as a breastwork, which was desperately contested.

Later, on the British left, Sir Thomas Graham—with the 1st and 5th Divisions, Pack's and Bradford's infantry brigades, a Spanish Division under Longa, and Anson's brigade of horse—had been equally successful in passing the desperately-defended Zadora and threatening the French right.

Some idea of the fighting on this flank may be gained from the terse account which was given of it by Lieutenant Campbell (afterwards to become Sir Colin, the hero of Lucknow, and Lord Clyde), who was then acting as orderly officer to Lieutenant-Colonel Crawford: " While we were halted the enemy occupied Gamara Mayor in considerable force, placed two guns at the principal entrance into the village, threw a cloud of skirmishers in front among the cornfields, and occupied with six pieces of artillery the heights immediately behind the village on the left bank. At 5 p.m. an order arrived from Lord Wellington to press the enemy in our front. It was the extreme right of their line, and the lower road to France, by which alone they could retire. Their artillery and baggage ran close to Gamara Mayor. The left brigade moved down in contiguous columns of companies, and our light companies were sent to cover the right flank of this attack.

"The regiments, exposed to a heavy fire of musketry and artillery, did not take a musket from their shoulder until they had carried the village. The enemy brought forward his reserves, and made many desperate attempts to retake the bridge, but could not succeed. This was repeated until the bridge became so heaped with dead and wounded that they were rolled over the parapet into the river below. Our light companies were closed upon the 9th, and brought into the village to support the 2nd Brigade. We were presently ordered to the left to cover the flank of the village, and we occupied the bank of the river, on the opposite side of which was the enemy. After three hours' hard fighting they retired, leaving their guns in our possession."

The battle now presented a magnificently imposing spectacle as the three divisions of Wellington's army, after having crossed the Zadora and beaten back their opponents from ridge to ridge, and from village to village, moved forward to a grand general attack. Here, again, Picton's "fighting villains" were ever to the front. Frequently the divisions on the right and left would see them charging into the very heart of the enemy's centre, and immediately after the enemy retreating in confusion. Napier wrote:

"Many guns were taken as the array advanced, and at six o'clock the enemy reached the last defensible height, one mile in front of Vit-

toria. Behind them was the plain on which the city stood, and beyond the city thousands of carriages and animals and non-combatants, men, women and children, were crowding together in all the madness of terror; and as the English shot went booming overhead, the vast crowd started and swerved with a convulsive movement, while a dull and horrid sound of distress arose. But there was no hope, no stay for army or multitude. It was the wreck of a nation. However, the courage of the French soldier was not yet quelled; Reille, on whom everything now depended, maintained his post on the upper Zadora; and the armies of the south and centre, drawing up on their last heights, between the villages of Ali and Armentier, made their muskets flash like lightning, while more than eighty pieces of artillery, massed together,

pealed with such a horrid uproar that the hills laboured and shook, and streamed with fire and smoke, amidst which the dark figures of the gunners were seen bounding with a frantic energy."

The French retirement was successively converted into retreat, flight, and headlong rout, followed by the scarlet masses of Wellington's victorious infantry from ridge to ridge, and from height to hollow. In the morning a superbly organised army, the French had by sunset become a wild and affrighted mob. King Joseph himself had a very narrow escape. The 10th Hussars galloped into the town just as he was leaving it in his carriage, and when Captain Wyndham dashed after him with a squadron, His Majesty only escaped by quitting his vehicle and mounting a swift horse. But the Hussars were rewarded by the finding of the greater portion of the king's regalia in his carriage. Another object, though less of value than of interest, that was captured, was Jourdan's baton of a field-marshal, which Wellington sent home to the prince regent as one of the trophies of his almost unparalleled victory—unparalleled by its military and political results, as well as by the immense amount of booty of all kinds which fell into the hands of the allies.

This consisted, among other things, of all the enormous amount of plunder which the French had rapaciously amassed in the course of their campaigning in Spain. To use the words of one of their commanders, Gazan, " They had lost all their equipages, all their guns, all their treasure, all their stores, all their papers so that no man could prove how much pay was due to him. Generals and subordinate officers alike were reduced to the bare clothes on their backs, and most of them were barefooted."

The work of fighting had scarcely ended when the work of plundering began. The camp of every Division was like a fair: planks were laid from waggon to waggon, and there the soldiers held an auction

through the night, disposing of such booty as had fallen to their share. Of five and a half million dollars alone, which were indicated by the French accounts to be in the money-chests, not one dollar was ever credited to the British public. The British private, however, had his fair share of all this immense spoil, and he had richly earned it by contributing to one of the most complete victories which had ever been won—a victory which, purchased by the allies at the comparatively small cost of 5,176 killed and wounded (that of the French being about the same), secured to the British arms the glory of having finally delivered Spain from the insufferable presence of its French oppressors.

True, the work of the war was not yet complete. San Sebastian had still to be stormed, and the battles of the Pyrenees fought. But, meanwhile, as Napier wrote:

"Joseph's reign was over; the crown had fallen from his head, and, after years of toils and combats, which had rather been admired than understood, the English general, emerging from the chaos of the Peninsular struggle, stood on the summit of the Pyrenees a recognised conqueror. From these lofty pinnacles the clangour of his trumpets pealed clear and loud, and the splendour of his genius appeared as a flaming beacon to warring nations."

July, 1813-February, 1814

The Battles in the Pyrenees

Major Arthur Griffiths

One of the most striking incidents in the long struggle for victory in the Peninsula was when Wellington met Marshal Soult, his great antagonist, face to face among the rugged mountains of the Pyrenees. It was at a critical moment. Soult had made a brilliant advance, and, by clever concentration of all his forces, was in greatly superior strength; he might count upon inflicting a crushing defeat upon the English opposed to him before their supports could arrive. Wellington was hurrying them up, with the consciousness that they were well placed and near at hand. How was he to gain time? Alone he rode up to the front and showed himself conspicuously to both friends and foes. His nearest troops, some Portuguese, raised a shrill and joyful cry at seeing him; it was taken up by the next regiments, and "soon swelled as it ran along the line into that stern, appalling shout which the British soldier is wont to give upon the edge of battle, and which no enemy ever heard unmoved." On the other side of the valley were the enemy, and at their head their great commander, Soult: he was so near that a spy at Wellington's stirrup pointed him out. The two generals plainly saw each other's features; and Wellington quickly drew his own conclusions as he carefully studied Soult's appearance. "Yonder," he said aloud, "is a great commander, but he is cautious, and will delay his attack until he can ascertain the cause of those cheers; that will give time for the 6th Division to arrive, and I shall beat him"—which he did, and handsomely, as we shall see.

This was in the early part of the great struggle in the Pyrenees—the longest, most arduous, most fiercely-contested campaign in the whole Peninsular War. It was fought out from first to last among the mountains; some of its most terrible episodes occurred at altitudes of five and six thousand feet. The warfare was incessant and greatly varied, comprising skirmish, combat, and set battle, the attack and defence of rocky positions, the forcing of narrow defiles, advance alternating with retreat, always by rugged flinty roads, by goat tracks and mountain paths, through crooked and winding valleys, across difficult hills intersected with deep glens and chasms and tremendous precipices, their flanks clothed frequently with impenetrable forests. To travel over such a country called for the greatest exertions from the troops. Marches were long and toilsome, more suitable to Alpine climbers than foot soldiers hampered with knapsacks, guns, and cartridges. Both sides were taxed severely, and were subjected to the most frightful hardships. The weather, even in the summer, was inclement; great heats were followed by terrific thunderstorms. As winter drew on, snow fell heavily; and the British, still in the hills, under tents or in the open, were exposed to great suffering. It was difficult to bring up the commissariat supplies; food was scarce; work—and such work!—had to be done constantly on a half-ration of biscuit, eked out with such morsels as the starving soldiers could forage for themselves in a poverty-stricken district and only by setting discipline at defiance, for the hangman's rope certainly awaited every detected marauder.

Here is a graphic picture, drawn by an officer of the Light Division, at the end of a long day, when his men, now in pursuit of the flying French, had marched nearly forty miles, mostly up hill, and for nineteen consecutive hours.

"We had nearly reached the summit of a tremendous mountain, but nature was quite exhausted; many of the soldiers lagged behind; many fell heavily on the naked rocks, frothing at the mouth, black in the face, and struggling in their last agonies, whilst others, unable to drag one leg after the other, leaned on the muzzles of their firelocks, looking pictures of despair, muttering in disconsolate accents that they had never fallen out before."

Down below were the French. The same officer records:

"We overlooked the enemy at stone's throw, and from the summit of a tremendous precipice. The river separated us, but the French were wedged in a narrow road, with inaccessible rocks on the one side and the river on the other. Confusion, impossible to describe, followed: the wounded were thrown down in the rush and trampled upon; the cavalry drew their swords and endeavoured to charge up the pass

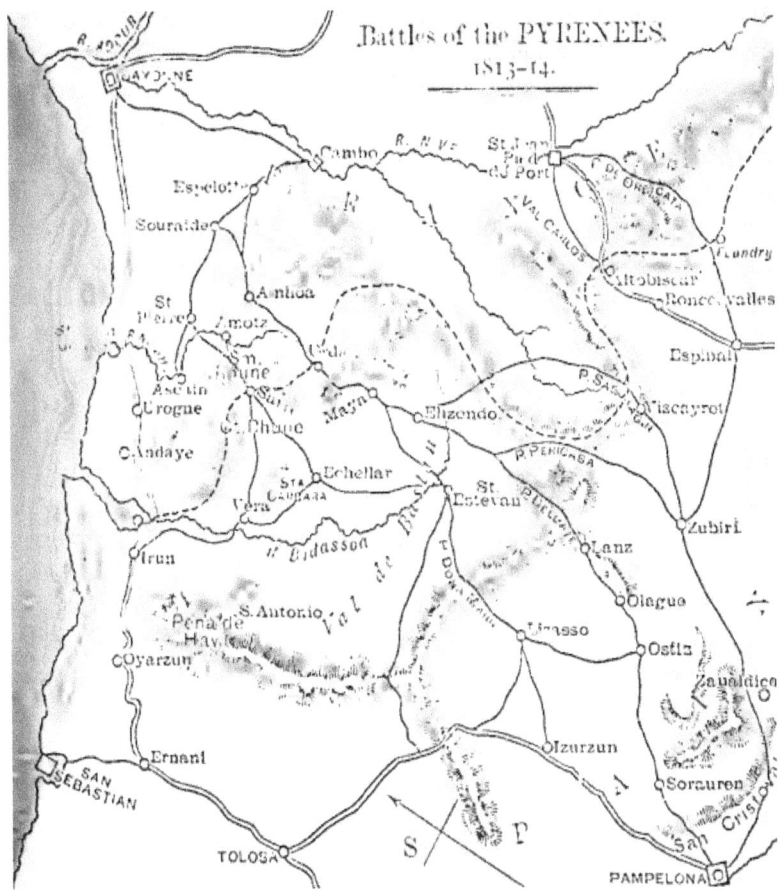

of Echellon [Echellar], but the infantry beat them back, and several, horses and all, were precipitated into the river; some fired vertically at us, while the wounded called out for quarter, and others pointed to them, supported as they were on branches of trees, on which were suspended great-coats clotted with gore, and bloodstained sheets taken from different habitations to aid the sufferers."

"On these miserable supplicants brave men could not fire," Napier says speaking of this incident, and thus doing due justice to the chivalrous spirit which animated both British and French alike in this campaign. They had so long faced each other, had met in so many sharp encounters, that mutual respect and a certain noble *camaraderie* had sprung up between them. They were foes, pledged to fight in their masters' quarrel, but having no special enmity of their own. A hundred stories could be told in proof of this—of friendly hobnobbing at the outposts, the interchange of compliments, of water-bottles, even of grog and wine. There was a regular code of signals between the picquets; when one side intended to advance or to occupy ground further forward, notice thereof was given by tapping the musket-butt, and, unless a serious move was expected, the other side withdrew. Sentries never fired wantonly or causelessly. One stormy night Colonel Alexander, when going round the advanced picquets, missed his way, and his horse fell over an unexpected obstacle with much noise. Instantly a French sentry near at hand cocked his musket, and Alexander, hearing the ominous click, called out quickly: "Don't fire! It is only the English field-officer of the day."

"All right, *mon Colonel*," quickly responded the gallant Frenchman. "I only hope you're not hurt."

The same Colonel Alexander was able to do a kindly turn for another French soldier, to whom his attention was called by one of our own sentries. It was a bright moonlight night, and the French sentry was plainly seen to be sound asleep on his post—an offence punishable in the French army with death. Colonel Alexander at once went across, and, first taking possession of the man's musket, waked the sleeper, who was, naturally, much terrified to find himself disarmed and in the hands of an English officer. The poor fellow soon expressed the deepest gratitude at finding he was still to go free, and that he had escaped the terrible retribution that must have overtaken him if he had been caught by his own people. He was yet anxious to excuse his unsoldierlike conduct by declaring that he had been put on outpost duty after a long and most fatiguing march. Another pleasant story may be told before passing on to the sterner operations of war. When the Light Division, after the march above mentioned, regained the heights of Santa Barbara, in front of the pass of Vera, they came upon two Frenchmen left behind in the retreat. One was a corporal, whose leg was broken; the other a comrade who had stayed with him to protect him from the knives of the implacable Spaniards. He had, however, no fear of the English, and cheerfully resigned his friend, for whom he had risked his life, to their care. Then, shouldering his musket, he walked off—of course, unmolested—with a parting "*Au revoir, bons camarades Anglais.*" Such incidents as these do much to brighten the inevitable horrors of war. To proceed now with the narrative of military events in the Pyrenees.

After the crushing defeat of Vittoria, Napoleon, although sorely pressed elsewhere, was resolved to make a last desperate stand on the frontiers of Spain and France. Unable to take command in person, he sent thither his most trusted lieutenant, Soult, the doughtiest antagonist—except Masséna—that Wellington, in his own judgment, had ever encountered in Spain. Marshal Soult travelled post-haste, and reached Bayonne early in July, where, with characteristic energy, he strained every nerve to reorganise his shattered forces. He gathered up reinforcements as he went, hurrying troops forward by every kind of conveyance, and soon got together upwards of 100,000 men. Marshal Suchet, it must be remembered, was yet in the eastern province of Spain, so that the French could still make a good show. Wellington at this time was in about equal strength with Soult; but his army, as usual, was made up of three nationalities—English, Spanish, and Portuguese. Of the first-named he had little more than 30,000 infantry, with some 7,000 cavalry. According to the muster-rolls, the numbers actually facing each other, although not always available, in the Pyrenees were, roughly, 82,000 under Wellington, against 78,000 under Soult. The latter could also count upon a number of foreign battalions and a large body of National Guards, all fierce and hardy mountaineers.

Soult, as has been said, was a man of indomitable and indefatigable activity. Within four days of his arrival at Bayonne he had worked out a new plan of operations on the boldest and most extensive scale. He was now resolved to take the offensive—that is to say, he meant to attack, not await attack—and his scheme was very admirably and elaborately devised. The initiative or first move gave him, as he knew, a very distinct advantage: he could choose his own line of advance, moving along it in strength, while his enemy, until fully alive to his direction and meaning, could not safely risk concentration to meet him. Wellington's position in the Pyrenees, it must be understood, was at this time defensive. He held all the passes along this long range of mountains, being obliged thus to cover the two sieges he had in progress—those of San Sebastian and of Pampelona, sixty miles apart. To hold passes in this way is considered the most hazardous undertaking in war. The only safe plan is to concentrate well to the rear of the passes, only leaving at them strong bodies to check the advancing enemy and give time to collect against him wherever he shows in strength. The run of the mountain ridges southward from the great central chain forbade this by cutting off lateral communication, or making it too tedious to be quickly effected. Soult believed, and rightly, that if he could throw his whole weight upon the centre or either end of the long line of English defence before he was expected, he would gain an early and signal success. He could do this by good beaten roads. All he had to consider was the best line of advance—right, centre, or left.

He decided to move by the last-named, and he came to this conclusion partly because he feared for Pampelona on this side, and partly because he knew or hoped that San Sebastian upon the other could long hold its own. Moreover, he knew that Wellington's principal force was gathered towards San Sebastian, and held on that side singularly strong positions of defence. The English centre could also more quickly reinforce its left than its right: two marches would suffice for the first, three long days for the last. Again, the English right, although posted in the mountains, was in more or less isolated bodies; while, as has been said, the support of the centre and left could not be obtained for three or more days, and then much further to the rear. Wherefore Soult resolved to move with all his available force by his own left against Wellington's right, counting, and with reason, upon being much stronger there than his opponent. Great consequences would follow a first success. He expected to easily overbear all resistance, to succour Pampelona, then seize the great road that came from Bayonne through Irun, Tolosa, Lecumberri, and Izurzun. Here he would be firmly established directly in the rear of the English, and could operate with marked advantage against each British division piecemeal, as it came tumbling back from its now hazardous position in the advanced passes and foremost hills.

A full comprehension of the close and intricate fighting now imminent can only be gained by studying the map, and acquiring an exact knowledge of the positions occupied by the troops, on either side at the outset of the campaign. Then the movements should be followed as they occurred, and I propose to give these briefly in a more or less military way.

The general position of the English was along the whole of the Western Pyrenees from opposite St. Jean Pied de Port on the extreme right, through the valley of the Bastan by the line of the Bidassoa River to Irun and the sea, on which rested the left. Speaking more in detail, and taking the forces as they stood from right to left, there were—

1.—Byng's British brigade in front of the pass of Roncesvalles in the main chain of mountains.

2.—Next, Campbell's brigade of Portuguese was in the Alduides on the north side of the chain.

Behind 1. and 2. was Sir Lowry Cole with the 4th British Division

at Viscayret, in the valley of Urroz, south of the chain. Farther to the rear was Sir Thomas Picton with the 3rd Division at Olague, in the valley of Lanz.

3.—The pass of Maya was held by the 1st Division, under Stewart, and part of the 2nd, under Sir Rowland Hill.

4.—The pass of Vera, in front of Echellar and the mountains of Santa Barbara, was held by the Light and 7th Divisions, under C. Alten and Lord Dalhousie.

Behind 3. and 4. stood the 6th Division at St. Estevan, in a central position, ready to move in support to either side.

5.—On the southern bank of the Bidassoa the Spaniards took up the line of defence from Lesaca to the sea at Irun.

Behind them Sir Thomas Graham, with the 5th Division and the Portuguese, was in support and carrying on the siege of San Sebastian. Pampelona was blockaded by a Spanish force. The British cavalry and the heavy guns were held about Tafalla, a long way to the rear of Pampelona.

Recapitulating briefly: the allied Anglo-Portuguese right was about 12,000, counting advanced troops and supports; the centre, 24,000; the left, including the troops besieging San Sebastian, 21,000. This was in the middle of July, just before Soult began his advance.

Let us take the French next. Soult had formed his forces into three principal bodies, or *corps d'armée*, as we should call them nowadays.

First Corps: Clausel's, at St. Jean Pied de Port, destined to operate against Roncesvalles.

Second Corps: Reille's, withdrawn from the line of the Nivelle towards Clausel, whom he was to reinforce and second in his move against the English right.

Third Corps: D'Erlon's, occupying a central position at and about Urdax. He was first to cover the concentration at St. Jean Pied de Port; then when Clausel and Reille, under the supreme direction of Soult in person, had driven back the English right, he was to force the pass of Maya, and manoeuvre to his left, so as to join hands with Soult.

At the same time a Fourth corps of reserve, under Villatte, stood firm on the Bidassoa, so as to occupy and distract Wellington's attention with threatenings of laying bridges and of vigorous attack on this side.

Heavy rains and floods delayed the march of the French, which began on the 20th July, and lasted four days. It was not until the 24th, therefore, that Clausel, Reille, and D'Erlon were ready, 60,000 men in all, to operate in overwhelming strength against the relatively weak right and right centre of Wellington's defensive line.

We will now follow the movements with the map, day by day.

25th July.—Clausel fell on Byng, in front, 16,000 against 1,600. At the same time Reille attacked his right, and sought to cut him off from Campbell. Byng stood fast; Campbell came up on his flank, where he encountered and stoutly resisted Reille, until Sir Lowry Cole arrived with the 4th Division in support. That night Cole drew off, surrendering the passes and his hold on the main chain, reaching Zubiri next day, where he halted and offered battle.

26th July.—Clausel followed Cole, but slowly; Reille, detained by mists and want of guides, made little progress. The English, however, were not yet concentrated; Picton, although at no great distance, had not come up, nor had Campbell made good his retreat. For about five hours Cole was in some danger. Alone and unsupported he might have been obliged to withstand Soult's whole strength. But the French marshal delayed his attack till next morning, and by that time the whole of the English forces in this direction had effected a junction.

Meanwhile, on the 25th and 26th, D'Erlon with 18,000 had been on the move, but in a dilatory fashion; yet he was at first successful. On the 25th he forced the pass of Maya, whereon Hill retreated to Vellate, a pass in the main chain of the Pyrenees. D'Erlon should have followed up his advantage, manoeuvring, as instructed, to his left towards Soult; but he paused to incorporate new reinforcements, and only followed Hill on the 28th, too late to be of service in the forward movements.

So much for Soult: now for Wellington.

The English general-in-chief was at San Sebastian when he first heard of Soult's general advance, and fully understood its purport. His proper place now was with his fighting divisions; and on the 26th, as he rode rapidly to the right, he ordered everyone he met to march towards Pampelona by the valley of Lanz. He counted upon Picton holding his ground in front of that fortress, and so instructed him, promising to come up with all possible support at once.

27th July.—The 6th, 7th, and Light Divisions were moving from St. Estevan, Echellar, and Vera respectively, towards Pampelona. It was a general retreat, very demoralising, and the confusion was greatly increased by vague rumours of terrible disasters everywhere. Picton, however, had turned, as Wellington expected, on the steep ridge of St. Christoval, and there assumed a strong position, which Cole, now un-

der Picton's orders, rendered more secure by seizing some heights on his right. Soult, who was now up with his advanced troops, promptly decided that he must assail Picton at once in front and on both flanks.

This was the movement he suspended on the sudden advent of Lord Wellington in the manner already described. The great English general, a splendid horseman, had come up from Lanz literally at racing speed, and with unerring instinct had fathomed the dangers that threatened, had dismounted, written his own orders, hurrying everyone forward, had despatched them by the only staff-officer still with him, Lord Fitzroy Somerset (afterwards the Lord Raglan of Crimean history), and ridden on, hoping to delay the action. In this he succeeded, as has been told.

28th July.—On this day was fought the first battle of Sorauren, a fierce encounter, when such great valour and determination were displayed on both sides that Wellington in his despatch called it "bludgeon work." About midday, Soult having heard that the English reinforcements were approaching, resolved to attack Cole and Picton without delay. Clausel's 1st Division turned the left, and would have gained the rear, when Pakenham, with the 6th Division—the first to come up in obedience to Wellington's pressing orders of the day before—appeared in strength over the ridge and delivered a counterstroke which has been compared to that of Salamanca. The French were caught on both flanks, and severely handled; nor could Clausel's other divisions, nor yet Reille's, restore the fight, although they behaved with superb courage, assaulting again and again the craggy heights occupied by the English. On the other flank Reille tried to dislodge the Spaniards on the Zabaldica hill; but they were reinforced by the British 40th, "that invincible regiment," which awaited in stern silence the French attack, then charged down and drove all before them. Four times the French remounted the steep slope, being at last so wearied that their officers were seen to drag up many by their belts; four times they were repulsed, and at last, "with thinned ranks, tired limbs, hearts fainting and hopeless from repeated failures, they were so abashed that three British companies sufficed to bear down a whole brigade."

29th July.—The whole of the British divisions, with the exception of the Light, which had gone astray in the mountains, were now well in hand, and Wellington was on the safe side. But Soult was feeling the pressure of events, and, realising that he must soon retire, had already sent off his guns, his wounded, and part of his cavalry to the rear. Now, however, he heard of D'Erlon's approach; 18,000 fresh troops had come up to Ostiz, within a few miles of him, and with these reinforcements he thought to extricate himself without entirely losing the reward of his bold advance. His plan was to hold his left in seeming strength about Sorauren, then under cover of" D'Erlon, draw off behind his right into the Bastan valley, where he would be once more in touch with the frontier and his reserves.

30th July.—Wellington was not to be outmanoeuvred. He quickly penetrated Soult's design to detain him with an inferior force, and, dashing forward at once with two divisions, attacked Sorauren in front and flank, thus bringing on the second battle of that name. It was hardly contested; but the determined gallantry of the British broke the French resistance, with frightful loss. Two French divisions were completely disorganised; a third, swollen with fugitives, was quite cut off from the main body. Meanwhile Soult had carried out the rest of his programme, and, acting against Hill's left, had opened for himself a retreat through the pass of Doña Maria which he threaded in safety, protected by a strong rear-guard. Now, however, Wellington's divisions, pushing steadily forward, drew closer and closer round the French, and Soult was nearly caught in a net from which there could be no escape but to surrender or disperse. It would be tedious to detail the various encircling marches made by the British, but on the 31st July, the situation was this:—Soult, with the remnant of his army, barely 35,000, many of them dispirited by defeat, occupied St. Estevan, a town in a deep narrow valley hemmed in by high hills, the exits from which were all closed. Wellington had three British divisions and one Spanish behind the mountains; the pass of Doña Maria was held by another; the Light Division, with more Spaniards, was blocking the pass of Vera, Byng that of Maya, Hill was in strength at Vellate. The French were in complete ignorance of their critical condition, and knew nothing of the dangerous proximity of Wellington. Now happened one of those small vexatious incidents that will mar the best dispositions in war. While the English general was still most anxious to hide his presence, forbidding all straggling or the lighting of any fires,: "Three marauding English soldiers entered the valley and were instantly carried off by the *gens d'armes*: half an hour afterwards the French drums beat to arms and their columns began to move out of San Estevan towards Sumbilla. Thus the disobedience of three plundering knaves, unworthy of the name of soldiers, deprived one consummate commander of the most splendid success and saved another from the most terrible disaster."

Soult escaped, but his further retreat was a rout: he was torn and harassed at every step, and when he at last regained the comparative security of the frontier it was in great disorder and after incalculable losses. His invasion of the Pyrenees, with its nine days of continual

movement and ten serious engagements, had cost him from 13,000 to 15,000 men killed and wounded, and 4,000 taken prisoners. On the other side the allies—British, Spanish, and Portuguese—lost 7,300 killed, wounded, and taken. Wellington himself was nearly included in the latter; for on the very last day's fighting, near Echellar, the English general was closely studying his map under the protection of a half-company of the 23rd, when the French came upon him suddenly and sent a party to cut him off. He was only saved by the intrepidity of an active young sergeant of the escort, Blood by name, who, "leaping, rather than running, down the precipitous rocks," warned him of his danger, and he galloped away, followed by a volley from the enemy, now close at hand.

Soult was beaten badly, but not cowed. In the weeks that followed his first disasters in the Pyrenees he strove hard to restore strength and spirit to his scattered forces, Wellington the while being busily employed on the now renewed siege of San Sebastian. Nearly a month so passed; and as the condition of that fortress grew more and more critical, the French commander felt constrained to strike a fresh blow for its relief. Soult in his weakness was not very hopeful of success; but he assumed a bold demeanour, and made a very desperate effort to raise the siege. For this, after all, it was only necessary to reach Oyarzun, behind the great mountains south of the Bidassoa and on the royal road from Bayonne and Irun.

Three days before the second storming of San Sebastian he embarked upon this momentous enterprise.

Soult resolved this time to concentrate against the English left. He thought to gather here, as he had previously done upon the right, more quickly than his enemy, and forestall him, with 40,000 men all told, upon the line of the lower Bidassoa.

30th August.—Clausel with 20,000 men and 20 guns was behind the hills above Vera; Reille with 18,000, and having Foy with 7,000 in reserve, was posted in rear of high points on the north of the river. D'Erlon farther back held Sarre and Ainhoa, whence he could check any wide outflanking movement by Wellington, or reinforce Clausel and Reille.

Wellington's army was at this time stationed as follows:—

1.—The Right—composed of the 2nd, 3rd, and 6th Divisions—at Roncesvalles, Maya, and in the valley of the Bastan.

2.—The Centre, of the 7th and Light Divisions, had the first-named at Echellar, the second occupying the heights of Santa Barbara, facing Vera.

3.—The Left, on the lower Bidassoa, was entrusted to the Spaniards in the position of San Marcial—heights that rose abruptly from the river-bank, and so steep that an eyewitness declared they could only be mounted by swinging from bough to bough. Behind San Marcial rose a four-ridged mountain called the Peña de Haya, and upon its lower slopes on the right were more Spaniards under Longa, while two British brigades were in support on the left. Higher up the Peña de Haya the 4th Division, of both British and Portuguese, stood in reserve; and as the mountain was so enormous that all these troops were insufficient to guard it, a brigade of the 7th Division was also brought across for the purpose from Echellar.

31st August (the day of the capture of San Sebastian).—Reille, covered by artillery fire, crossed the fords of Biriatu and stormed San Marcial. Clausel was to attack Vera simultaneously, and the two French corps, uniting on the Peña de Haya, were to force their way forward, driving the allies from ridge to ridge until they reached their objective point, Oyarzun.

Reille, moving out at daylight, attacked the formidable heights with great intrepidity, and, although the Spaniards fought well, they were near defeat when Wellington appeared in person. His presence was acknowledged by loud shouts, and, acting as an incentive to renewed and more gallant efforts, encouraged the Spaniards to drive the French down headlong. Soult stiffened his columns by drawing up his reserves, but forbore to renew the attack until that of Clausel was further developed.

On the side of Vera, Clausel sent three heavy columns across by the fords and up against the Portuguese, fighting his way forward amidst the asperities of the Peña de Haya but very slowly, so that it was two in the afternoon before he had gained much ground. But now Wellington had strengthened the defence of this mountain by the rest of the 7th Division, while the whole of the Light threatened Clausel's left flank and rear. Fearing for his communications, that general now paused and informed Soult of his condition. This was the turning-point of the action. Almost at the same moment news from D'Erlon reached Soult that he was threatened by the whole weight of Wellington's right wing.

The English general, with true military sagacity, had penetrated Soult's intention from the first. Seeing that his left was to be attacked in force while his right was held in check by D'Erlon, he promptly resolved to throw his right forward, and so disturb Soult's plan. On the 30th he directed three lines of attack against D'Erlon, and these were made with such fierceness that that general believed a great movement was in progress against Bayonne. Wellington had in reality no such aim: it was only a masterly strategical move, which, by unsettling Soult, changed the face of the battle at the most decisive point. The French commander at once drew Foy's division from Reille to reinforce D'Erlon, and ordered Clausel to withdraw behind the Bidassoa. Reille himself was still on our side of the river, under the position of San Marcial, and opposed only by the Spaniards, who were losing heart; but any fresh engagement was rendered impossible by the outburst of a terrific storm of wind and rain, in the teeth of which no man could stand, while the thinnest streams swelled rapidly into raging torrents. Reille retreated under cover of and uninjured by the elements; but Clausel's last division was half-drowned at the fords, and the rest were nearly cut off at the bridge of Vera.

Next day, the 1st September, Soult learnt that Wellington's advance towards Bayonne was only a feint, and he was disposed to organise a fresh attack upon San Marcial. But now came the news that San Sebastian was captured, all but the citadel, and it was deemed hazardous to continue the forward movement. Already Soult had lost, in the five different combats of the 31st August, some 3,600 men, and many generals and other officers. In the seven last weeks he had fought in all twelve battles, and he felt now that the tide was turning against

him, that he must relinquish offence for defence, and limit himself to a stubborn resistance. He was well placed strategically for defensive warfare, and his army held many strong positions; moreover, "his vast knowledge of war, his foresight, his talent for methodical arrangement, and his firmness of character peculiarly fitted him" for operations of this kind. We enter now upon the second great period in the Pyrenean conflict, when the initiative passed from Soult to Wellington, and the English general, at the head of the allied troops, invaded France.

All through September and into the first days of October the opposing armies remained inactive. Both sides were reorganising, replenishing, regaining strength. It was an especially trying time for Wellington and his troops, most of whom were still among the mountains, exposed to the wet and cold of an inclement autumn, while down below the fertile plains of France glittered in the warm sunshine, a veritable Promised Land. Duty was severe and unremitting, the outposts were ever on the alert, and a most stringent, irksome discipline was always maintained. The troops were discontented and lost heart; desertions became frequent; the provost-marshal was kept constantly busy; the halberds and the gallows found many victims. The forward move came not a day too soon, and was hailed with delight by all ranks as a prelude to brighter days.

All this time Wellington was being continually worried by the politicians to invade France, and so hasten the overthrow of Napoleon, now sorely pressed on every side. But the English general was reluctant to advance; the time was not yet ripe. Soult, undismayed, with abundant forces, stood based upon two fortresses, Bayonne and St. Jean Pied de Port, holding strongly-entrenched positions between them. Another French marshal, Suchet, was in Catalonia with an army of 60,000, ready to act against Wellington's flank and rear if he made any forward move. There was much to impose caution; yet the English general, yielding at length to the persistent pressure from home, resolved at least to place his left in a menacing attitude within the French territory. His right and centre, occupying the passes from Roncesvalles to Maya, were already well situated for attack, and it was on this side that Soult naturally looked for the next move.

To deceive your enemy is one of the first and most important of all military maxims, and Wellington did everything to encourage Soult's idea, although he had no intention of so acting. He continually disquieted Soult with feints in this direction, while he was preparing serious operations in the other. His plan was to move by his left, to force the passage of the lower Bidassoa, to drive the French out of their entrenchments there, and at the same time move to the right, attack and, if possible, capture the Great Rhune mountain, a rocky peak rising some three thousand feet above the sea. This enterprise has been justly deemed by the historian to be "as daring and dangerous as any undertaken during the whole war." Let us now see how it was accomplished, briefly considering first the positions of the opposing armies.

Taking the French first from left to right, from Pied de Port to the sea: Foy was at that town and fortress, having, however, power to reinforce the right by the bridge of Cambo; D'Erlon stood next at Ainhoa, with an advance at Urdax and his right at the bridge of Amotz, on the Nivelle; then came Clausel, reaching as far as Serres on the same river, while redoubts covered his left front, and his right flank was behind the Great Rhune; finally, Reille occupied two long ridges that ran from the main chain of La Rhune towards the sea, one constituting the northern bank of the Bidassoa and rising sheer above the river's bed, the other in rear of it, and both crowned with many formidable earthworks. Behind all, about Ascain, was Villate in reserve and keeping up the connection between Reille and Clausel.

Wellington, on the other hand, kept his extreme right still at Roncesvalles, but with a preponderating weight towards his centre about Maya, where was Hill with the 2nd Division, having the 3rd a little to its left front. The 7th Division was at Echellar, with the 6th in support. More to the left was Giron's Spanish Division, backed up by the Light

Division, and that again by the 4th, on the heights of Santa Barbara. Beyond Vera and on the farther or southern side of the Bidassoa were Longa's Spaniards, while the rest of the river was held by the 1st and 5th Divisions, with Freyre's Spaniards and two independent brigades, Aylmer's British and Wilson's Portuguese. This was the plan of battle. Giron was to take the right of the Rhune mountain, with Alten next and in the centre, while Longa, crossing by the ford of Salinas and the bridge of Vera, was to assail the left. These troops numbered 20,000 in all, and they had much stiff climbing with hard fighting before them. Wellington held 24,000 more for a perhaps tougher job, the passage of the river lower down, where it was unbridged and where its few known fords were raked by artillery placed on purpose in entrenchments strongly garrisoned. But Wellington had heard of other fords, three of them secretly discovered near the mouth of the river; and it was on the existence of these that he based the main part of his hazardous operation. These last-named fords were only practicable at low water. The tide hereabouts rose and fell sixteen feet; but when quite out, it left broad sands firm for half a mile, good going, but in full view of the French positions on the northern shore. To cross so near the mouth of the river was deemed impossible, and the French were thus lulled into false security, never dreaming of attack on that side. They had in consequence established themselves most strongly about the centre, where the Bildox or Green Mountain overlooked the known lords. Soult was himself deceived. He had been warned by spies and deserters of the movement contemplated, yet he would not believe it, and his subordinate generals were as negligent as he was incredulous.

The 7th of October was the day fixed for the passage, and just before daylight a terrific storm burst over the French positions, which with tempest and darkness helped to cloak Wellington's movements. He had left all his tents standing, so as to further deceive the enemy; and his seven columns of attack, embracing a front of five miles, approached their several points of crossing without being observed. The 1st and 5th Divisions took the sands at the lowest fords—pointing the one towards the great redoubt of "*Sans Culottes*," to the right rear of the French position, the other towards Andaye, on the right flank. Both passed the river before a shot was fired; then the English signal went up—a rocket, fired from the steeple of Fuentarabia— the English guns began to play, and the remaining columns entered the water. Now the French awoke and gathered slowly, but all too tardily, to the defence. Their artillery in the nearest redoubts— the "Louis XIV," the

"*Café Republicain*," and the "*Croix des Bouquets*"—opened fire, and the struggle commenced. The 1st British Division, with Halkett's Germans and Wilson's Portuguese, quickly drove the French out of the two first named redoubts into the third, which was really the key to the position, and here the fight raged fiercely. Both sides brought up guns and troops in reinforcement, but the day was gained by Colonel Cameron at the head of the 9th Regiment, who charged with such astonishing courage and impetus that he carried all before him. Meanwhile Freyre with his Spaniards had gone up against the Bildox and neighbouring heights, had gained them, and thus turned the French left; while the unopposed advance of the 5th Division towards the "*Sans Culottes*" equally compromised the French right. Reille, who was now in chief command, found himself beaten in the centre and menaced on both flanks. A precipitate retreat followed; only the arrival of Soult with some of Villatte's reserves saved the flight from degenerating into a disastrous rout.

On this lower side Wellington triumphed easily; his losses were trifling, his success extraordinary. Yet with less masterly skill in disposition, less unhesitating boldness in execution, this "stupendous operation," as Napier calls it, might have had a far different ending. Had Soult guessed Wellington's real design and prepared to meet it, he could have opposed him with 16,000 men securely posted and protected with artillery sufficient to resist, or greatly delay, the passage. Any prolonged check would have been fatal, "because in two hours the returning tide would have come with a swallowing flood upon the rear."

The attack on the Great Rhune has still to be described; and here, although the French were also taken unawares, the fight was closer, more nearly balanced, and much more prolonged. The French general Taupin occupied the long saddle from the Rhune to the river, and had in his front a lesser hill, called the Bear's Back, which must be taken first. It was carried most gallantly by Colborne of the 52nd, who passed on to attack Taupin's right; while Kempt's brigade and, farther back, Freyre came up on the left, and all pressing forward, in spite of the steep incline and the enemy's desperate courage, succeeded at length in driving the French out of their entrenchments. Meanwhile Giron, higher up, had assailed the Great Rhune, where he was met with a stout resistance, and might have been repulsed but for the intrepid bravery of a young Englishman, Havelock, General Alten's *aide-de-camp*, who came to Giron with a message, and staved to see the fight through. Havelock., seeing the check, nobly pushed to the front, and gave the Spaniards fresh spirit; with loud cries of "*El Chico Blanco!*" ("The fair-haired boy!") they willingly followed him, and were led on to victory. Now the French drew higher up the mountain, where bold staring crags just below the summit had gained the name of The Hermitage, and in this impregnable fastness made a last determined stand all through the night. Next day Wellington ordered a flanking movement, a strong demonstration by the Sixth Division round the rear of the Rhune, whereupon Clausel, fearing for his communications, abandoned the mountain and drew off entirely behind the Nivelle. Later on he vindicated his position and again occupied the Lesser Rhune, movements that had an important bearing upon the next battle.

Wellington had now entered France, but he was still in the Pyrenees; victory had improved his military situation, but his troops, posted mainly on high bleak mountains, suffered terrible privations. Supplies came up with such difficulty that the men were often half-starved; their clothing was insufficient, and their tents but poor protection against the snow and cold on the hills. Many reasons urged Wellington forward; the politicians were still clamorous for advance, but a stronger argument was the necessities of the troops. The next great effort promised great reward.

"The plains of France, so long overlooked from the towering crags of the Pyrenees, were to be the prize of battle; and the half- famished soldiers in their fury broke through the iron barrier erected by Soult as if it were but a screen of reeds."

For Soult, after the passage of the Bidassoa, was more than ever limited upon a strict defensive, hoping, behind a strong line of fortifications, to revive the spirit of his troops. Since the loss of the Bidassoa he had taken up a more concentrated position between the Nive and the sea, and had strengthened it to the utmost with redoubts and forts and entrenched camps. These formidable works, hardly inferior to Wellington's celebrated lines of Torres Vedras, which had stopped Masséna in Portugal in 1810, had been thrown up with incessant labour and at great expense; they were strongly armed, and held by 60,000 men. To understand the situation and follow the operations on both sides it is once more necessary to examine the positions of the opponents with the aid of the map.

Souk's line of defence was in three great portions, the Right, Centre, and Left, all more or less inter-dependent, although each French commander had a special position assigned to him.

1.—The Right, under Reille, in front of St. Jean de Luz, was nearly impregnable in strong fortifications upon the lower ground, extending from the sea towards Ascain.

2.—The Centre, under Clausel, occupied a range of hills from Ascain to the bridge of Amotz, and as the Nivelle described a great curve behind him, both his flanks rested on that river. In front a brigade held the Lesser Rhune, and another the redoubts of St. Barbe and Grenada, both of which acted as advanced posts, covering his front and his entrenched camp at Sarre.

3.—The left, under D'Erlon, was beyond the Nivelle, on its right or northern bank, and between that river and the Nive, so that his flanks rested also on rivers. His right connected with Clausel at the bridge of Amotz, his left was on the Mondarrain mountain, and in between these he had two lines of defence—the first, and most forward, a continuation of the Mondarrain range; the second was a broad ridge farther to the rear, its right flank at Amotz, where it touched upon Clausel.

Souk's weakest point was at this junction, between D'Erlon and Clausel, and Wellington knew it—knew that from the lie of land it could not be so strongly fortified as the rest of the line; knew, too, that if he could smash in there with considerable numbers he would separate these commanders, turn the right of one, the left of the other, and by the sole direction of this victorious march oblige Reille on the right to retire by taking him in reverse. This was how it struck the great strategist, and his adoption of this, the true line of movement, was no less a mark of his military genius than were his masterly dispositions to give it due effect. Throughout the intricate combinations which followed he showed himself Soult's superior in war, and a most successful exponent of its unalterable principles.

It is a leading axiom in generalship to bring masses to bear on an enemy's fractions; and whenever and wherever the allies had met the French, Wellington had always the advantage of numbers on his side at the decisive point.

All through October the English general had been minded to attack Soult's entrenched camps, which he realised were growing stronger day by day; but want of supplies had delayed him, and then the weather. It was not until the first week of November that he began his movement, by drawing Hill from the right to the centre behind the pass of Maya. It should be mentioned here that, in anticipation of the coming offensive operations, the whole allied force had been organised anew into three great army corps, composed and commanded as follows:—

1.—The Right Corps, under Sir Rowland Hill, with whom were the 2nd and 6th British Divisions, also Morillo's Spaniards, Hamilton's Portuguese, and some light cavalry.

2.—The Centre, under Sir William Beresford, an two bodies—the 3rd, 4th, and 7th Divisions composing the right; while the left was made up of the Light Division, Freyre's and Giron's Spaniards, and the cavalry under Victor Alten.

3.—The Left, under Sir John Hope, consisting mainly of the troops who had forced the lower Bidassoa—namely, the 1st and 5th Divisions, with Aylmer's British and Wilson's Portuguese. Wellington's plan being to thrust in at the centre, as already described, he collected some 40,000 men for the purpose on the night of the 9th November. Hill, with the 2nd and 6th Divisions, was to go against D'Erlon, striking him on his right or inner flank in the direction of Ainhoa and Amotz; Beresford, with the 3rd, 4th, and 7th Divisions and Giron's Spaniards, assembled on the mountains from Zagaramadi to the slopes of the Greater Rhune on the left, was to aim at the entrenched camp of Sarre and press on against Clausel's left, where it was strongly posted in redoubts above Amotz; C. Alten with the Light Division (part of Beresford's corps) were designed to attack Ascain and Clausel's right, and were to be aided therein by the Spanish generals Longa and Freyre. On the far left, beyond the range of the principal engagement, Hope had the less glorious but vitally important *rôle* of occupying Reille and Villatte all day, thus preventing them from working to their left to reinforce Clausel.

The battle began at daylight, when Alten, who had gained his positions during the darkness, sprang forward to assail the Lesser Rhune, the capture of which must necessarily precede any movement against Ascain. The 43rd went forward at a run, but were exhausted before they gained the summit; pausing there to recover breath, they pressed forward and drove all before them. The 52nd next turned the flank of the Rhune, and gained the Star Fort behind. Meanwhile Cole with the 4th Division had advanced with scaling-ladders to the attack of Sarre, which, with the advance redoubt of St. Barbe, was speedily abandoned by the French, and then, the 7th Division joining in, the whole pressed forward against the main position and line of redoubts above. Hill with the 2nd and 6th Divisions, after a difficult night march, neared the enemy about 7 a.m.; the 2nd Division soon drove the French out of Ainhoa, while the 6th Division aimed at D'Erlon's right on the bridge of Amotz. Three divisions in all now attacked D'Erlon in his second and rearmost position, and the defence was but feeble. D'Erlon was, in fact, feeling the pressure of events on the other side of the river, where Clausel's approaching extremity was uncovering and weakening D'Erlon's right. Beresford's 3rd Division, under Colville, had edged away to the right, while the rest assailed the front, and, aiming at Amotz, joined hands with the 6th Division, the two thus forming the wedge thrust in between the French commanders at the most vital and decisive point. Now D'Erlon yielded, and, fearing to be cut off, retreated upon St. Pé, where he was no longer of value in the fight.

But Clausel was not yet beaten, and still showed a bold front. He had two divisions intact: Morransin's, which held fast to the front of the redoubt Louis XIV., but, being attacked in front and flank, was presently hurled headlong down the ravines; Taupin's, still firm on the right. With the latter Clausel essayed to form a new battle around the signal redoubt, and drawing his reserves to him from the right beyond the river. Now Alten with the Light Division, whom we left on the inner slopes of the Lesser Rhune, had shot forward to his front and smote Taupin, who tried to stand; but the Spaniards, under Freyre and Longa, had made an enveloping movement round by Ascain, and the noise of their battle in the rear struck Taupin's men with such panic that many fled. Clausel made a last unsuccessful effort, to withdraw his garrison from the signal redoubt, and then left it to its fate. Through the mistake of a staff officer the 52nd were wasted in useless attacks upon this redoubt, which presently surrendered to Colborne. This was the last hostile act in the fight; the French were in full retreat; and although Soult came up with reserves and tried to rally the fugitives, the victory could no longer be withheld from the allied troops. In the night Soult availed himself of the darkness to draw off Reille from the right, a delicate manoeuvre impossible in daylight, for Hope would have pressed the retreating columns, and Wellington could have struck with effect upon their flank.

The Battle of the Nivelle was, strictly speaking, the last fought among the Pyrenees. It was a decisive defeat, very costly to the enemy, who lost 50 guns, 4,000 killed and wounded, and 1,500 prisoners. On our side there were but 500 killed. No doubt this brilliant result was mainly due to good generalship. Wellington had superior numbers, but he wielded them with superior skill. Yet he was ably seconded by the bravery of his troops; no others would have so easily won works which Soult confidently expected would have repelled them or cost them at least five-and-twenty thousand men to force. As to the French, it was no discredit to troops dispirited by successive disasters that they should be overmastered when both outnumbered and outmanoeuvred.

Other battles were still to be fought, and soon; but they hardly belong to the campaign in the Pyrenees.

Early in December Wellington felt constrained to throw his army across the Nive river, in order to have access to the more fertile country beyond. Hill moved by the fords at Cambo and the bridge at Ustaritz, followed by Beresford; while Hope, still occupying the left, advanced close under the walls of Bayonne. Soult was now well placed in the centre, and could act by the radii of a circle, on the outer circumference of which the allies were distributed at some distance apart. He sought to profit boldly by this advantageous position, and sallied forth in strength to first overwhelm Hope. Foiled in this, after a hard-fought engagement, he turned next upon Hill, whom he hoped to find isolated upon the north of the River Nive. Wellington, anticipating this attack, had sent reinforcements across; but Hill's situation was for a time critical, and he had to stand the shock alone. The Battle of St. Pierre, which he fought and won on the 13th December, was generally agreed by both French and English to have been one of the most desperate in the war.

"Wellington said he had never seen a field so thickly strewn with dead; nor can the vigour of the combatants be well denied, when 5,000 men were killed and wounded in three hours upon a space of one mile."

After this the opposing armies went into winter quarters; the allies occupied cantonments, the French withdrew behind the lines of Bayonne, and nothing of interest occurred till the middle of February, when the spring weather returned.

MARCH 8-9, 1814
Bergen-op-Zoom
Colonel Percy Groves

After the defeat of the French at Leipzig, on the 16th and 18th of October, 1813, and the consequent advance of the allied armies towards the Rhine, the Emperor Napoleon found himself compelled to withdraw a considerable number of his troops from Holland and the Low Countries. Seizing this opportunity, the Dutch resolved to make an attempt to free themselves from the yoke of France; and on the 15th of November the inhabitants of Amsterdam rose *en masse*, with the cry of "*Orange Boven!*" hoisted the Orange flag, and proclaimed the *stadtholder*. The example of the Dutch capital was quickly followed by other towns, and in a few days the long-oppressed Hollanders were in open revolt.

On receiving intelligence of this rising, the British Government decided to afford material assistance to the Dutch, both in asserting their independence and in driving the remainder of the French troops from their country; so an expedition was organised, and several regiments received orders to hold themselves in readiness for immediate embarkation. This expedition, which consisted of some 8,000 men, including three battalions of the Foot Guards, was placed under the command of General Sir Thomas Graham (afterwards Lord Lynedoch), who had just recovered from an illness, on account of which he had been invalided home from the Peninsula.

The Guards' Brigade sailed from Greenwich on the 24th of November, and, disembarking at Scheveling early in December, marched to The Hague. Having seen the Prince of Orange firmly

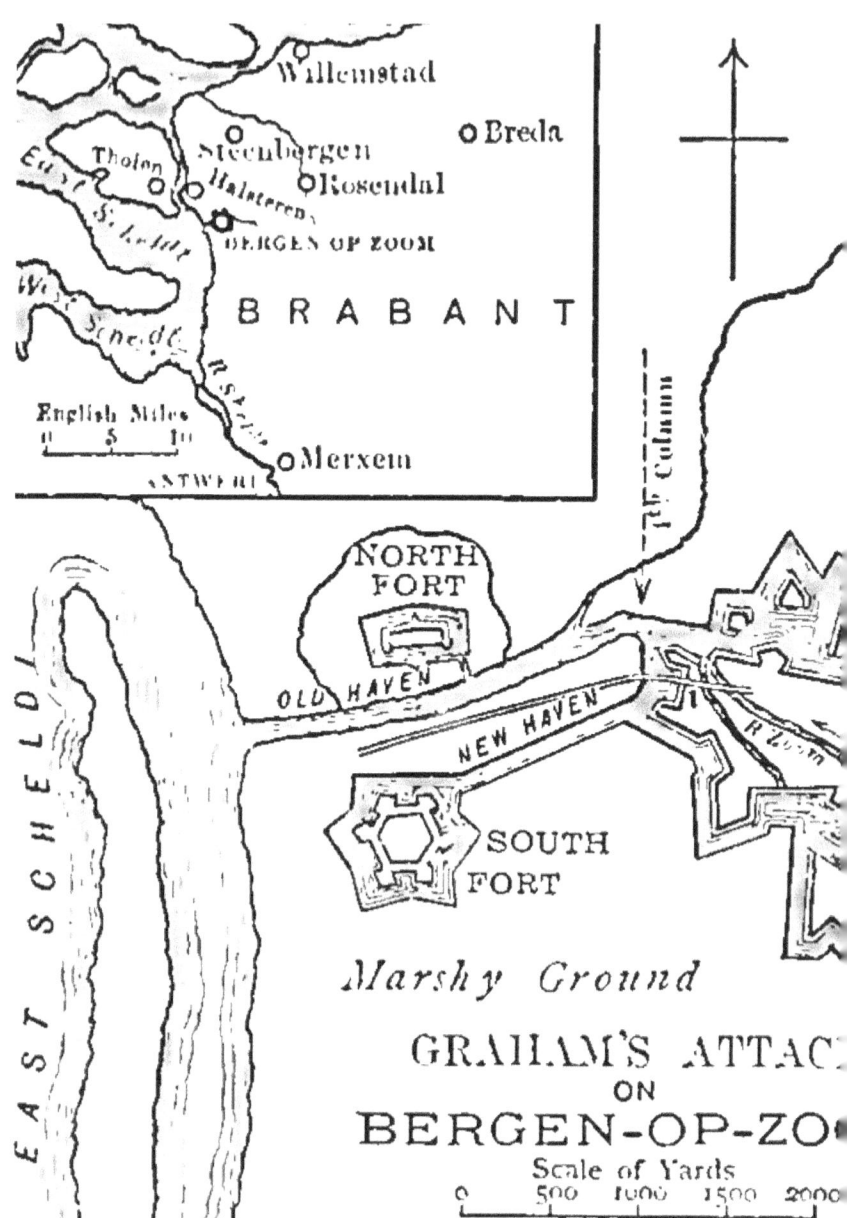

re-established on his throne, the Guards proceeded to Willemstad, and on the 9th of January, 1814, they reached Steenbergen—which lies a few miles north of Bergen-op-Zoom—where Sir Thomas Graham was enabled to effect a junction with the allied troops cantoned on his left at Oudenbosch and Breda. The weather at this

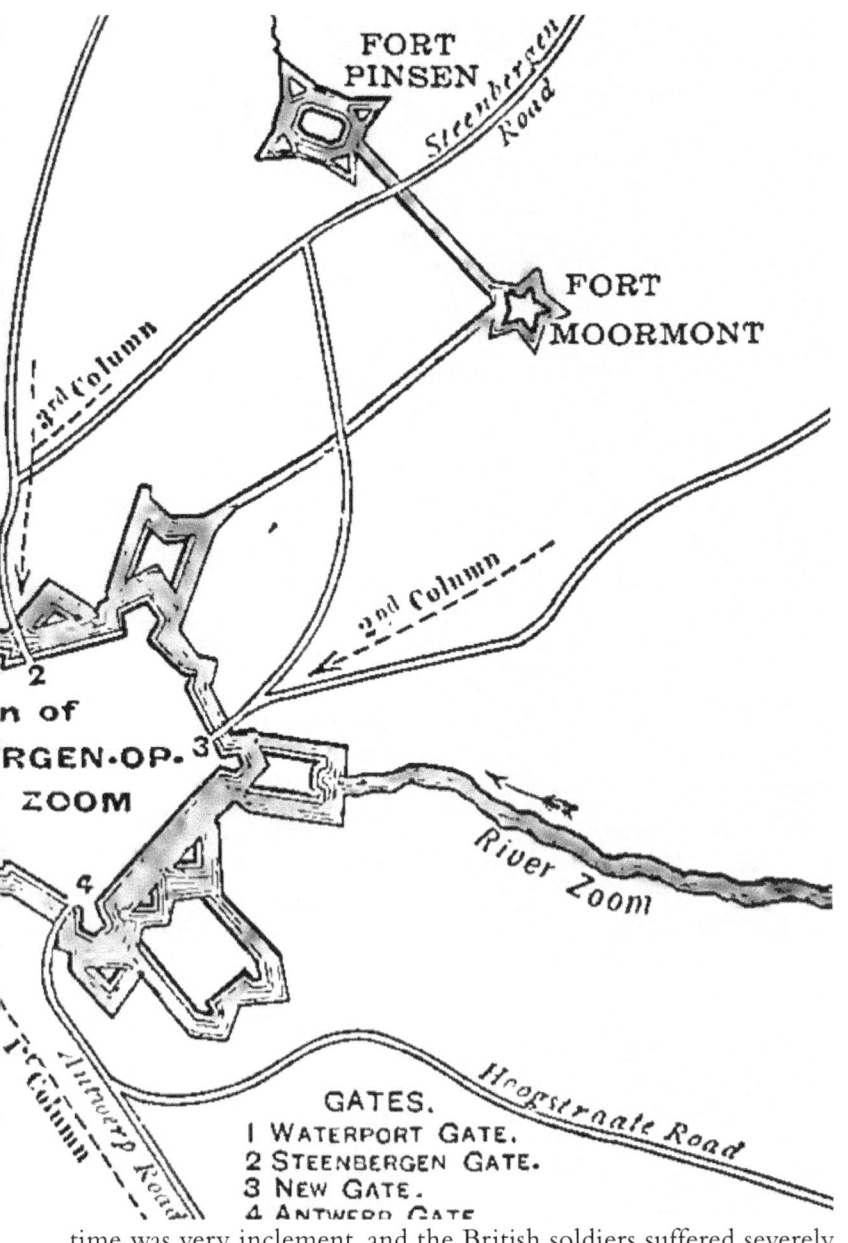

GATES.
1 WATERPORT GATE.
2 STEENBERGEN GATE.
3 NEW GATE.
4 ANTWERP GATE

time was very inclement, and the British soldiers suffered severely from the bitter cold.

Early in January, 1814, the French had assembled all their available forces at Antwerp, and, after various movements, Sir Thomas Graham, in concert with the Prussian general, Bülow, made an attack, on the

2nd of February, on Merxem, with the object of moving against Antwerp. The village of Braachstad was quickly captured, and next day batteries were erected and fire opened; but, unfortunately, the mortars and ammunition, which had been brought from Willemstad, proved so defective that after three days the troops returned to their cantonments. The investment of Antwerp was, however, continued.

While investing Antwerp, General Graham conceived a scheme for carrying, by a *coup de main*, the important fortress-town of Bergen-op-Zoom, which was held by a strong French garrison.

Bergen-op-Zoom, a fortified town of old Dutch Brabant, is situated on the right bank of the Scheldt, and derives its name from the little River Zoom, which, after supplying the defences with water, discharges itself into the Scheldt. It lies some five leagues north of Antwerp, and seven south-west of Breda. The old channel of the Zoom, into which the tide flows towards the centre of the town, forms the harbour, and is nearly dry at low water. There were four principal entrances into the town—three by land, through the Steenbergen Gate in the north face of the fortifications, the Antwerp Gate in the south face, and the New Gate in the east face; and one by a canal—which communicated with the river Scheldt, and, in fact, formed a part of the harbour—through the Waterport Gate, in the west face. The fortress was garrisoned by 5,000 or 6,000 French troops, under command of General Bizonet, a very able officer.

Sir Thomas Graham and his colleagues calculated that the severe frost would prevent the sluices from being used to raise or lower the water, and that the ice in the ditches of the fortress would only be partially broken; so Sir Thomas determined to carry into execution his plan, which was certainly a daring one, and well considered.

Graham's command had recently received reinforcements—including a strong draft for the Guards' Brigade; the 4th Battalion 1st Royal Scots, which had marched from the north of Germany, and was cantoned at Rosendal; and the 2nd Battalion Royal North British Fusiliers, stationed at Tholen.

Having decided on the attack, Sir Thomas lost no time in making the necessary arrangements, and on the 8th of March 4,000 troops were detached from the army investing Antwerp, and marched secretly to the neighbourhood of Bergen-op-Zoom. This force was told off into four "columns of attack," as follows:

1st Column.—Detachments of the Guards' Brigade (1,000), under Colonel Lord Proby, 2nd Battalion 1st Foot Guards.

2nd Column.—33rd (600), 55th (250), and 2nd Battalion 69th Foot[1] (350), under Lieutenant-Colonel Morice, 69th Foot.

3rd Column.—2nd Battalion 21st Fusiliers (100), 37th (150), and 2nd Battalion 91st Foot (400), under Brevet Lieutenant-Colonel Henry, 21st Fusiliers.

4th Column.—Flank Companies of the 21st and 37th (200), 4th Battalion Royal Scots (600), and 2nd Battalion 44th Foot (300), under Brigadier-General Gore and Lieutenant-Colonel the Honourable G. Carleton, accompanied by Major-General Skerrett.

Major-General George Cooke was in supreme command.

The 1st column, led by Cooke, formed the left of the line, and was destined to attack the works between the Waterport and Antwerp Gates. The 2nd column was to attack the right of the New Gate; while the 3rd column made a feint on the Steenbergen Gate, to call off the attention of the enemy from the more serious attacks, and to be disposable according to circumstances. The 4th—or right—column, accompanied by the gallant Skerrett—the former temporary Brigadier of the Guards in the Peninsula—was to force the entrance of the harbour, which was fordable at low water.

A detachment of the Royal Sappers and Miners—about forty men in all—provided with axes, saws, crowbars, and a few scaling-ladders, was distributed between the four columns.

As soon as the 1st (Guards) and 4th columns gained an entrance to the fortress, they were to push along the ramparts, and, having effected a junction, proceed to clear them of the enemy and assist the other attacks.

---

1. The 2nd Battalion 69th Foot.—This battalion was raised in 1803, and disbanded in 1816 or 1817. The 69th is now known as the 2nd Battalion the Welsh Regiment.—The 2nd Battalion 21st Royal North British Fusiliers (now Royal Scots Fusiliers), raised in Ayrshire in 1804, and disbanded in 1816.—The 2nd Battalion 91st Foot, raised in 1804 and disbanded in 1816. The 91st (raised as the 98th) is now styled the "1st Battalion Princess Louise's Argyll and Sutherland Highlanders." The 2nd Battalion 37th Foot (now "1st Battalion Hampshire Regiment"), raised in 1811 and disbanded in 1815-16.—The 4th Battalion 1st Foot, or "Royal Scots," embodied at Hamilton, North Britain, on Christmas Day, 1804, and disbanded at Dover on the 24th of March, 1816. This ancient regiment, which traces its origin to the Scots Guards in the service of the king of France in 882, was in 1684 styled the "Royal Regiment of Foot," and some years later was numbered the 1st of the British Line. In 1812 it was styled the 1st or "Royal Scots," and in 1821 the "Royal Regiment." The designation "Royal Scots" was restored to the regiment in 1871, and it is now known as the "Royal Scots (Lothian Regiment)."—The 2nd Battalion 44th Foot, raised in Ireland in 1803-4, and disbanded at Dover early in 1816. The 44th is now known as the 1st Battalion the Essex Regiment."

Such was the general plan of attack: we shall now see how it was carried out.

The hour for the assault was fixed for 10.30 on the night of the 8th of March, and at that hour the four columns advanced.

We will first follow the movements of the 4th column, of which the following graphic account is given by a subaltern officer of the 21st Fusiliers, who, having missed his own regiment, attached himself to the Royal Scots, and thereby came in for the very hottest of the fighting. This young officer in the *United Service Journal* for 1830 writes:

"We had all become thoroughly sick of the monotony of our duties at Tholen, when we received orders to march the next day (the 8th March, 1814). As the attack on Bergen-op-Zoom which took place that evening was, of course, kept a profound secret, the common opinion was that we were destined for Antwerp, where the other division of the army had already had some fighting.

"It was nearly dark when we arrived at the village of Halsteren, which is only three or four miles from Bergen-op-Zoom, where we took up our quarters for the night. On the distribution of billets to the officers, I received one upon a farmhouse about a mile in the country, where I was presently joined by four or five officers of the 4th Battalion Royal Scots, who told me that they believed an attempt to surprise Bergen-op-Zoom would be made that night.

"Learning from my new acquaintances that the grenadier company of their battalion, which was commanded by an old friend of mine (Lieutenant Allan Robertson) whom I had not seen for some years, was only about a mile further off, I thought I should have time to see him and join my regiment before they marched, should they be sent to the attack. However, the party of the Royal Scots whom I accompanied lost their way from their ignorance of the road, and we in consequence made a long circuit, during which I heard from an *aide-de-camp*, who passed us, that the 21st were on their march to attack the place in another quarter from us.

"In these circumstances I was exceedingly puzzled what course to take: if I went in search of my regiment, I had every chance of missing them in the night, being quite ignorant of the roads. Knowing that the Royal Scots would be likely to head one of the assaulting columns, from the number of the regiment, I took what I thought to be the surest plan, by attaching myself to the grenadier company of the Royal Scots under my gallant friend.

"After mustering the men, we marched to the general *rendezvous* of the regiments forming the 4th column: the Royal Scots led the column, followed by the other regiments according to their number. As everything depended on our taking the enemy by surprise, the strictest orders were given to observe a profound silence on the march.

"When we had proceeded some way we fell in with a picket, commanded by Captain Darrah, of the 21st Fusiliers, who was mustering his men to proceed to the attack. Thinking that our regiment must pass his post on their way to the false attack, he told me to remain with him until they came up. I, in consequence, waited some time, but, hearing nothing of the regiment and losing patience, I gave him the slip in the dark, and ran on until I regained my place with the grenadier company of the Royal Scots."

On nearing the point of attack, the column crossed the Tholendike, and entered the bed of the Zoom, through which our troops had to make their way before reaching the wet ditch. It was terrible work pushing through the thick deep mud of the river: the men sank nearly to their waists, and as they advanced, fell into some confusion—the various companies getting mixed up. Many poor fellows were trodden down and smothered in the mud, but the more fortunate pressed on, and a considerable portion of the column succeeded in passing through this veritable "Slough of Despond," and entered the ditch.

So far the French garrison had not taken alarm, but now some thoughtless men raised a cheer, probably to encourage their comrades. General Skerrett, who was at the head of the column, was furious with rage, and passed word to the rear for strict silence to be observed. Unfortunately, the mischief was done: that one cheer had alarmed the garrison, who at once opened the sluices and sent a torrent of water down upon their assailants, while almost at the same moment a brilliant firework was displayed upon the ramparts, showing up every object as clear as if it were daylight.

In spite of this, General Skerrett, with a good number of his men, cleared the bed of the river, and gained the ditch. The Fusilier officer continues:

"The point at which we entered was a bastion to the right of the harbour, from one of the angles of which a row of high palisades was carried through the ditch. To enable us to pass the water, some scaling-ladders had been sunk to support us in proceeding along the palisades, over which we had to climb with each other's assistance. So great were the obstacles we met with, that had not the attention of the enemy fortunately (or rather most judiciously) been distracted by the false attack under Lieut.-Col. Henry it appeared quite impossible for us to have effected an entrance at this point.

"While we were proceeding forward in this manner. Colonel Muller of the Royal Scots was clambering along the tops of the palisades, calling to those who had got the start of him to endeavour to open the Waterport Gate and let down the drawbridge to our right; but no one, in the hurry of the moment, seemed to hear him. On getting near enough, I told him I should effect it, if it was possible.

"We met with but trifling resistance on gaining the rampart: the enemy being panic struck, fled to the streets and houses in the town, from which they kept up a pretty smart fire upon us for some time. I got about twenty soldiers of different regiments to follow me to the Waterport Gate, which we found closed. It was constructed of thin paling, with an iron bar across it about three inches in breadth. Being without tools of any kind, we made several ineffectual attempts to open the gate: at last, retiring a few paces, we made a rush at it in a body, when the iron bar snapped in the middle like a bit of glass. Some of my people got killed and wounded during this part of the work, but when we got to the drawbridge we were a little more sheltered from the firing.

"The bridge was up, and secured by a lock in the right-hand post of the two which supported it. I was simple enough to attempt to pick the lock with a bayonet, but after breaking two or three, we at last had an axe brought us from the bastion, where our troops were entering. With this axe we soon succeeded in cutting the lock out of the post, and, taking hold of the chain, I had the satisfaction to pull down the drawbridge with my own hands.

"While I was engaged in this business Colonel Muller was forming the Royal Scots on the rampart where we entered; but a party of about one hundred and fifty men of different regiments, under General Skerrett—who must have entered to the left of the harbour—was clearing the ramparts towards the Steenbergen Gate, where the false attack had been made by the 3rd column under Lieut.-Col. Henry; while another party, under Colonel Carleton of the 44th Regiment, was proceeding in the opposite direction along the ramparts to the right, without meeting with much resistance.

"Hearing the firing on the opposite side of the town from General Skerrett's party, and supposing that they had marched through the town, I ran on through the streets to overtake them, accompanied by only one or two men; for the rest had left me and returned to the

bastion after we had opened the gate. In proceeding along the canal or harbour which divided this part of the town I came to a loopholed wall, which was continued from the houses down to the water's edge. I observed a party of soldiers within a gate in this wall, and was going up to them, taking them for our own people, when I was challenged in French, and had two or three shots fired at me. Seeing no other way of crossing the harbour but by a little bridge which was nearly in a line with the wall, I returned to the Waterport Gate which I found

Colonel Muller had taken possession of with two or three companies of his regiment. I went up to him, and told him that I had opened the gate according to his desire, and also informed him of the interruption I had met with in the town, and he sent one of his companies up with me to the wall already mentioned, ordering the officer in command of the company to drive the enemy away, and hold the wall and gate until further orders.

"On coming to the gate we met with a sharp resistance, but, after tiring a few rounds and preparing to charge, the Frenchmen gave way, leaving us in possession of the gate and bridge. Leaving the company here, and crossing the little bridge, I again set forward alone to overtake General Skerrett's party, guided by the firing on the ramparts. Avoiding any little parties of the enemy, I had reached the inside of the ramparts where the firing was, without its occurring to me that I might get into the wrong box and be taken prisoner. Fortunately, I observed a woman looking over a shop door on one side of the street. I asked her where the British soldiers were, and she told me without hesitation, pointing at the same time in the direction. I shook hands with her, and bade her 'good night,' not entertaining the smallest suspicion of her deceiving me; and, following her directions, I clambered up the inside of the rampart and joined General Skerrett's party.

"The moon had now risen, and though the sky was cloudy we could see pretty well what was doing. Here I found my friend Robertson, with the grenadier company of the Royal Scots, and I learned from him that the party—which was now commanded by Captain Guthrie, of the 33rd Regiment—had been compelled by numbers to retire from the bastion, which the enemy now occupied; and that Guthrie intended to endeavour to hold the one he was now in possession of, until he could procure a reinforcement. Robertson also told me that General Skerrett had been dangerously wounded, and taken prisoner, which was an irreparable loss to our party, as Captain Guthrie was ignorant of the general's intentions.

"In the meantime the enemy kept up a sharp fire on us, which we returned as fast as our men could load their firelocks. Several of the enemy who had fallen, as well as of our own men, were lying on the ramparts. We presently discovered a large pile of logs of wood on the ramparts, and these we quickly disposed across the gorge of the bastion, so as to form a kind of parapet over which our people could fire, leaving, however, about half the distance open towards the parapet of the rampart. On the opposite side of the bastion were two 24-pounders, raised on high platforms, and these guns we turned on the enemy, firing along the ramparts over the heads of our own party. But, however valuable this resource might be to us, we were still far from being on equal terms with the French, who, besides greatly exceeding us in numbers, had brought up two or three field-pieces, which annoyed us much during the night. There was also a windmill on the bastion the Frenchmen occupied, from the top of which their musketry did great execution among us.

"In the course of the night the enemy made several ineffectual attempts to drive us from our position; but on these occasions—of which we were always made aware by the shouts they raised to encourage each other—as soon as they made their appearance on the rampart, we gave them a good dose of grape from our 24-pounders, and had a party ready to charge them back. I observed our soldiers were always disposed to meet the enemy halfway, and the latter were soon so well aware of our humour, that they invariably turned tail before we could get within forty or fifty paces of them.

"The firing was kept up almost continually on both sides until about two o'clock in the morning, when it would sometimes cease for more than half-an-hour together. During one of these intervals of stillness, being exhausted with our exertions and the cold we felt in our drenched clothes, some of us lay down along the parapet together, in hopes of borrowing a little heat from each other, and presently fell into a troubled, dozing state, when I suddenly felt the ground shake under me, and heard at the same time a crash as if the whole town had been overwhelmed by an earthquake; a bright glare of light burst on my eyes at the same instant, and almost blinded me.

"A shot from the enemy had blown up our small magazine on the ramparts, on which we depended for the supply of the two 24-pounders which had been of such material use to us during the night. This broke our slumbers most effectually, and we had now nothing for it but to maintain our ground in the best way we could, until we received a reinforcement from some of the other parties.

"Immediately after this disaster the enemy, raising a tremendous shout, or rather yell, attempted to come to close quarters with us, in hopes of our being utterly disheartened; but our charging party, which we had always in readiness, made them wheel round as usual. In the course of the night we had sent several small parties of men to represent the state of our detachment and endeavour to procure assistance; but none of them returned, having, we supposed, been intercepted by

the enemy. Discouraged though we were by this circumstance, we still continued to hold our ground until the break of day."

While the events described in the above narrative were taking place, the main portion of the 4th column had also met with disaster: after all their toil and gallantry, the Royal Scots and their comrades of the 33rd—which regiment had been sent to reinforce Colonel Muller during the night—saw the prize which they had gained at such frightful cost snatched from their grasp.

We have already seen how Colonel Muller, with the battalion companies of the Royal Scots, took possession of the ramparts round the Waterport Gate. Before very long the battalion found itself exposed to a murderous grape and musketry fire from a couple of howitzers, and a small detachment of French marines stationed in the vicinity of the arsenal. Colonel Muller at once detached two companies to keep the enemy in check, and these detached companies—which were relieved every two hours—were actively engaged in this arduous service from 11 p.m. until daybreak, when the enemy made a furious attack in strong columns which bore down all before them.

The detached companies were now quickly driven in by overwhelming numbers, while the battalion, being exposed to a terrible fire from the guns of the arsenal, was forced to retire by the Waterport Gate, only to receive the fire of a detached battery. Finding himself thus placed between two fires, with a high palisade on one hand and the Zoom filled with tide on the other, Colonel Muller preferred to surrender rather than throw away the lives of his soldiers. The colours of the battalion were first sunk in the River Zoom by Lieutenant and Adjutant Galbraith; the battalion then surrendered, on condition that the officers and men should not serve against the French until exchanged, and on the following day it marched out of Bergen-op-Zoom "with all the honours of war."

In this disastrous affair the 4th Battalion Royal Scots lost 4 officers and 37 non-commissioned officers and men killed; 4 officers and 71 non-commissioned officers and men wounded.

The 33rd also suffered severe losses.

******

We left the small party, under Captain Guthrie of the 33rd, holding the position they had so gallantly won, and hoping against hope that, sooner or later, they would be relieved from the terrible predicament in which they found themselves; but the first dawn of day plainly showed the devoted men the utter hopelessness of their situation. By this time the firing had entirely ceased in other parts of Bergen-op-Zoom, and so, in absence of all communication, Guthrie and his comrades could only believe that the British troops had been driven from the place, and that there was nothing for them but to surrender, or die where they stood. The former alternative, however, does not appear to have entered their minds. The French now brought an overwhelming force against them, but they still hoped, from the narrowness of the rampart, to be able to hold their own. In this they were deceived. The bastion was extensive, but only that portion of it near the gorge was furnished with a parapet. At this spot, and behind the logs which Guthrie and his men had piled up, the now greatly diminished party was collected. Keeping up a hot fire, in order to divert attention, the French detached part of their force, which, skirting the outside of the ramparts, and ascending the face of the bastion occupied by Guthrie, suddenly opened a murderous fire on his left flank and rear. From this fire Guthrie's men were entirely unprotected, while the French were sheltered by the top of the rampart. Lieutenant —— continues:

"The slaughter was now dreadful, and our poor fellows, who had done all that soldiers could do in our trying situation, fell thick and fast. Just at this time my friend Robertson, under whose command I had put myself at the beginning of the attack, fell. I had just time to run up to him, and found him stunned from a wound in the head, when our gallant commander, seeing the inutility of continuing the unequal contest, gave the order to retreat.

"We had retired in good order about three hundred yards when poor Guthrie received a wound in the head, which I have since been informed deprived him of his sight. The enemy, when they saw us retreating, hung upon our rear, keeping up a sharp fire all the time, but they still seemed to have some respect for us from the trouble we had already given them. We had indulged the hope that, by continuing our course along the ramparts, we should be able to effect our retreat by the Waterport Gate, not being aware that we should be intercepted by the mouth of the harbour, and we were already at the very margin before we discovered our mistake and found ourselves completely hemmed in by the French; so there was no alternative left to us but to surrender as prisoners of war, or to attempt to escape across the harbour by means of the floating pieces of ice with which the water was covered.

"Not one of us seemed to entertain the idea of surrender, and in the despair which had now taken possession of every heart we threw ourselves into the water, or leaped for the broken pieces of ice which were floating about.

"The scene that ensued was shocking beyond description! The canal, or harbour, was faced on both sides by high brick walls, and in the middle of the channel lay a small Dutch vessel, which was secured by a rope to the opposite side of the harbour. Our only hope of preserving our lives, or effecting our escape, depended on our being able to gain this little vessel. Already many had, by leaping first on one piece of ice and then on another, succeeded in getting on board the vessel, which they hauled, by means of the rope, to the opposite side of the canal, and thus freed our obstruction; but, immediately afterwards being intercepted by the Waterport redoubt, they were compelled to surrender. Among the rest, I had scrambled down the face of the canal to a beam, running horizontally along the brick-work, from which other beams descended perpendicularly into the water, to prevent the sides being injured by the shipping. After sticking my sword into my belt (for I had ' thrown the scabbard away the previous night), I leaped from this beam—which was nine or ten feet above the water—for a piece of ice, but, not judging my distance very well, it tilted up with me, and I sank to the bottom of the canal.

"However, I soon came up again, and after swimming to the other side of the canal, and to the vessel, and finding nothing to catch hold of, I returned to the piece of ice upon which I had first leapt, and, swinging my body under it, managed to keep my face above water. I was not the only survivor of those who had got into the water: several men were still hanging on to other pieces of ice, but one by one they let go their hold and sank as their strength failed, until only three or four, besides myself, remained. All this time some of the enemy continued firing at us, and I saw one or two poor fellows shot in the water near me.

"So intent was everyone on effecting his escape, that though they sometimes cast a look of commiseration at their drowning comrades, no one thought for a moment of giving us any assistance. The very hope of it had at length so completely faded in our minds that we ceased to ask the aid of those who floated past us upon fragments of ice; but Providence had reserved one individual who possessed a heart to feel for the distress of his fellow-creatures more than for his own personal safety. The very last person who reached the Dutch vessel was Lieut. McDougal of the 91st Regiment, and by his assistance I, too, succeeded in getting on board.

"While assisting McDougal to save two or three soldiers who still clung to pieces of ice, I received a musket-ball through my wrist; for the enemy continued deliberately firing at us from the opposite rampart, which was not above sixty yards from the vessel. After this I went down to the cabin, where I found Lieut. Briggs of the 91st[2] sitting on one side with a severe wound through his shoulder-blade. The floor of the cabin was covered with water, for the vessel had become leaky from the firing. I managed to bind up my wounded wrist with my neckcloth so as in some measure to stop the bleeding, and we remained, cold and miserable, in the cabin for several hours. During that time the water continued to rise higher and higher, until it reached my middle.

"Fortunately, the vessel grounded from the receding of the tide, and, escape in our condition being now quite out of the question, my companion and I were glad, on the whole, to be relieved from our truly disagreeable position by surrendering ourselves prisoners of war." [3]

---

2. Lieutenant James Briggs, 91st (afterwards Major Sir James Briggs, K.H.) exchanged to the 63rd Foot, and retired in 1837. He was reported killed.
3. The officer who wrote the above narrative was taken to a hospital in the town, where his wounds were dressed. He was subsequently released, and rejoined the 2nd Battalion 21st Fusiliers at Wouw. We cannot, with any certainty, identify this officer; but as only two subalterns of the 21st appear in the casualty list as wounded and taken prisoners at Bergen-op-Zoom, he must have been one of the two—namely, 2nd Lieut. J. W. Dunbar Moody, or 2nd Lieut. David Rankine. The 21st lost nine officers killed, wounded and missing, including Brevet Lieut.-Col. Henry, who commanded the 3rd column.

******

Having described the disasters which befell the 4th column, we will now turn to the movements of the 1st, 2nd, and 3rd columns, whose efforts, unfortunately, met with no better success.

The 1st, or Guards, column, under Colonel Lord Proby, was, as we have already stated, destined to attack the works between the Waterport and Antwerp Gates. Between the point of attack and the Antwerp Gate the enemy had a strongly entrenched camp. At the appointed hour the Guardsmen, accompanied by Major-General Cooke, advanced from the Antwerp road, and, skirting the salient of the *lunette* of the entrenched camp, they reached the broad wet ditch of the unrevetted fronts (between the Waterport Gate and the *lunette*)

without being discovered by the enemy. So far all had gone well; but now it was found that, owing to the rise and fall of the tide, the ice at the point where the ditch was to have been crossed was not sufficiently thick to stand the passage of the column. Lord Proby at once reported this untoward circumstance to General Cooke, who ordered him to move his men more to the right, towards the ditch of the "Orange Bastion," where a *batardeau*, preventing the action of the tide, allowed the ice to form strong enough to support them.

This spot reached, the advanced and ladder parties of the Guards, under Captain Rodney and Ensigns Gooch and Pardoe, quickly crossed the frozen ditch, followed by the rest of the column. Under the direction of Lieutenant-Colonel Smyth, R.E., and Captain Sir G. Hoste, the ladders were placed against the *demi-revetment* (seventeen feet high), and the Guardsmen, swarming up, gained possession of the ramparts without meeting with much opposition beyond a slight musketry fire from the flanks. Major-General Cooke, with the officers commanding Royal Artillery and Engineers, entered the place with the Guards.

Owing to the delay caused by the unavoidable change in the point of attack, it was 11.30 p.m. before the 1st column established itself on the ramparts of Bergen-op-Zoom.

Though surprised by the first assault, the French garrison was not thrown into confusion, and was soon again in a position to resist the British troops.

Suspecting from the quiet that reigned at the French posts opposite the other intended points of attack that the several columns had not yet entered, Cooke formed the Guards on the ramparts in column of sections, and also occupied some houses in front, and in the adjoining bastion, from which his men might otherwise have been seriously annoyed. The ladders by which the Guards had entered were left standing against the scarp, so that a ready communication with the exterior was ensured.

A strong patrol was now despatched to the left, towards the Waterport Gate, to ascertain whether the 4th column had entered; and a detachment of the 1st Foot Guards, under Lieut.-Col. Clifton, was sent along the ramparts to the right, with orders to secure the Antwerp Gate, and to support, or at least gain some intelligence of, the 2nd column under Lieut.-Col. Morrice. General Cooke in his despatch of the 10th March, 1814, writes:

"Lieut.-Col. Clifton reached the Antwerp Gate, but found that it

could not be opened by his men, the enemy throwing a very heavy fire upon a street leading to it. It was also found that they occupied an outwork commanding the bridge, which would effectually render that outlet useless to us. I heard nothing more of this detach-

ment, but considered it as lost, the communication having been interrupted by the enemy. Lieut.-Col. Rooke, with a party of the 2nd Foot Guards, was afterwards sent in that direction, and driving the enemy from the intermediate rampart, reached the Antwerp Gate;

but he found it useless to attempt anything, and ascertained that the outwork was still occupied."

Rooke was thus compelled to rejoin the main body of the column, after his party had been pretty severely handled, without having gleaned any tidings of the missing detachment, whose fate, as we shall see, was learned later on.

After making a most gallant charge on the enemy, and capturing a field-piece at the point of the bayonet. Colonel Clifton and his men had found themselves cut off by a very superior force. The Guardsmen offered a most determined resistance, but being exposed to a destructive fire on all sides, which placed many officers (including Clifton himself) and men hors dc combat, they were at length obliged to surrender. Amongst the officers taken prisoner was Lieut.-Col. Jones, upon whom the command of the ill-fated detachment devolved after the gallant Clifton's fall.

While the Guards were engaged in their attack the 2nd column had made an unsuccessful attempt on the works to the right of the New Gate, in which it lost upwards of 200 men killed and wounded, including its leader, Lieut.-Col. Morrice, and Lieut.-Col. Elphinstone, of the 33rd Foot.

The 33rd, 55th, and 69th were driven back in some confusion, but they quickly re-formed, and, leaving the left wing of the 55th to remove their wounded, they moved off to the support of the 1st column. It will be remembered that the scaling-ladders used by the 1st column had been left in position, and by this means the men of the 33rd, 55th, and 69th gained the summit of the ramparts, joined the 1st column, and were formed up to the left of the Guards, who still held their position, though they had for hours been exposed to a galling fire from those houses which still remained in possession of the enemy.

Though thus reinforced. General Cooke—who was still uncertain as to how matters were going on in other quarters of the town—did not think it expedient to make any further attempts to carry points which he might not be able to maintain, or to expose his troops to certain loss by penetrating through the streets; but on receiving intelligence that Colonel Muller was holding the Waterport Gate against heavy odds, he sent the 33rd to his assistance.

Throughout that long night the French garrison kept up a hot fire upon General Cooke's position, and at one time they held an adjoining bastion, from the angle of which they completely commanded his communication with the exterior. They were, however, charged, and driven away from this point of vantage in a very spirited style by the 55th and 69th, under Majors Hogg and Muttlebury.

At length, finding that matters were becoming serious, and being still without any certain information from other quarters, General Cooke determined, at the suggestion of Lord Proby, to let part of the Foot Guards withdraw, which was done by means of the ladders at the point where they entered. At daybreak, the enemy again possessed themselves of the bastion commanding the communications, from which they were again driven by Hogg and Muttlebury with their weak battalions. About 6 a.m. the enemy directed their first attack in force upon the British troops holding the Waterport Gate, and General Cooke had now the mortification of witnessing the Royal Scots and the 33rd retire from that position without being able to render them any assistance. At the same time the French gunners opened a heavy cannonade upon the Guards and the 55th and 69th, who still remained on the open ramparts.

Seeing that all was lost. General Cooke ordered the rest of the Guards to retire. The retreat was conducted in the most orderly manner, covered by the 69th and 55th; the latter corps, led by the general in person, repeatedly driving the enemy back. These weak battalions as they crossed the ditch were so much exposed to an incessant concentrated fire of musketry and artillery, that the general saw it would be impossible to withdraw them; and he was contemplating a surrender, when Lieut.-Col. Jones, of the 1st Foot Guards—who had been taken prisoner after the destruction of Clifton's detachment—arrived on the scene, accompanied by a French officer, with a flag of truce. Cooke, in his despatch says:

"Lieut.-Col. Jones informed me that Lieut.-Col. Muller and the troops at the Waterport Gate had been obliged to surrender, and were marched prisoners into the town. I now also learnt the fate of Lieut.-Col. Clifton's detachment and of Major-Generals Skerrett and Gore and Lieut.-Col. Carleton (Major-General Skerrett was dangerously wounded; Brigadier-General Gore, of the 33rd, and Lieut.-Col. the Hon. G. Carleton, of the 44th, were killed); and that the troops who had followed them had suffered very much, and had been repulsed from the advanced points along the ramparts, where they had penetrated to. I was now convinced that a longer continuance of the contest would be a useless loss of lives, and I therefore consented to adopt the mortifying alternative of laying down our arms."

It is strange that no mention is made in the despatches of either Generals Graham or Cooke of the movements of the 3rd column, and we can find no details of the part it played in the attack—beyond the fact that it made a feint on the Steenbergen Gate. Whether Lieut.-Col. Henry turned this false attack into a real one. or whether he joined the 4th column, we cannot say for certain; but it is evident that the 3rd column entered Bergen-op-Zoom, and was hotly engaged, for Lieut.-Col. Henry and his second- in-command, Lieut.-Col. Ottley, were both wounded, and the corps (21st, 37th, and 91st), composing the column, suffered heavy losses.

The total loss of the British in this disastrous affair was about 300 killed and 1,800 prisoners, many of the latter being wounded.

******

Thus ended the memorable attack upon Bergen-op-Zoom, in which, though defeated, the troops engaged were not disgraced. The failure of the enterprise was due, in a great measure, to circumstances over which General Cooke had no control: unforeseen difficulties cropped up which would have tended to frustrate the very best concerted plan of operations; and however much the disastrous termination was deplored, it was freely acknowledged that there had been few occasions during the long war with France in which the courage and energies of British soldiers were put to a more severe test, or were met by a more gallant and successful resistance on the part of the enemy.

1814-16
The Gurkha War

Lieutenant-Colonel Newnham-Davies

The thunders of the cannon of Waterloo were in the ears of Englishmen when Ochterlony beat to their knees the pluckiest soldiers in Asia. In the supreme excitements of Napoleon's struggle and overthrow and the great game of "grab" that followed afterwards at Paris, men had scarcely time or patience to follow the fortunes of the armies which on the north-eastern frontier of India, in one of the most difficult countries in the world, faced by the bravest hill-warriors who ever crossed steel with us, and dogged by the deadly Terai fever, won a great stretch of country for India and changed the fiercest of enemies into the staunchest of friends. Whenever and wherever in our Asiatic wars the stress has been greatest, whenever the bugles have shrilled for some desperate charge, side by side and shoulder to shoulder with the British soldiers rejoicing in the joy of battle, the little Gurkhas have charged with our men.

On the eastern shoulder of India the long line of the Himalayan snows—those peaks that are giants amongst the mountains of the world—thrust up their white towers and pinnacles to the sky; and from this great barrier ridge after ridge of smaller mountains dip to the *dhuns*—fertile valleys that lie between the Himalayan foot-hills and an outer barrier of hill, known as the Sandstone range to the south and the Suwaliks further north. Between this outer barrier, through the ravines of which come tearing down the mountain-rivers, and the broad sun-kissed plains of India lies the slope of the Terai, a great grass jungle where it touches the plains—the finest tiger-preserve in the world—and, towards the line of hills, a forest of great trees, where the

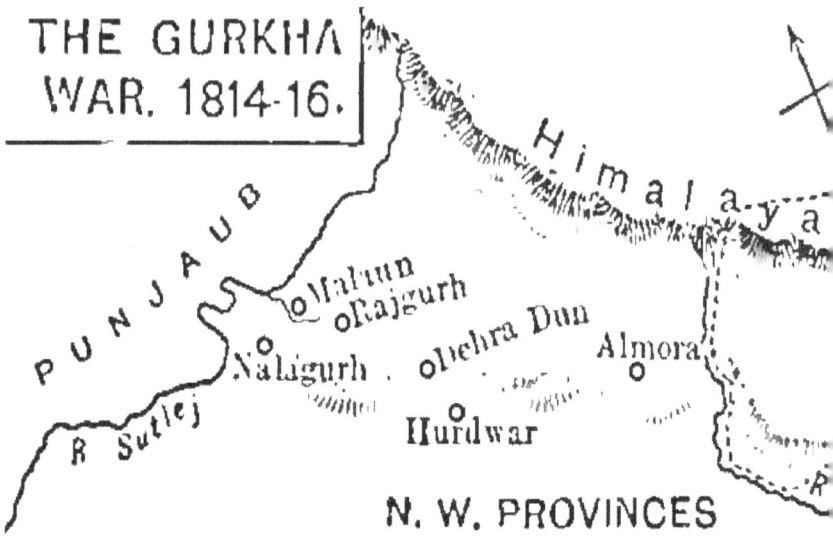

trunks are so close to each other that the foliage closes overhead and the glades are as dim as the aisle of a great cathedral; where the foot of the traveller sinks deep into the cushion of decaying leaves; where the song of a bird is never heard. It is a silent forest, a dread place where in the hot months a fever almost as deadly as a cobra's bite claims as a victim anyone who sleeps in its shade.

From where the Sarda foams round its rocks, rushing from the snows to join the mighty Gogra, to Darjeeling, the British hill-station that looks across the deep valley to the great peak of Kinchinjunga, towering in mid-air, is now the kingdom of Nipal—*terai* and *dhun* and mountain; but when the British bayonets clashed with the Gurkha *kukris* the conquering Nipalese generals had won a broader stretch and held the mountain land as far north as the Sutlej.

Nipal is the hermit kingdom of the world. The great ones of the European world who travel in India in the cold weather are asked as the guests of the king of Nipal to shoot tigers in the *terai*, and at Khatmandu, the capital, a British Resident, like a caged bird, is held in his walks and rides to the limits of the valley; but, excepting the resident and his suite and occasional visitors to the capital, who are allowed to journey by one path only, no white man passes that first barrier of sandstone hills.

But every year in the spring the little Gurkhas, the Nipalese hillmen—jovial little fellows, broad-chested, and big-limbed, short in stature, with Tartar eyes, noses like pug-dogs, and great good-natured

gashes for mouths—flock down to enlist in our regiments. Brave as lions, vain as peacocks, faithful as dogs, with few prejudices in peace and none in war, the Gurkhas are the special friends and companions of our men. The stately Sikh throws away his food if a white man's shadow falls on it, and between Mohammedan and Christian is always the bar of religion; but on a campaign the Gurkha eats his food with as few formalities as Tommy Atkins, drinks his rum, and is good company at the camp fire.

When Captain Younghusband, travelling on the Pamirs with an escort of Gurkhas, met the giant Russian explorer, Gromchefski, the native officer of the little men asked leave to speak to Younghusband. "Tell him," he said, pointing to the big Russian, "that though we are small men, all the rest of the regiment are taller than he is." When, after the assault of Bhurtpore, where the Gurkhas raced with the grenadiers of the 59th for the breach, the British soldiers praised them for their bravery, they returned the compliment by the following characteristic remark:—"The English are as brave as lions; they are splendid *sepoys* and *very nearly* equal to us."

Those are examples of the vanity of the little men. The mutiny, the Ambeyla campaign, every frontier expedition, have proved their loyalty and gallantry, and when Lord Roberts, the hero of Cabul, had to choose "supporters" for his arms, he placed on one side a private of the Highlanders, on the other a Gurkha *sepoy*.

But if we are brothers and friends now with the Nipalese, it was not until after a tremendous bout of fisticuffs that we became so, and so well did the Gurkhas hold their own that they very nearly brought down on us all the great disaffected princes of India.

The Nipalese highlanders, the men of the Gurkha kingdom, a nation of conquerors, looked down from their hills on to the Indian plains, and, conscious of their own strength, longed to try their mettle against the army of India. The cause for a war was soon found. There were some lowlands in dispute. We established police posts to protect our rights, and the Gurkhas came down and murdered our officials and policemen. Lord Hastings, the governor-general, declared war in the autumn of 1814, the beginning of the cold season. Both sides knew exactly what was coming, and both were prepared.

In the sea of razor-backed hills and single peaks, west of what is now the summer capital of India—Simla—Umar Sing, the best general of Nipal, had his troops. It was the northernmost portion of the Nipalese kingdom, a country of great grassy slopes of a marvellous steepness with rocks breaking through the grass and here and there broad patches of treacherous shale, with on the sheltered slopes stretches of forest, and, where the streams race down the hillside and tumble in cascades over the rocks, strips of undergrowth like an English copse.

A strangely mixed array Umar Sing had under him, long-nosed Brahmins as well as the pug-nosed little Gurungs and Magars, men in scarlet coats of the cut of those of our infantry and turbans, men in their loose native garb with the little lop-sided cap that is character-

istic of Nipal, but all armed with firelocks which put them nearly on an equality with our troops, and with that deadliest of weapons the *kukri*, the blade of which looks like a crooked laurel-leaf, all fighting on familiar ground, all intensely patriotic.

Opposite to him, with six thousand men—all natives, except the artillery—was General Ochterlony, the man of the campaign.

"Ould Maloney," as the Irish soldiers used to call him—"*Loniata*," as the natives jumbled his name—had behind him in his career the bad dream of Carnatic prisons, had been most desperately wounded, had in a memorable siege thrust back Holkar from the walls of Delhi, and, now seeing further with his one eye, so the men said, than any other general in India, cautious when generalship and not the mettle of his troops had to win the day, splendidly audacious when rashness was necessary and he had tried troops under him, "Ould Maloney," with his sepoys of the plains, was going to try conclusions with the best fighting hillmen of the East.

Further south, facing the hills where the lightest-hearted of the Anglo-Indian world now dance and flirt at Missouri, was Gillespie, as daring a man as ever wore the British scarlet, with Her Majesty's 53rd, some dismounted dragoons, some artillery, and 2,500 native infantry. Bulbudhur Sing, Umar's best lieutenant, was in the hills with 600 men waiting for the hot-headed soldier who, single-handed, had galloped a few years before to help the besieged residents of Vellore.

Further south again, facing the passes which lead to the richest towns and most productive country of Central Nipal, was Major-General John Sullivan Wood with her Majesty's 17th and 3,000 natives; and further south still, threatening the passes which lead to the capital—Khatmandu—was Major-General Marley with a force of 8,000 *sepoys*, stiffened by Her Majesty's 24th.

Ochterlony and Gillespie were to open the ball, and Wood and Marley were to thrust their forces through the passes later on.

Gillespie, with characteristic hot-headedness, was going to be first in the race. Lord Hastings had warned the handsome devil-may-care soldier against knocking his head against fortifications when there were Gurkhas behind them; but Gillespie believed in dash, and the Indian army was used to victory, so he disregarded the governor-general's little lecture, and made his rush forward. He seized a pass in the first range, the Suwaliks, pushed through the valley beyond, the Dehra Dun, and occupied the little town of Dehra at the foot of the first slopes of the Himalayas.

On a hill thrown out from the higher slope, some five miles from Dehra, was a stone fort. It was of the simplest type, four stout stone walls, loopholed, with here and there towers to give flanking fire. It stood some 600 feet above the ground that sloped up to the first rise of the hills and commanded the path up which Gillespie intended to take his men into the higher mountains.

Bulbudhur Sing with his 600 men waited here for Gillespie's advance, strengthening the primitive fort by outside stockades.

Gillespie was only too anxious to try conclusions with the Gurkhas and their leader; so, after reconnoitring the position, he made his scheme for an attack on the last day of October. Four columns were to make the attack on the little fort, which was first to be battered by field-pieces to prepare for the assault. The field-pieces were carried up in the darkness by elephants to a little table-land which commanded the fort and was within range, the four attacking columns, each with a company of the 53rd to lead, were in position, and as soon after 10 o'clock as the guns had done their work, a signal given by gunfire was to set all four columns racing up the hill at once.

Gillespie, impatient and hot-headed, stood by the guns, and watched the shot striking the thick stone walls and making no impression. The little brown faces of the enemy looked through the embrasures and laughed at him; some of them danced on the tops of the walls. The general grew angry, angry at the futile cannonade and the mocking enemy. His men lying all round, close against the lower slopes, had scaling-ladders, then let them use them! And so, an hour before the time fixed, the gun signal for an attack was given. Only one of the waiting columns heard the signal and acted on it, though another followed later. Up the steep grass slope went the company of the 53rd that led, slipping and scrambling, the pioneers who carried the scaling-ladders tugging desperately at the heavy weights. A hail of lead came from the loopholes that had framed the little grinning faces, and by mischance the pioneers stumbled into the shelters of dry grass under which the Gurkha garrison slept. The grass took light, and the pioneers to save themselves dropped the ladders. A flaming hillside, a hail of lead, no ladders, the assailants had no chance, and the first column and the second, which had begun its advance, slid back down the slippery hillside to shelter leaving many red-coats lying on the slope.

The general's blood was up. Three more companies of the 53rd had come up, and a battery of the Bengal Horse Artillery. He ordered a second assault and determined to lead it in person.

In the rear face of the fort there was a little door, and Gillespie intended to be the first man in through that. The 53rd out their backs to the work and hauled up two of the galloper-guns by drag-ropes on to the ridge at the back of the fort, a light stockade that barred the way was hacked at and kicked and shaken till it gave way, and the two guns were brought close to the door. The general, with some dismounted dragoons about him and the 53rd crowding behind, went with the guns, while the other columns again started up the slopes.

The light guns fired a couple of rounds at the stoutly-barred door and did not shake it, and from the walls and loopholes came a blaze of fire in response. The general fell shot dead, the bullets ploughed into

the closely-packed mass, and when the attack had definitely failed, as it did, the British carried out of action 4 officers and 29 men killed, and 15 officers and 213 men wounded. First blood to the Gurkhas.

Meanwhile, Ochterlony was making his way into the hills, but with all requisite caution. Passing without difficulty the outer range of hills, which here are small and have many gaps in the chain, he encamped at Plassea, facing the Himalayan foot-hills. The mountain country into which he had to win his way is a series of broken ridges running north-north-west, and each ridge forms a strong position.

On the outermost ridge was the fort of Nalagur—a stout stone fort with towers for flanking fire, and its outpost, the little square fort of Taraghur. The slope of this outside ridge was covered with bamboos and thorny shrubs, and the only paths up were along the stony beds of dried-up torrents.

Behind the first ridge was the Ramghur ridge, crowned with stone forts, and behind that again towered the Malaun heights.

A corps of reserve of the light companies of the different battalions, and the 3rd Native Infantry, under Colonel Thompson, cut off the communication between the fort and the outpost, and Ochterlony occupying all the surrounding heights got his guns with infinite difficulty into position, and battered away at the stone walls of the fort. The Gurkhas had only *jingals*—throwing balls of three or four ounces—to reply with; and Chumra Rana, who was in command, came to the conclusion that resistance was hopeless, and surrendered with a hundred of his men, the rest of the garrison having slipped away by night to join Umar Sing.

A night march anticipated any resistance that might have been offered on the way, and on the 8th of November Ochterlony faced the centre of the Ramghur position.

The fort of Ramghur was the right of the Gurkha position, their left rested on a fortified peak called Rotka Tiba.

Ochterlony moved on to the Gurkha left flank, but sent his battering-train, with one battalion, to keep the Gurkhas employed at Ramghur.

Then came the second reverse that Ochterlony's troops sustained during the campaign.

The battery before Ramghur shelled a stockade, which defended the road, without effect, and Lawtie, the field-engineer, took a hundred *sepoys* under a British officer to reconnoitre the ground before he brought his guns nearer. The *sepoys* dislodged the Gurkhas from a small breastwork they found in their advance. To quote an eye-witness of the affair:

"Thus far had the spirit of the officers actuated their men. But when the enemy, getting reinforced, came back with superior numbers to retake their post, the *sepoys* could not be prevented from wasting their ammunition by keeping up a useless fire as their opponents were approaching. The upper layer of their cartridges being at last expended, some voices called out for a retreat, alleging as a reason that

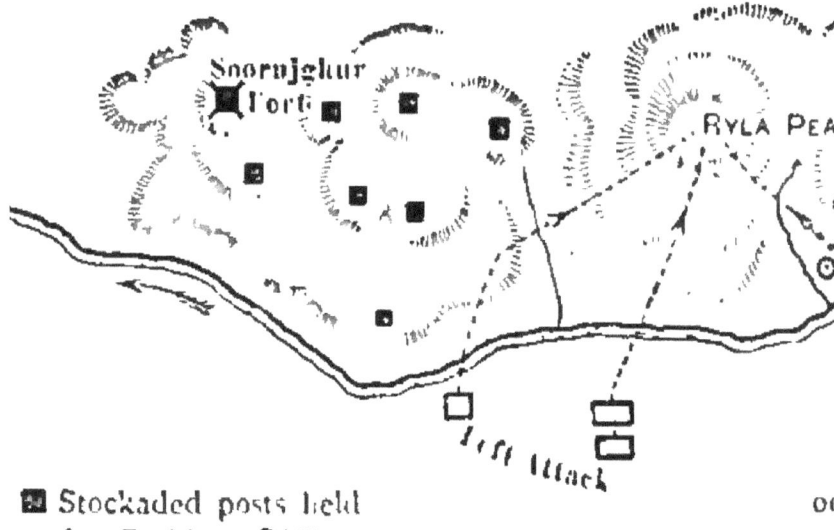

they would not have time to turn the boxes. The place appeared tenable with the bayonet; the Gurkhas, however, were now at hand, and arguments, threats, entreaties, proved equally vain to avert the disaster which ensued. Our men broke in confusion and turned their backs: the enemy, plunging among the fugitives, cut to pieces all whom their swords could reach."

But worse news still was to reach Ochterlony from the column which Colonel Mawbey, of the 53rd, now commanded in the place of the dead Gillespie. Bulbudhur and his Gurkhas still held to the fort and heavy guns had been sent for from Delhi. When they arrived the fort was bombarded. On the 27th of November a practicable breach was made, and on the 28th the two flank companies and one battalion company of the 53rd and the grenadiers of the native corps, under Major Ingleby, tried to storm it. Lieutenant Harrison and some men of the 53rd got into the breach, but penetrated no further, and the storming column withdrew with 4 officers, 15 Europeans, and 18 natives killed, and 7 officers, 215 Europeans, and 221 natives wounded.

It was said that the men of the 53rd were discontented, and that, though they mounted the breach, they would go no further; and later on, as a sequel to this most misfortunate day, some duels were fought between the officers of the two battalions of the 53rd.

The fort was afterwards beleaguered and its water supply was cut off,

The Battle of MALAUN.

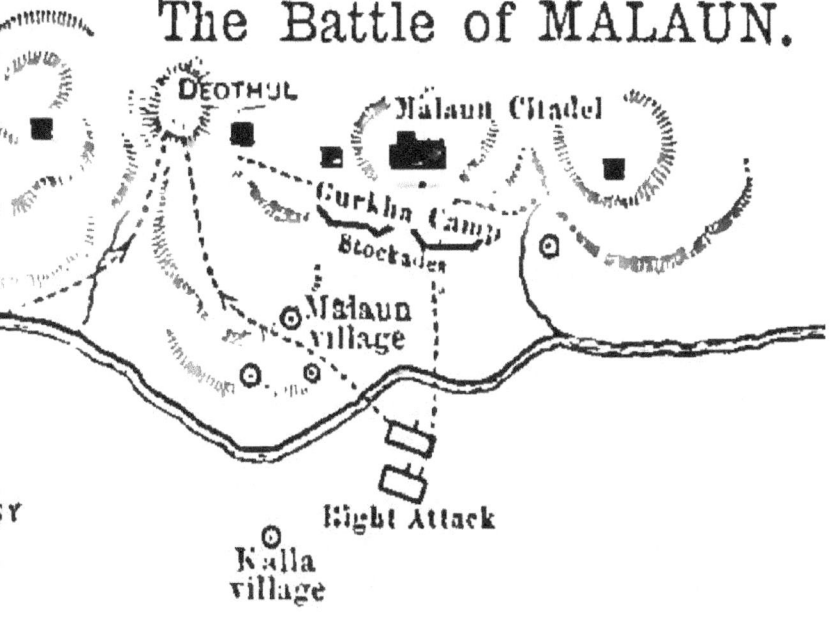

when Bulbudhur Sing, refusing to surrender, cut his way through the cordon surrounding him, and left the fort, with a ghastly garrison of dead and desperately wounded, to Mawbey and his men. Ochterlony knew the mettle of his enemy and how skilful a strategist he had to meet in Umar Sing, and he played the game of war with the greatest caution, drew away Umar Sing's allies from him, made roads, reduced outlying forts, cut the Gurkha lines of communication, and intercepted their supplies. Umar Sing, as each position became untenable, retreated to another, and at last took his stand on the Malaun ridge. It was April now, and if the campaign was to close successfully, Ochterlony had to gain a decisive victors, for the other three columns had fared badly.

Major-General Martindell had been appointed to the command of the force which had received such a check from Bulbudhur Sing and his gallant six hundred. Runjoor Sing, the Gurkha general, a son of Umar Sing, opposed to him had, following Umar Sing's tactics, fallen back upon a strong position at Jytuk, striking hard at our forces whenever he got a chance; and Martindell was irresolutely investing him there. Further south and east .again Major-General John Sullivan Wood had advanced through the forest towards Butwal, where, on the jungle-covered sandstone range, a fort and some shelter-trenches guarded the first pass on the road to the towns of Central Nipal.

Through the dense silent forest the advance-guard of men of the light company of the 17th, on elephants, made their way, and the column followed as best it could. When the men of the advance-guard were close upon the far edge of the forest, fire was opened upon them from a breastwork, the *mahouts* could not control the frightened elephants, and they rushed back crashing through the forest. It was difficult in the dense dark forest to tell friends from foes, for the Nipalese were wearing red coats like our men, and for a little all was confusion;

but Captain William Croker with his company drove the enemy up a rocky, wooded spur which ran down from the hills on the right of the breastwork, killing Sooraj Thappa, one of their leaders, and the enemy were streaming away from the breastwork, when the 17th, pushing on eagerly, were intensely disappointed to hear the "retire" sound.

General John Sullivan Wood judged the hill behind Butwal too strong a position to attack, and with the light company covering their retirement, the disappointed troops withdrew.

Later in the cold weather General J. S. Wood made another reconnaissance to Butwal, but without penetrating the hills.

Further south and east again, where the passes lead from the plains to the capital, Khatmandu, Major-General Marley had two advanced detachments at Summunpur and Persa surrounded and overpowered, and Major-General George Wood, who succeeded him in command, judged the season too late to attempt any important operations.

A gleam of encouragement came from Kumaon, where Colonel Gardner with some Rohilla levies and Colonel Jasper Nicolls, who was afterwards to be commander-in-chief in India, won success after success, and finally captured Almora, the chief fort in those parts.

The success or non-success of the campaign lay then with Ochterlony, who was now at close quarters with Umar Sing, the best of all the Gurkha generals, who had under him as his chief lieutenant Bucti Thappa, whose deeds are sung to this day throughout Nipal as the bravest of the brave.

The Malaun position, where Umar Sing waited for Ochterlony, is a range of bare hills with peaks at intervals. The citadel of Malaun guarded the Gurkha left, the fort of Soorujghur their right, and the peaks between were held as stockaded posts—all but two, the peak of Ryla towards the enemy's left and the peak of Deothul almost under the guns of Malaun.

Ochterlony, who throughout the campaign had been consistently cautious, knew now that the time had come to risk everything.

During the night of the 14th April, Lawtree, the field-engineer, stole up to the Ryla peak, and, seizing it without difficulty, set about stockading it with the few men he had with him.

At daybreak on the 15th five columns were sent out. Three moved on Ryla, two under Colonel Thompson marched on Deothul and seized those positions without difficulty, for the attention of the Gurkhas was distracted by an attack on their stockades below the citadel of Malaun, an attack which cost us many lives—amongst them that

of a gallant officer, Captain Showers, who in single combat, in view of the two forces, killed his opponent, a Gurkha leader, before he was himself shot—but answered its purpose well.

There was desultory fighting about Deothul all through the day, but our men held their own and busied themselves erecting stockades. Two field-pieces were sent up to Colonel Thompson, and through the night shots were exchanged with the Gurkhas, while the men finished their work at the stockade, which became a strong work with embrasures for the guns.

During the night Bucti Thappa slipped away from the fortified position he held between the peaks in possession of the British,

and joined Umar Sing at Malaun. Both the Gurkha leaders knew that, unless Deothul was recaptured, the game was up. An attack was planned for next morning, and Bucti, who was to lead it, swore a solemn oath in the durbar-hall, before all the higher officers of the Gurkha force, to conquer or remain dead on the field. He warned his wives to prepare for the funeral pile, gave his son over to the protection of Umar Sing, and then went down to take command of the 2,000 Gurkhas, who in the darkness were forming in a semicircle at the base of the Deothul hill. Colonel Thompson had inside his stockade two native battalions and two guns.

With daylight the great trumpets of the Gurkhas sounded, and the attack began. The hill blazed like a sheet of flame with the Gurkha musketry. The hillmen strove to get to close quarters, reserving their fire till they were within pistol shot; but grape and canister and musketry fire struck away the Gurkhas charging kukris in hand. No man turned, but the attacking force was swept out of existence. The trumpets sounded again, and a second body charged and went down like corn before the wind, and then a third.

Though it was a forlorn hope, Bucti Thappa gathered some men together, and for a fourth time tried to charge up that desperate hill on the slopes of which lay dead the flower of the Gurkha army, and Thompson, knowing that the victory was gained, led out his men to meet him.

The battle was decisive. They counted 500 of the Gurkha dead, and our men had some 300 killed and wounded. Our two guns suffered terribly, and at the end of the day Lieutenant Cartwright, with the only unwounded man of the gun detachments, served one gun, while Lieutenant Armstrong, of the Pioneers, and Lieutenant Hutchinson, of the Engineers, worked the other.

When the last remnants of the attacking force were hurled down the hill, our men found the body of Bucti Thappa amongst the slain; and Thompson, honouring a noble enemy, had it wrapped in a shawl of honour and sent it to Umar Sing. Next day a funeral pile was built in the valley between Deothul, where the victorious British stood to their arms, and Malaun, where what was left of the Gurkha army crowded round the grey walls of the fortress.

From the gate of the citadel a sad little party, headed by Brahmins, wound down the hillside. The smoke rose from the pyre, and, to accompany the Gurkha hero to paradise, two of his wives dared the fire with him and died on the funeral pile.

Umar Sing sulked. His men and his allies were deserting him day by day, but it was not until the walls of Malaun began to crumble under the fire from the British guns that he would consent to sign a convention, which gave to the British all the land between the Sutlej and the Sarda. Those of the Gurkhas in that part of the country who did not come over to us retreated across the latter river, and Umar Sing himself, with his son Runjoor, retired to Khatmandu.

The fierce old warrior, beaten and brokenhearted, gave to the Nipalese *durbar* his advice never to make peace with the Christians, and then retired to a temple he had built, and died soon after the Gurkha defeats of the next year ended the war.

******

Malaun, though three-quarters of the Englishmen who read of battles have never even heard its name, was second only to Plassy in asserting the dominancy of the European in India, for all the wolves were afoot thinking that the lion was very sick indeed; and, if Ochterlony had failed before that Himalayan ridge, we might have found ourselves in worse straits than even the mutiny brought us to.

*****

Diplomacy failed where the sword had been successful. The Nipalese *durbar* haggled, chaffered, and temporised; but old Umar Sing's advice was very much to the liking of the council presided over by the Prime Minister, and though the great nobles hoped to spin out the cold weather in negotiating, on one point they had thoroughly made up their minds—they would have no British Resident in Khatmandu.

Ochterlony had struck, in 1814-15, where the capital scarcely felt the blow; Lord Hastings determined that this time, in 1816, the blow should reach the heart of Nipal.

Without waiting for a formal declaration of war, Sir David Ochterlony was ordered to make his advance against the capital, and as he led his brigades through the *terai* he was met by the Gurkha emissary bringing down the declaration of war from Khatmandu.

It was now February, 1816. In a month the fever that haunts the *terai* would make a campaign impossible.

Sir David Ochterlony was a K.C.B.—a reward for his services in the last campaign. He had under him nearly 20,000 fighting-men; he had a reputation that he could not fall short of.

Beyond the deserted jungle and the dense, deadly forest, where he was assembling his force, there lay the labyrinth of hills of the sandstone range, jungle-covered, with long walls of precipices facing towards the plains. The few passes that led through to the *dhuns* were all as difficult as Nature could make them, and all were stockaded. And towering above the lower range were the Himalayan foothills, which would give an army as much trouble and more than the first range.

He divided his force into four brigades. Colonel Kelly, with the first brigade of 4,000 men, all native infantry except his own regiment, Her Majesty's 24th, was despatched to Ochterlony's right to force a passage by the gorge of the Bagmatti or some neighbouring pass; Colonel Nicholl was sent off to Ochterlony's left, with her Majesty's 66th and some 3,800 natives, to find his way up the valley of the Rapti—a small river that flows into the majestic Gandak; Sir David

Ochterlony with the 3rd and 4th brigade, Her Majesty's 87th, and seven-and-a-half native regiments, 8,000 men in all, appeared before the Bichiakoh pass, the direct road to the capital.

Other columns from Gorakpur and the newly-captured Almora were to keep the Gurkhas employed further north-west; but as they had no effect upon the war we need not trouble- about their doings.

On the 10th of February, 1816, Sir David had his men safely through the dreaded forest of the *terai* and camped within sight of the first Gurkha stockade in the pass. On the 11th, Nicholl and Kelly began their marches; but for four days Ochterlony left his men in camp and did nothing. The hotheads amongst the

officers began to grumble and to ask to be allowed to try their luck against the stockades before them. But Sir David knew that the stockaded defences of the Bichiakoh were impregnable, and had called on his Intelligence Department to find him some path by which he could turn the position. Captain Pickersgill found him one. This very active officer in his search along the range met some smugglers of salt, and they, being heavily bribed, agreed to show him the path they used into Nipal—a path unknown to any Nipalese officials.

On the night of the 14th, as the men were preparing to turn in, a whisper went through the camp of the third brigade to fall in; and leaving all tents standing, and all provisions and baggage, at nine o'clock, just as the moon rose in a cloudless sky, the column—a long, dark snake—wound out of the camp northwards and into a dark gap in the hillside, the gorge of the Balu stream. First went the light company of the 87th, and next Sir David, on foot like the rest, led the long column on its desperate enterprise.

It was a daring venture for so cautious a player of the game of war, for if the column had been discovered in the gorge by the Gurkhas not a man would have escaped.

The men moved in single file, scrambling as best they could over the rocks, sometimes high in the air, sometimes deep down in what seemed to be a pit. An historian of the war says:

"Through five miles of this passage three thousand men moved with the silence of a funeral procession. The lofty banks being clothed with trees, their branches from opposite sides in some places intermingled above, in others the clear moonlight showed tremendous rocks at a great height, rising over the column in cliffs and precipices. The only sounds which interrupted the stillness were caused by the axes in removing some trees which had grown or fallen across the way."

When the grey of dawn came, those behind in the narrow watercourse could distinguish the "Light Bobs" scrambling up a final three hundred yards of hillside almost as steep as the side of a house, holding on to the shrubs and grass, being pulled up by the officers' sashes, which were unwound for the purpose.

The rest followed, and by seven in the morning the third brigade was on the ridge of the sandstone range, and the Bichiakoh pass was turned. They marched five miles further to bivouac by a stream, and then came two bad days, while the pioneers made the path practicable for elephants, during which there was no food for the troops: for there had been a muddle, and the three days' provisions ordered had not been served out to them before starting.

The Irish boys of the 87th took it all right cheerfully: they cut down boughs of the trees and made shelters for the general and staff as well as themselves. Barefooted, cold, foodless, on constant harassing

outpost work, these gallant fellows knew that they had won the first move in the game; and as the stern "Auld Maloney" came striding round the pickets, the men, setting discipline for the moment at defiance, greeted him with an Irish yell of triumph.

******

The fourth brigade joined Sir David, marching up through the

Bichiakoh pass, which the Gurkhas had deserted when they found that Sir David was in rear of them, and as the hot-headed young officers who were so keen to attack passed the stockades, they were forced to admit that to assault them would have meant certain defeat. Colonel Kelly had crossed the first range without opposition, and was facing the fort of Huriharpur, where Runjoor Sing, General Martindell's old opponent, was in command. Colonel Nicholl, also unopposed, was marching up the valley of the Rapti. On the 27th February the third and fourth brigades marched through the tree-covered *dhun* to where the brick fort of Mukwanpur towered on a hill to the east—our right—and from this a long broken ridge, jungle-covered on the upper slopes but naked on the lower, led down to a fortified village on our left.

The slopes of the hill were strongly stockaded, and there was a force of Gurkhas in the village.

At breakfast time on the 28th two of the men of the 87th were brought up before the colonel of that corps for straying beyond the pickets. They had been for a walk, and, seeing none of the enemy about, had gone into the fortified village, where they found only an old woman.

"Fall in, the light company!" shouted the colonel, and the men ran to their arms. "Ould Maloney" was on the spot at once, and the gallant " Light Bobs"—the two culprits of the morning with them—went off for the village at the double, and the light company of the 25th Native Infantry were sent after them in support.

The village was deserted, as the men had said; and Pickersgill, taking Lieutenants Lee of the 87th and Turrell of the 20th Native Infantry, a volunteer, and some twenty men, began to reconnoitre the Mukwanpur hill. He posted two parties on the wooded ridge to cover his retreat, and went on with one or two men higher up the jungle-covered slope towards the fort.

Meanwhile the Gurkhas in Mukwanpur had seen what had happened, and the original garrison of the fortified village was sent down to retake it. They swept away Pickersgill's two parties, driving them down the narrow footpath, killed Lee, and were only prevented from hacking to pieces the other officers by the splendid gallantry of Corporal Orr and Private Boyle, who, fighting coolly with the bayonet, held the rocky path as a rear-guard.

Sir David had thrown reinforcements into the village, and the 87th came up the hill to help their retiring comrades, and checked the advancing Gurkhas where a glen cut through the ridge.

In the stockades the great trumpets were blown, and down the hill, bringing some guns with them, streamed a shouting torrent of some two thousand Gurkhas. From the camp Sir David sent more men across to the village, till on our side we had one European and two native battalions before the village commanding the glen. From the camp the artillery pounded at the Gurkhas swarming down the ridge.

It was bayonet against *kukri*. Again and again the Gurkhas charged over the open slope up from the glen, and again and again those not swept away by bullets and shells perished on the bayonets of the 87th, who yelled, in answer to the Gurkha shouts, as they charged to meet the rush of the little, brown demons.

The Gurkha gunners, finding that they could not make any effect on our men before the village, turned their guns on the camp. The shot came hurtling through the tents, and Sir David's old servant, who stood inkstand in hand by his master, where the general, in front of the camp, was directing the fight, was killed by a ball. A lucky shot blew up the enemy's reserve ammunition, and the Gurkhas began to charge less resolutely.

The action had lasted since ten in the morning, and it was now near five. Sir David sent the 8th Native Infantry to finish the fight be-

fore sunset. They deployed and with a shout swept up the hill, capturing the Nipalese guns and sending the beaten Gurkhas flying through the thickets, leaving their wounded and dead upon the ground.

It was a horrible sight that the setting sun went down upon. Ensign Shipp, of the 87th wrote of it:

"The dying and wounded lay in masses in the dells and the ravines below. In our own company we had, I think, eleven killed and twenty wounded, our total number being eighty only. As long as it was light, we could plainly see the last struggles of the dying. Some poor fellows could be seen raising their knees up to their chins and then flinging them down with all their might. Some attempted to rise, but failed in the attempt. One poor fellow I saw get on his legs, put his hands to his bleeding head, then fall and roll down the hill to rise no more."

******

The fight at Mukwanpur broke the Gurkha power, and hard on the heels of the messenger who brought the news to Khatmandu came others telling that Kelly had routed Runjoor Sing, who had fled, leaving his picked guard, the Band of the Moon—the men with silver crescents on their turbans—defeated and disheartened, behind the walls of Huriharpur, and that Nicholl, come safely through the Rapti valley, had joined Ochterlony.

On the 4th of March, 1816, in full *durbar*, at the general's camp in the valley of Mukwanpur, with the *vakeels* of all the great princes of India to witness, Chunda Seka, the Nipalese envoy, on his knees presented to Sir David Ochterlony a treaty which gave to the British everything that they claimed.

Here let us leave the stout old veteran at the moment of his supreme triumph. It is better to think of him as the brilliant commander of 1816 than as the politician of 1824, rebuked and superseded, and dying like his great antagonist, Umar Sing, of a broken heart.

JULY 25, 1814
Lundy's Lane

Angus Evan Abbott

Lundy's Lane! Strange, savage struggle; struggle in which Briton, Canadian, American, Iroquois, and Huron all met in chaotic deadly grapple on the bank of the great river, and by the side of the thundering falls whose veil of white spray hung from heaven like a winding-sheet. Lundy's Lane! where the red man's war-whoop mingled with the frenzied shout of the white, where the sharp crack of the musket cut the sullen roar of the cataract as lightning slashes the black cloud; fight of the early evening, of the long gloaming, of the night, dark before the moon hung m the sky. And when her pale face looked down between the slowly-drifting clouds, although her light fell upon many a blanched face, she saw crowds of maddened men still slashing with sabre, thrusting with bayonet, swinging their clubbed muskets around their heads as they battered a path, this way and that, for the possession of the field. It was the battle of battles in the War of 1812, Lundy's Lane. The sides that fought were blood-brothers. Their officers cried their orders in the same tongue, the men cheered the same cheer; the same courage, the same determination, the same unconquerable spirit animated all who fought the fierce fight across the narrow highway, Lundy's Lane, that led into pastoral Ontario.

Besides its being famous as a fight, Lundy's Lane has some peculiarities. Looked at from a purely military standpoint, the battle was in a way lacking in brilliant points and movements, being in fact a fair and square stand-up bit of slogging on both sides, the British holding a position and the American general, by repeatedly hurling his full force

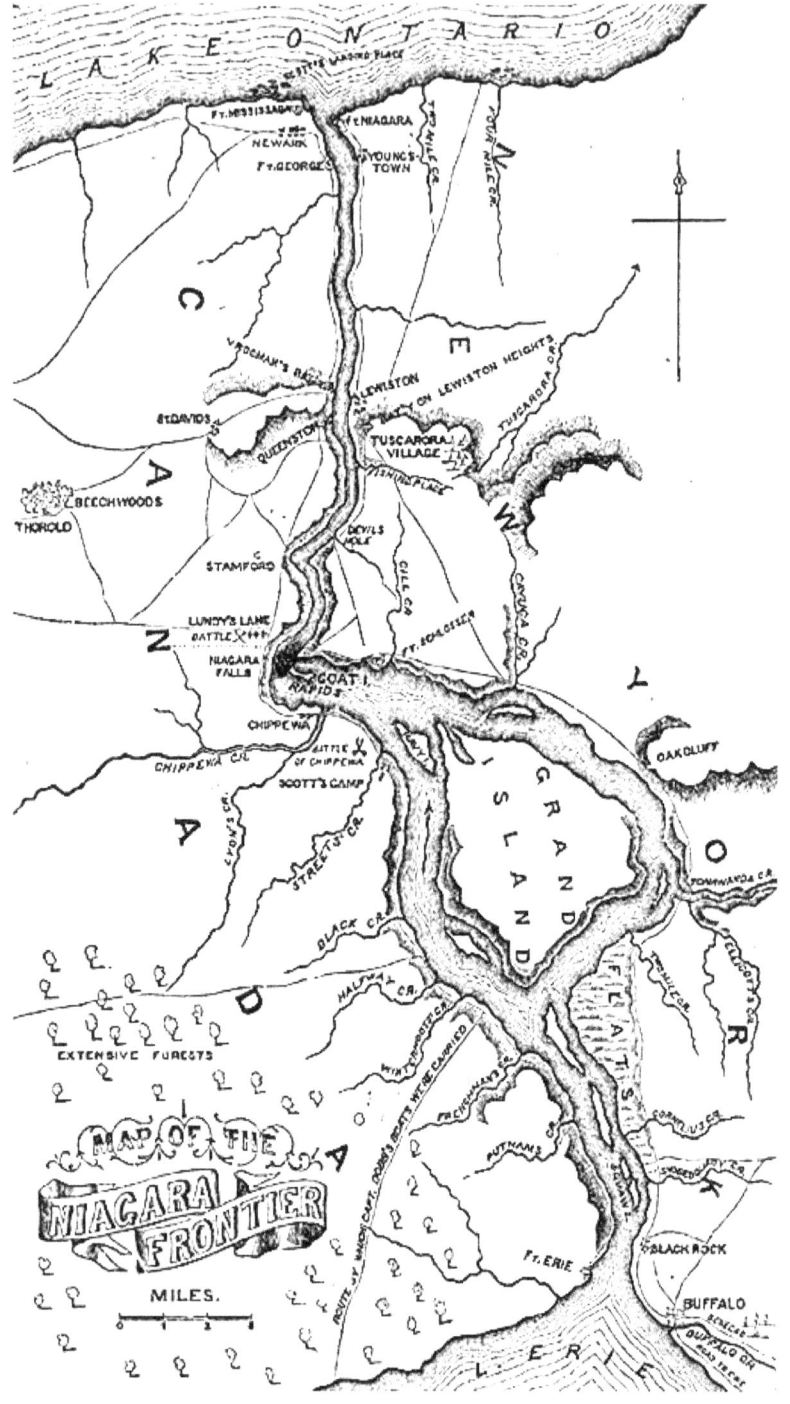

against the red-coats, attempting to carry the position. The peculiarities to which I now refer lay outside the actual fight.

In the first place, the battle can be called by any one of three names. The Canadians have named it Lundy's Lane, the Americans Bridgewater, and some few Canadians and British, and a good many American writers, refer to it as the Battle of Niagara Falls. Seeing that the fight took place on Canadian soil and across Lundy's Lane, it may be as well to accept the name the Canadians have given it. Certainly they should know best. They had everything to lose had the battle gone against the Union Jack, as at one point appeared not at all improbable, and the ground over which the fight raged is to them sacred ground. Another strange feature of the battle is that each side claimed a decisive victory. Search the histories of Canada and the United States and victory is credited to British or American according as the history is written by an Englishman or an American. Now, a battle can scarcely be won by both sides competing. One may be drawn, but that actual victory can never be won by both the opposing forces is certain; and with all due respect to the Americans, and the evidence their writers bring forward to support their contention, an impartial student of the battle will find great difficulty in discovering much logic in their claim. The American army came very near to winning a brilliant victory, but that they did not win is quite evident from a recital of the undisputed facts of the fight. Admittedly the Americans captured the British guns—the key of the whole position—and admittedly they drove the British back and secured for a time possession of the position, and it looked as if all was over for the army of Drummond. But the British and Canadians charged again, regained the guns—this was all done in the dead of the night; and when the morning's sun rose the British army was in exactly the same place as it had been when the battle began, and the American army had retired to Chippewa. But subsequent events placed beyond all question where victory really rested. The next morning after the battle the British moved *forward* and the American army *fell back*, General Drummond finally cooping the Americans securely in Port Erie. The fact of the matter seems to be that the Battle of Lundy's Lane was, as a fight, a duplicate on a grand scale of the Battle of Chippewa, which immediately preceded it. At Chippewa the British attempted to carry a position, found the task an impossible one, and retreated to Lundy's Lane. At Lundy's Lane the Americans attempted to carry a position, found the task an im-

possible one, and retreated to Chippewa. No British writer claims Chippewa as a victory, and no American writer has any substantial grounds for looking upon such a reversal as the American army received at Lundy's Lane as a victory.

Lundy's Lane was fought on July 25th, the evening and the night of that date, 1814. Three summers had this cruel war dragged its course, and the little army of Canada, sorely battered on many an occasion, losing its ablest generals, and, moreover, far more of the rank and file than it could well afford, still fought grimly against the invading Americans, who swarmed to the borders to overrun the British possessions and to add another star to their flag by annexing Canada to the Union. The war had dragged horribly. The people of Canada, a country then of only some 300,000 souls, were suffering intensely. Every man, young or old, who could bear arms and could be spared, had been drafted to the defence of his country, and women found that it fell to their lot to do the work that formerly had been done by husband or son, now stationed at the various forts along the American frontier. Up to the year of the battle of Lundy's Lane Canada expected and, indeed, received but little assistance from the Mother Country, for Waterloo had not yet been fought, and all eyes were turned to the great danger that threatened England from the Continent. So it came about that the war with such a powerful nation as the United States pressed gallingly upon the Colony. But all the suffering was not confined to Canada. The people of the Republic, too, had suffered. Taxes grew to enormous proportions, their foreign trade completely died out, their ships rocked and rotted in the harbours, and their pride had suffered blow after blow, for their armies of born fighters had been kept in check and repeatedly defeated by small numbers of British and Canadians, the latter fighting fiercely for their homes. Nor does this convey anything like a complete idea of the difficulties America found herself in. Many of the New England States totally disbelieved in the war, and threatened to withdraw from the Union if an arrangement with Great Britain was long delayed. The American generals who first had power put into their hands almost without exception turned out to be incapable, and the soldiers, although true fighters, when they came to battle were lacking in discipline, and on more than one occasion their insubordination and grumbling caused their leaders to rush in when prudence cried caution. During the summers of 1812-13 there had been much fighting and little progress, and when the winter of the latter year closed down on the land and put a stop to hostilities, each side set its heart on doing something decisive before the summer of 1814 passed over.

All the winter there were great goings on in the harbours around the lakes. British and Americans each strained every nerve to build a fleet that should sweep the other from the lakes, and the war-cry sounded from village to village, and floated into many a quiet farmhouse, into many a rude log cabin in the woods calling for volunteers to the cause. Even in the *wigwams* of the red men the martial note was struck, and many a warrior sat over the fire of a cold winter's night polishing his flintlock, whetting his scalping knife, and hefting his tomahawk, while his squaw, muffled in blankets, sat as silent as a heathen idol, her black eyes fixed upon the glowing coal. Tecumseh was slain, but other chiefs had led out their bands to thirl the wood in search of scalps. Canada had been fortunate in her Indians. She had Tecumseh, Brant, Norton, and many other steadfast fighters. But now she was no longer to have it her own way in this respect.

Sa-go-ye-wat-ha, or to give him the name by which he is known to the white man—Red Jacket—one of the most famous Indian orators of history, great chief and *sachem* of the Senecas, had been wooed and won to the American cause, and his orations addressed to his tribesmen were not long in setting the hot blood coursing through the veins of the Iroquois. His ringing appeals, addressed in the proper tone and rich in metaphor and legend, thrilled the minds of the bucks, and soon the Six Nations—the most fearless fighters that ever trod the American forests, whose war-whoops had rung on the air at many a stubborn contest between British and French—took up the hatchet and threw in their lot with the "Long Knives," as they called the American soldiers.

During the summer of 1814, at Chippewa, Lundy's Lane, Fort Erie, and many other bitter fights, the tomahawks of Seneca, Mohawk, Oneida, Cayuga, Onondaga, and Tuscarora whirled through the air at the heads of their old-time allies the British. Red Jacket, although in all conscience a feeble-hearted warrior, still was able to apply the torch of oratory to the brands that lay *ready* for the fire in every Indian's breast. The fever for the fight ran from *wigwam* to wigwam like fire through autumn leaves, and when the campaign of 1814 opened, the Iroquois painted their cheeks with ghastly colours, danced the war-dance before the great tent, and set their faces to the north to confront their Redskin brothers who fought under the Union Jack.

The campaign of 1814 opened early. Indeed, the frost had not relinquished its hold on the continent when the American troops were set in motion for their various points of concentration near the Canadian border. March is proverbially a harsh month in that part of North America through which the border line runs; but through the frost and snow the Americans trudged on their way. Four thousand troops—a woefully large number for the small forces in Canada to hold in check—under General Wilkinson, were the first to commence action at a little place known as Lacolle Mills. To reach this place the Americans had to cross Lake Champlain on the ice. This rather startling enterprise ended in disaster to the Americans, and General Wilkinson's military career closed. Some of his troops were forwarded to Buffalo, to fight under General Brown, on whose shoulders was placed the responsibility of making yet another attempt to conquer Canada.

After two years of fighting it was only natural that those officers who held command but lacked the necessary ability to conduct a campaign should be found out, and officers of the true metal placed in their stead. The Americans at first were wretchedly officered. But now Dearborn and Van Renssalaer, who had opened the war, were in retirement—there is reason to believe that they were men of real capacity but were hampered by public opinion and the unmilitary independence of their picturesque troops; Hull and Hampton had left the service in disgrace; Winder, Winchester, and Chandler were prisoners in the hands of the British; and now Wilkinson was relieved of command. So it came about that the troops

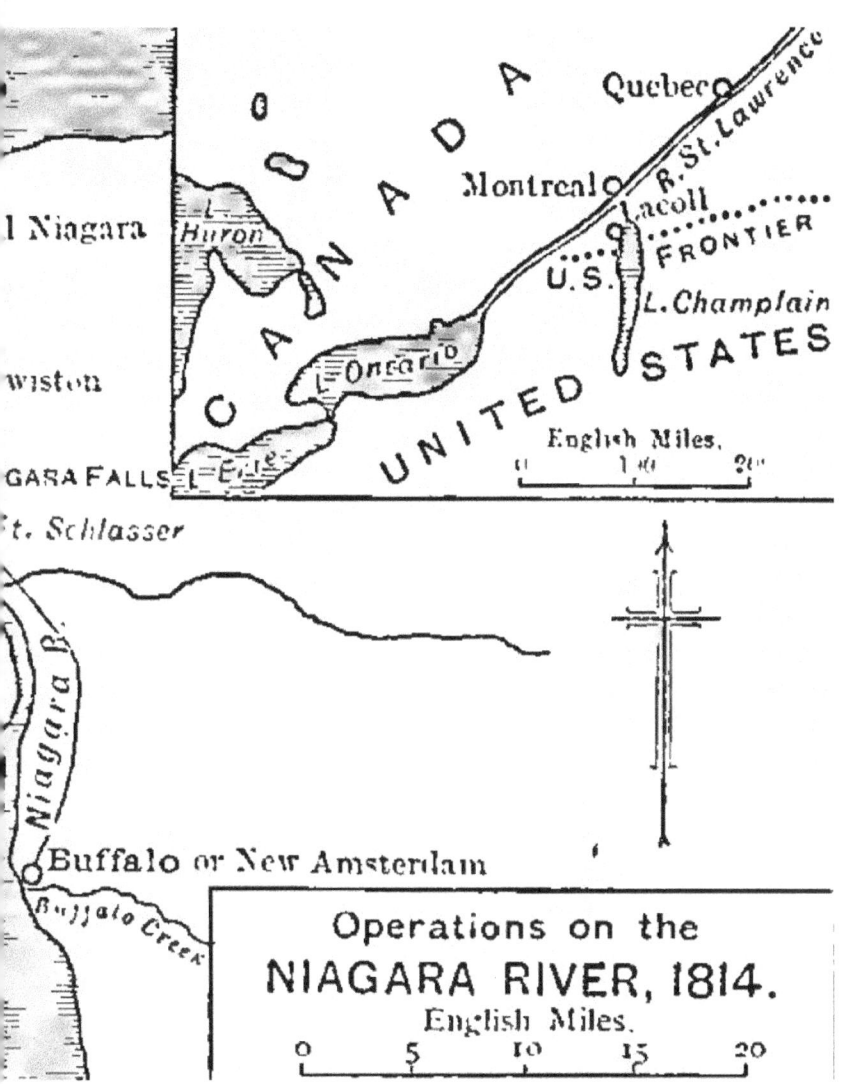

Operations on the
NIAGARA RIVER, 1814.

concentrated at Buffalo were placed under the charge of General Jacob Brown, who led them against the British at Lundy's Lane.

Brown was then a man of about forty. He had been a county judge in New York State, and in 1809 was made colonel of militia, advanced to brigadier-general in 1810, and in 1812, at the declaration of war against Great Britain, was given command of the frontier from Oswego to Lake St. Francis, a strip of country some two hundred miles in length. So satisfactory to his government were all his doings, that in January, 1814, he was placed in charge of the army of Niagara, with rank as major-general. Rapid promotion this, but Brown seems to have merited all the good things that fell into his lap. He proved to be a man of considerable executive ability and decision, and earned the confidence and respect of his officers and his men.

Under him he had a sound officer in Brigadier-General Winfield Scott, who, with untiring perseverance, spent the winter in drilling the troops, so that when they took the field no higher disciplined soldiers ever marched on the American continent. The very first battle these troops took part in proved their efficiency—their cool and soldier-like behaviour at the Battle of Chippewa surprised their own leader quite as much as it did the British.

And now for the third year in succession Canada was to be invaded. On the previous occasions the Americans, officers and men alike, had set out with a light heart, looking upon the task of overrunning the country as a simple one. But events had shown that there was to be no walk over.

Early in July Brown set his army in motion. Brigadier-Generals Scott and Ripley marched their men to the Niagara River at a point where it receives the waters of the upper lakes to tumble them over the great falls, and successfully landed on the opposite shore, their feet once more upon the threshold of Canada. Without opposition, there being no sufficient force to offer any, the Americans took possession of Fort Erie. The news of this movement spread like the wind through Canada: horsemen galloped the well-worn roads, canoes rippled the waters of many a forest stream, and the couriers ran through the woods to apprise the people of their danger, and to speed fencibles, militia, and all to the front. That this invading army was an extremely dangerous one all very well knew.

General Riall commanded the British forces on the Niagara frontier. He, too, was an officer of great parts, and when the news reached him that General Brown had taken the initial step he energetically prepared to fight. His force in comparison with Brown's was ridiculously small. But during this war small armies well led had done wonders, and Riall made up his mind to fight without losing a moment. There can be no doubt that he underestimated the Americans somewhat as regards their numbers and woefully as regards their discipline, and he suffered a severe repulse as a consequence of these mistakes. On Independence Day, July 4th, Brown quitted Fort Erie and marched his army down the Niagara to Chippewa. The troops held close to the river, while the Iroquois crept by their side, dodging behind the bushes and trees, and completely scouring the country. On July 5th the Americans reached Chippewa. This was as far as Riall had any intention they should proceed before he offered them battle.

Riall's force consisted of 1,500 regulars. 600 militia, and 300 Indians. Brown had 4,000 well-trained Americans occupying a strong position. But up to this time the Canadians had won so many fights against well-nigh overwhelming numbers that Riall determined to strike without waiting for reinforcements. The British troops charged in splendid order, and with a fierceness that was characteristic of this war. But the Kentucky riflemen stood firm as a rock, the Iroquois, too, fought with all their old-time bravery, and Riall found he was but smashing his head against a stone wall. Consequently, after a vicious little battle lasting an hour, Riall drew off defeated in his attempt to carry the Americans' position. But he retired his force in perfect order without losing a gun or a prisoner. He retreated to Twelve Mile Creek, where, meeting with reinforcements, he ceased his rearward march and returned to take up a position at Lundy's Lane, the Americans all this time remaining inactive at Chippewa. Chippewa was an effective repulse rather than a defeat, if such a distinction be allowed.

Riall was not destined to lead the British at Lundy's Lane. The chief in command was yet to arrive. Sir George Gordon Drummond, lieutenant-general and second in command in Canada to Sir George Prevost, heard of the invasion of the Americans when he was at Kingston, and at once set out for Niagara.

Drummond, like most of the British officers who commanded in Canada, had studied the art of war on many a hard-fought field. He was a Canadian by birth, and entered the army as ensign in the Royal Scots in 1780, joining his regiment in Jamaica. Rapid promotion placed him in charge as lieutenant-colonel of the 8th or King's Liverpool regiment, a regiment with which he was closely connected all the remainder of his life. With it he served in the Netherlands in 1795-6, he was with Sir Ralph Abercromby in the West Indies, and, promoted to the colonelship, he fought in Minorca and Egypt, greatly distinguishing himself at Cairo and Alexandria. To Jamaica again, and in 1808 transferred to the staff in Canada, he was made lieutenant-general in 1811. His life had been a bustling one, and the generals he fought under were the brilliant teachers of an apt pupil. Drummond, when he heard of Brown's across-river movement, lost not a moment, but made all speed to Lundy's Lane.

His arrival at Niagara, as a matter of fact, brought about the bat-

tle of Lundy's Lane. Brown and his army still lay at Chippewa, satisfied apparently that a serious rebuff had been given to the defenders of the country and looking forward to a campaign of little difficulty. Riall lay at Lundy's Lane, and only a few miles of broken country,

wooded in places, stretched between the opposing forces. It seems not to have been the intention of either side to strike at the other, at least not for some time. But when Drummond reached Niagara, and before he knew the exact state of affairs, he sent Colonel Tucker with a small force alone; the Republican soldiers. Couriers rode in hot haste to General Brown, and told him that the British army was marching upon Lewiston. When the American general heard this, he jumped to the conclusion that his supply *depôt*, Schlasser, was to be subjected to an attack. Nothing could save his stores, he felt sure, if it was really the purpose of the British to make a general movement against them. To call back the British by attacking the forts at the mouth of the river was the best plan that presented itself to Brown. With this object in view he ordered Scott to at once move his brigade down the river and to set about the forts in good earnest. How badly Brown must have been served by his scouts is shown when it is told that drawn up right across Scott's proposed route of march were the full available British forces prepared for battle. Scott had pushed on his troops not more than a mile or so when he got a great surprise. Instead of on the opposite bank of the river, there on the top of a slight eminence, drawn up in splendid strategical position were the regulars, militia, and Indians—the British army—under Drummond. Scott seems to have been within musket-shot of the British before he made the discovery. He had gone too far to turn back.

The Queenston road skirts the Niagara River on the Canadian side. It was along this road Scott marched his brigade. From the road and at right angles to it, and but a short distance down the river from the great Falls, shoots out Lundy's Lane, a narrow highway making from the Falls to the shore of Lake Ontario. Near to where Lundy's Lane joins the wider Queenston road it runs over a small hill, rather a bit of slightly rising ground. This elevation is about 200 yards from the river. On the top of this knoll Drummond had instructed Riall to station his little army—there were only 1,600 in position when the battle began—so as to form a shallow crescent. On the brow of the knoll were planted seven small guns. Behind these as a support lay the Royal Scots, the 89th Regiment, and the light companies of the 41st. The left wing, resting on the Queenston road, consisted of a detachment of the 3rd Buffs; the right wing was formed of the Glengarry Light Infantry. In the rear lay a squadron of the 19th Light Infantry. The position taken up was as strong a one as could be found in the neighbourhood, but the force at the disposal of Drummond was altogether inadequate for the occasion. Reinforcements to the number of 1,200 were in the immediate vicinity, and these arrived before the

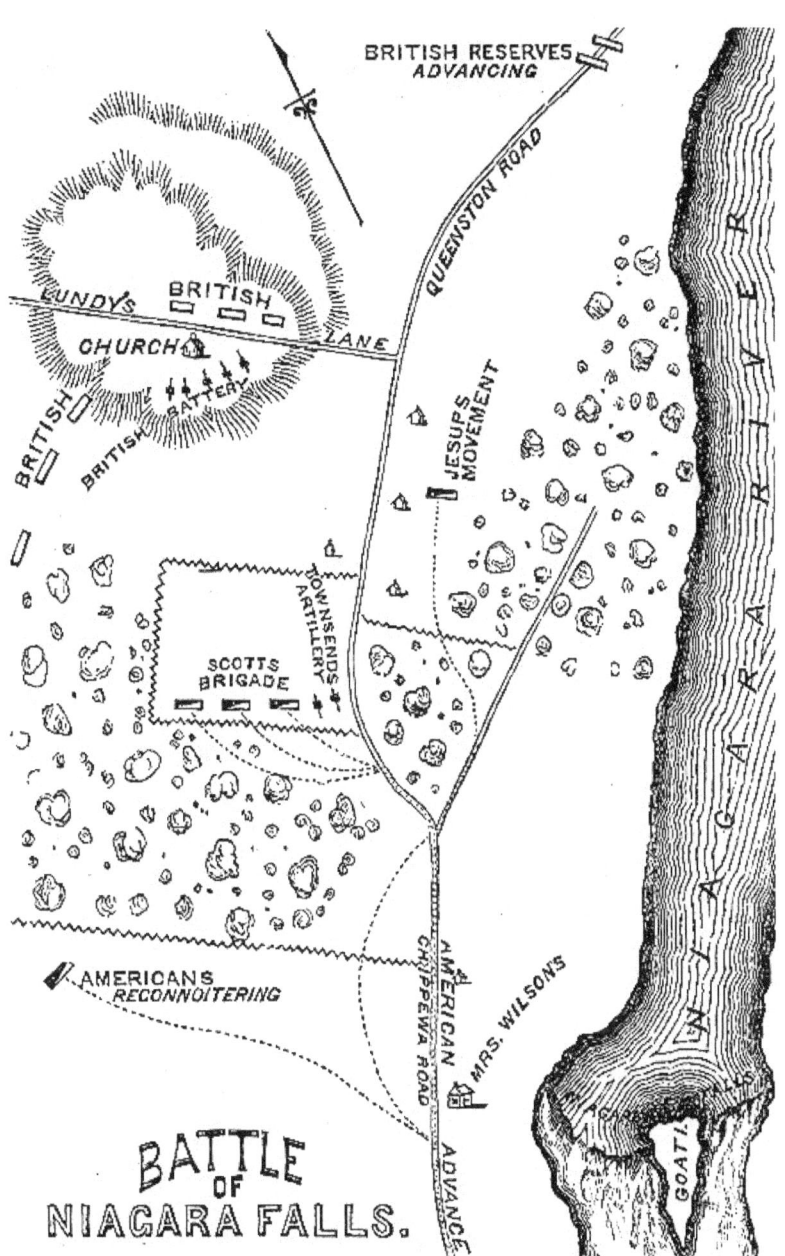

battle had ended. At best General Drummond had less than 3,000 troops to fight Lundy's Lane. The American army numbered close upon 5,000 soldiers.

Scott halted his brigade—he had 1,800 in his personal command—

when he found himself confronted by the British. He rapidly summed up the situation. Although he had not been looking for a fight at the moment, he saw that retreat would probably demoralise his soldiers. To stand there was equally out of the question. There was nothing for it but to "pile in." Hastily despatching a messenger to inform his commanding general of the true state of affairs, he without loss of time began the battle, opening fire on the slender line of British and Canadian soldiers who stood so grimly still and silent along the crest of the knoll.

The fierce July sun had now sunk far into the west, splashing the heavens with crimson and glorious gold; not a zephyr stirred the parched grass, lazy clouds scarcely moving in their course hung in the blue; the birds that all the day had sat in the deep shades of the bushes to escape the blistering heat, now hopped to the topmost twig and sang farewell to the light, and all the time the floods from Superior, Michigan, Huron, and Erie poured over the stubborn ridge of rock and fell to the level of Ontario with a hoarse sullen roar as of distant thunders.

It was a sultry evening. Nature herself seemed to pant for breath. Even before the battle began the perspiration stood on the brows of the gallant men who confronted each other. Seemingly, the only cool beings were the red men, who already were snaking their way through the long grass on the alert for an unexpected dash upon their foe.

In his swift glance round General

Scott noted that the strip between the Queenston road and river was unoccupied by British troops. It occurred to him that if a force could secretly occupy this territory and unexpectedly fall upon the Buffs, the British left might be turned. He hurried orders to Major Jesup, commander of the 25th Regiment, ordering him to creep under the shelter of the bushes, occupy the position, and wait his opportunity. This Jesup did most successfully.

The battle began. Both sides opened fire at the same moment; a steady fire it was all along the line, Scott moving his men forward cautiously, carefully, and all the time keeping a sharp watch for any opening likely to lead to a successful storming of the knoll, the British remaining stationary in the position which, by its strength, enabled them to oppose a much larger force with prospects of withstanding the onslaught. Early in the engagement it was clearly seen that the little battery which hung on the brow of the slope was destined to play a large part in the fight. From the mouths of the half-dozen and one guns fire shot wickedly out, and grape swept down the slope and into the ranks of the Americans, with results altogether disastrous to the assailants. Suddenly General Scott called upon his men to charge, and helter-skelter they broke from their semi-cover and, with a shout, bounded forward for the height. But it proved a disastrous move. The Royal Scots, the Buffs, the Glengarry men, regulars, fencibles, and Indians, each and every one stood grim and immovable, and fired volley after volley into the ranks of the Republicans. Before the foot of the slope had been gained, the Americans' charge was checked, and the soldiers rapidly fell back to a more respectable distance. This proved to be the first of a series of desperate charges, which resulted in regiments on both sides being shot to pieces.

During the hot fight in front Jesup's flanking regiment had not been idle. The Americans of the 25th Regiment had been steadily making their way around to the rear, and one company, pushing on much further than the others, fell in with a stroke of great good fortune. This was nothing less than the capture of General Riall, second in command of the British, and his escort. It came about curiously enough. Riall, at the very outset of the fight, received a bad wound. His escort closed around him and hurried him through the British lines to the rear. Suddenly the aides with the wounded general in their charge came upon a company of soldiers, which they took to be Canadian reinforcements, and one of Riall's attendants shouted,

"Make room there, men, for General Riall." Now this request, as it turned out, was addressed to the adventurous company of the 25th, who with the greatest alacrity "made room" as requested, and captured the whole party. Delighted with their good luck, the American captain called upon his men, and, with General Riall in their midst, they charged unexpectedly right through the British left and rejoined their command. Riall was hurried into the presence of General Scott, who treated him with every consideration.

From sundown to close upon nine o'clock the battle raged. Scott, furious at being checked, charged time after time, only pausing long enough after each repulse to form for a fresh onslaught. Already the slope was thickly strewn with the dead and dying. But over all the Kentucky riflemen and the New England volunteers made their way, firing as they ran, in a vain attempt to capture the guns. On a number of occasions the leaders got so close as to bayonet the artillerymen as they served the field-pieces, but, struggle as they might, they were rolled down the slope by the red-dripping bayonets of the regulars and volunteers who fought under the folds of the Red Cross of St. George.

Close upon nine o'clock a hush fell upon the field. General Brown had just arrived from Chippewa, bringing with him Ripley, Porter, and their men, and, strangely enough, at exactly the same moment Colonels Gordon and Scott, with their commands, consisting of parts of the 103rd and 104th Regiments, and the Royal Scots, in all about 1,200 men, reached the battlefield to the reinforcement of the sorely-pressed defenders of Lundy's Lane.

After the clamour of battle the stillness was appalling. Once again the hollow sound as of the beating of gigantic wings came rolling across from the Falls; and from the slope, from the top of the knoll, and from the level plain arose the piteous appeal of the stricken for help and for water. Only a few yards distant water enough to quench the thirst of the world growled over the precipice, but not one drop of it fell on the parched tongues of the poor fellows who lay on the ground through that sultry July night.

Brown's first order was that Ripley's men should relieve Scott's. The latter had fought a fatiguing fight, and the weary men fell back while the fresh men from Chippewa stepped into their places. Drummond's men were not so fortunate. The British general's force was too small to admit of any being spared from the front. With the newcomers Drummond strengthened his line.

The short calm was truly in this instance to be followed by a furious storm. Brown determined to force the position and to sweep back the British without a moment's delay. On top of the knoll the little army lay prostrate from fatigue. Men dropped to the ground where they had stood panting and putting their cheeks to the cool earth. The gunners leaned against their guns, matches alight, but muscles relaxed. The night was black, and for the most part it was impossible for foe to see foe. General Brown called Colonel Miller to him, and ordered the colonel to take his regiment, the 21st, and capture the guns.

Colonel Miller first spoke to his men, ordering that complete silence be observed in the ranks and discovering to them his plans. At the order every man of them dropped, to earth, and began an exciting crouching crawl for the slope. Close to the ground the blackness was intense. Over the dead and among the wounded the 21st made its way, noiseless as serpents, steadily on. Half-way up the slope the Americans caught a sight of the guns looking like blotches of black against the sky, and by them, as silent as ghosts stood the artillerymen, weary, but alert for the slightest sound, their matches glowing in the murk like fireflies.

Miller halted his men. Before him zigzagged a rail fence. Across this the riflemen lay their guns, aimed with cool deliberation, and at a signal a sheet of flame cut the night air. It is told that every gunner leaped into the air and fell below his gun.

The next instant Miller and his men were among the guns. Ripley's whole battalion, too, sprang forward up the slope, and down upon the Americans came the Royal Scots, the Glengarry men—every man indeed in the British ranks. Guns were clubbed, bayonet thrust, war-

whoop and cheer rang together. Officers, realising that no order could be heard, sprang into the mass and slashed with sword and sabre, all joining in one savage *mêlée*, fighting for the position on the hill.

Half the British force that fought that night across Lundy's Lane were Canadian volunteers, and when the news of the battle spread, from the knobs of many a door, town-house, and log-cabin fluttered the long strip of crape that told of death.

The Royal Scots and the 89th lost more than half their men in the frightful scramble on top of the hill, American regiments were cut to tatters on the slope, General Drummond had his horse shot under him, and, while fighting on foot, was shot in the neck and dangerously wounded. Colonel Morrison of the 89th had to be carried from the field. Generals Porter and Scott were also badly stricken, and General Brown himself so severely wounded that he had to relinquish his command and leave Ripley to look after the American interest.

The last hour was an indescribable jumble and tussle hand to hand round the guns. There could be no definite formation in the darkness, and every man fought for himself. At length the Americans began to waver. Ripley saw this, and, finding the task of holding possession of guns and field an impossible one, gradually and in order withdrew his men from the fight, taking with him as a souvenir of the hardest-fought battle of the War of 1812 one six-pounder.

The Americans retreated to Chippewa that night, and the British slept under the stars on the hard-held field.

On the field lay so many dead that Drummond's little force was unable to bury them, and word had to be sent to the Americans to come and assist in the work. For some reason the Americans did not do this, and the British were obliged to burn a large number of bodies of the slain. July's fierce sun admitted of no delay.

The official report of the losses were given as follows:—American losses: 171 killed, 570 wounded, 117 missing; total, 858. General Drummond's report: 84 killed, 559 wounded, 193 missing, 42 prisoners; total, 878.

April 10, 1814
Toulouse
D. H. Parry

The day before Waterloo a Peninsular veteran of the 52nd was overheard to remark, "There'll be a great battle tomorrow," and when questioned by an officer as to his meaning, said, "All the Duke's great battles are fought on a Sunday!"

To a large extent the man was right: Vimiera, Fuentes d'Onoro, Ciudad Rodrigo, Orthez, were all waged on the Sabbath day, and Toulouse, as desperate an engagement as any in the war, was fought on Easter Sunday. It was a last stand by a brave general, turning at bay before the gates of the third city of his country, ignorant that the cause for which he struggled was already lost, and that his master had abdicated several days before.

Standing in the centre of a flat and pastoral country, liable to frequent inundations from the streams that intersected its meadows and cornfields, the city of Toulouse was protected on three sides by the River Garonne and a large canal, and girdled by a massive old wall flanked at regular intervals by pointed turret towers, above which rose a forest of spires and the quaint gables of the houses, many of them built of wood. Soult lost no time in raising works and strong bridgeheads, and did all that skill and ingenuity could accomplish in seventeen days to make the place impregnable. Its natural features offered every facility for the purpose, and he compelled the somewhat reluctant citizens to assist in forming redoubts on the heights to eastward, which heights ran for two miles roughly parallel to the city wall, between the canal and the swollen Ers, all of whose bridges, save one at Croix d'Orade, were purposely broken or mined.

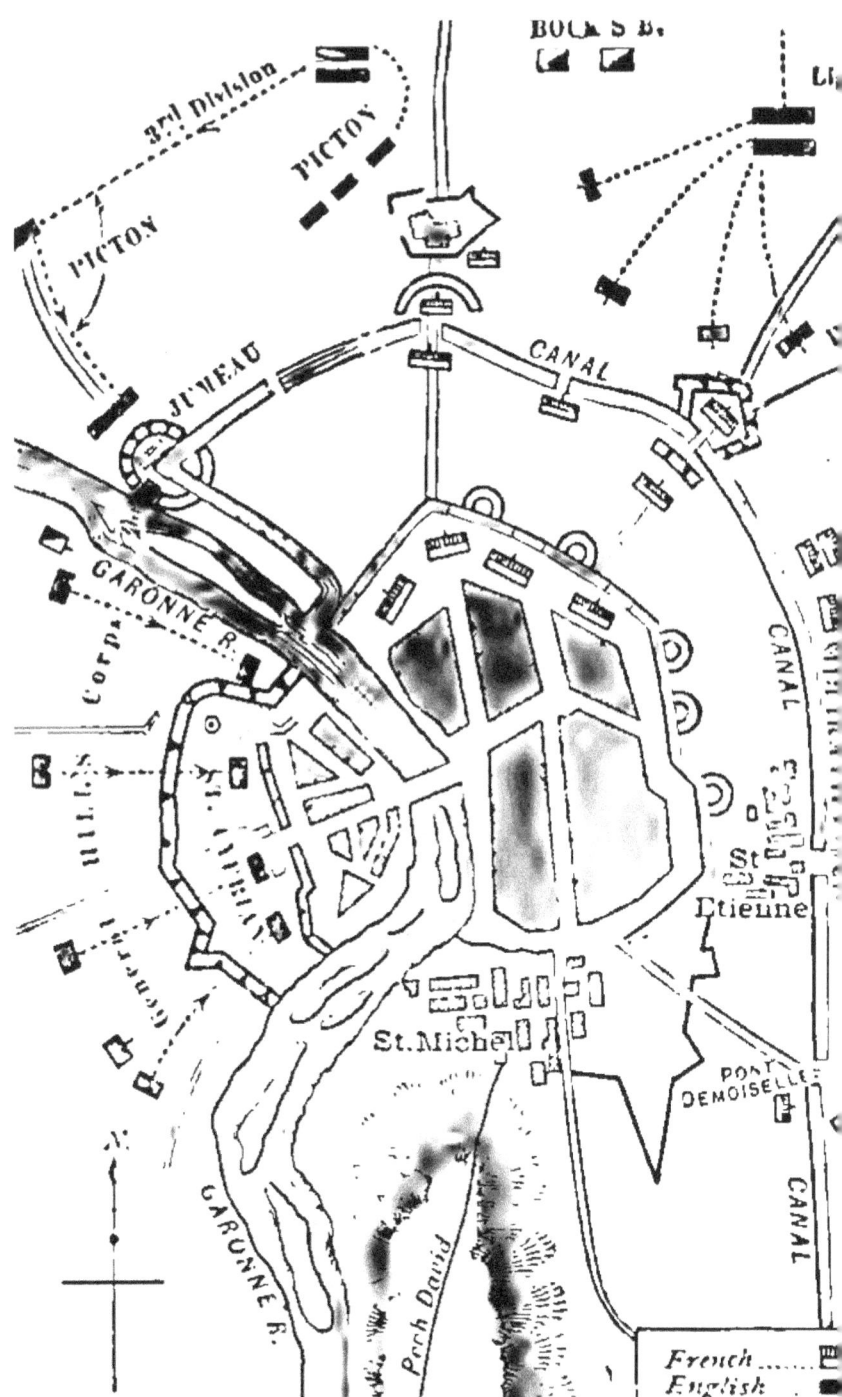

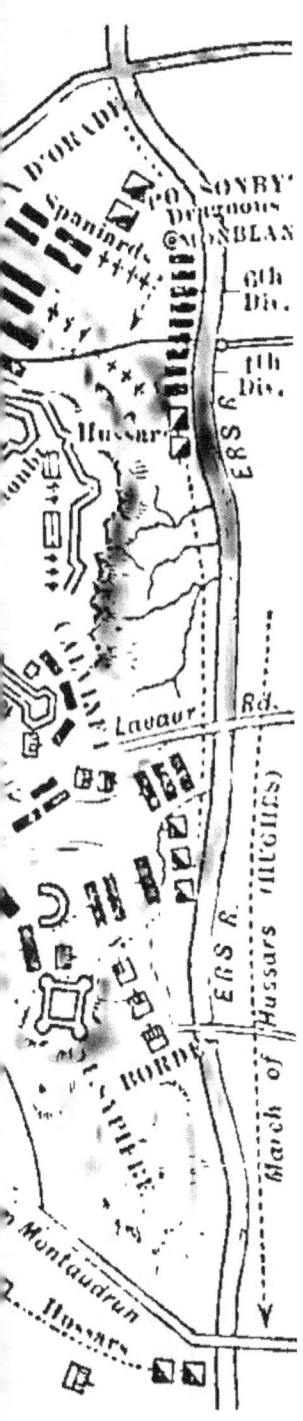

On the west the Garonne formed a strong barrier, with the outlying suburb of St. Cyprien beyond it. The canal, lined with troops, curved from the Garonne round the north of the city, and then along its eastern side, where several clustering suburbs were capable of being strongly garrisoned, so that the only weak spot was to the southward, and even there another suburb was full of troops. The walls were manned with guns. The heights—divided by the Lavaur road into two distinct elevations or platforms, the Calvinet and St. Sypière—were steep, and held by Harispe's division. Darricau defended the canal; Reille occupied St. Cyprien; and a detached hill between the northern end of the heights and Croix d'Orade, called the Pugade, was garrisoned by St. Pol.

Artificial inundations covered the approaches in many places, cavalry were on the lookout about the River Ers, and the roads themselves were no contemptible allies, sodden by the heavy rains. In an unpublished journal I have before me, kept by an officer of the 2nd Queen's (Lieutenant, afterwards Captain, J. A. Wilson), the following entry occurs:

"Roads actually up to my middle in mud; walked into a river to wash my clothes!"

Under these conditions, and to oppose this formidable resistance, Wellington attacked St. Cyprien on the 28th of March, and made several attempts to cross the Garonne *above* Toulouse. The floods, however, retarded us, and it was not until the 4th April that Beresford passed over, fifteen miles *below* the city, with the 3rd, 4th, and 6th Divisions and three brigades of cavalry, the 4th Division crossing the pontoons first, their bands and drums playing "The British Grenadiers," and the sun coming out as they halted on the enemy's bank to sponge arms and loosen ammunition.

They marched to La Espinasse without opposition, the French patrols retiring at the first passage of the river, and a large body of cavalry menacing us without coming to blows. To quote the above-mentioned journal:

"At four o'clock our regiment sent with the Rocket Brigade to support the cavalry. At eight o'clock got squeezed into some poor houses, having been forty-eight hours without resting to sleep."

"*April 8th.*—Marched at three in the afternoon. At five my company sent on picquet. Ordered by the general to load and go to a church, where I should find a picquet of the French, and to drive them out and keep the church. A company of the 53rd sent to support me . . . Found the French had just retired, and left both doors of the church open for me, for which I was much obliged to them."

Napier has cleverly shown how Soult left the bridge intact at Croix d'Orade to entice Wellington into the marshy ground between the heights and the river Ers, and then he shows what Wellington did when he got there, which was not at all what the French marshal anticipated.

On the 8th the 18th Hussars made a brilliant dash at the bridge against the French dragoons, after a pause on both sides.

The advance of our infantry set them in motion simultaneously. The trumpets rang out the charge together; but our fellows in blue and white were too sharp for the brass helmets, and jamming the dragoons between the stone parapets, broke them after a moment's sabring, and spurred over in pursuit led by Major Hughes, Colonel Vivian being incapacitated by a carbine bullet.

Wellington wished to attack on the 9th, but owing to the removal of the pontoon bridge closer to Toulouse, it was necessary to postpone until the day after. The allied army occupied a peculiar position, and one which indicated in a marked degree the place Napoleon had won in the hearts of his people.

In the north, where the population had suffered more severely from the ravages of war, from the conscription, and the devastating passage of troops, the peasants rose and helped the tottering emperor; but in the hot, impressionable south they not only refrained from armed resistance, but welcomed the "perfidious" English; and Soult, fighting a last battle for the cause, fought it unaided by his countrymen, who were even reluctant to help him dig his trenches, and had probably more sympathy with the success of the invaders than with that of the bayonets that upheld the Tricolour.

The weather had improved a little, but there was still much water out over the country, and the Garonne, flowing swiftly in a deep channel, threatened our pontoons as it foamed on its way to the Atlantic.

Wellington's plan, the result of personal observation carried out with great care the previous days, was to deliver two feint attacks, one by Sir Rowland Hill against St. Cyprien across the Garonne, the other upon the outposts along the canal north of Toulouse under Picton, while Frevre's Spaniards carried the isolated hill of Pugade, and Marshal Beresford stormed the French right on the hilly platform of St. Sypière, the cavalry moving along each side of the Ers to watch Berton, whose horsemen roved over the marshy fields before and beyond St. Sypière.

At two o'clock on the morning of the 10th April our troops mustered under arms in the darkness, and the hussars passed to the head of Beresford's columns, which they were to precede on their toilsome two-mile march along the front of the enemy's position. After many halts, until everything was in proper order, the army got under weigh about six o'clock, and with the sun shining on its war-worn ranks, stepped boldly forward to begin that useless and unnecessary battle.

While Hill began his attack against St. Cyprien, and Picton, seconded by Baron Alten, opened on the French skirmishers in front of the canal, the Spaniards advanced under a fire from two guns and took speedy possession of the Pugade St. Pol having orders to fall back to the Calvinet, the first of those two platforms which formed the main strength of Soult's position; while Beresford, leaving his clattering batteries in the village of Monblanc, turned to his left, and soon clearing the protecting barrier of the Pugade, marched ahead under a terrible flank fire between the platforms and the river.

Advancing in three columns through the swamps, the heights on their right became alive with smoke and flame, and we learn from the journal already quoted that the men had to run by companies to escape the fire, the soft mud having one advantage—that it put out the falling shells, and when a round shot struck it did not rise again.

Still the 4th and 6th Divisions suffered severely in their long tramp, and were destined to suffer more before the day closed, the 6th especially, the "Marching Division," as their comrades of the war designated them.

The Spaniards occupying the Pugade, the Portuguese guns were dragged up the hill and opened on the Calvinet, keeping up a thunderous roll against the enemy across the valley; and about an hour

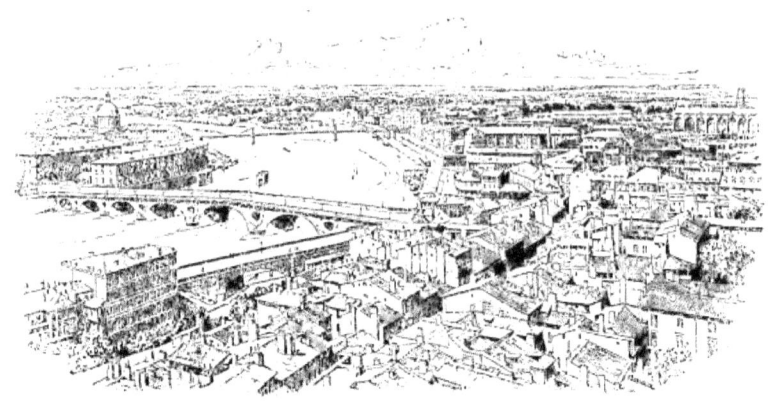

before noon, while Beresford was still splashing on through the mud and mire, an unfortunate mishap befell.

Don Manuel Freyre, flushed with his first success, descended into the gorge below and attacked the hornwork on the Calvinet platform in two lines with a reserve in his rear. Advancing boldly at first, they soon came under a withering fire of artillery and musketry, a battery on the canal also raking their right flank; and, turning to an officer beside him, Wellington is reported to have said, "Did you ever see nine hundred men run away?"

The officer addressed admitted that he had never done so, and Wellington said, "Wait a minute, you will see it now." As he spoke, the right wing wavered, and the leading ranks flung themselves into a hollow road, twenty-five feet deep, for a shelter it could not afford them. Leon de Sicilia's Cantabrians alone stood their ground somewhat sheltered by a bank; but the left wing and the second line turned and fled helter-skelter, a terror-stricken mass, the French rushing forward with triumphant yells and firing down into the hollow road, which was soon a hideous lane of dead and dying.

The Spanish officers with great courage rallied their men and led them back again, but the sight that met their gaze as they reached the edge of the hollow put the finishing touch to their valour, and breaking rank they fled for the open country, hotly pursued by the enemy, who were only brought within bounds again by the reserve artillery and Ponsonby's Heavy Dragoons, a battalion of the Light Division taking the fugitives" place in splendid order.

More than fifteen hundred Spaniards were killed; but Wellington, as he sat on his charger Copenhagen, afterwards to carry him at Waterloo, had more serious news brought to him.

General Picton, whose eagerness for combat was so well known that his orders had been given to him both verbally and in writing, had disobeyed them, and turning his feint attack into a real one, had been defeated for the moment.

Successful at first, the Fighting 3rd Division had driven the French outposts back about three miles on to the Jumeaux bridge; but their fiery leader, not content with this, sent six companies of the 74th Highland Regiment—a corps which had lost the "garb of old Gaul" five years before, and had then twice as many Irish as Scots in its ranks—against the palisade at the bridgehead across an open stretch of plain.

Brevet-Major Miller and Captain McQueen led them bravely forward; but the work was too high, and they had no ladders, and although the whole brigade made the attempt, they were heavily repulsed, losing nearly four hundred officers and men, among them Colonel Forbes, of the "Old Stubborns," killed, and General Brisbane, who was wounded.

It was a severe repulse, and, taken together with the Spanish failure, might have proved serious, for Wellington had now no reserves. Hill was checked by the second line of entrenchments at St. Cyprien, and the French marshal was able by these reverses to withdraw about 15,000 men to reinforce the rest on the platforms, where Beresford now had victory or defeat in his own keeping.

On the other side of the Ers our cavalry made two bold dashes—one against the bridge of Bordes, which sent Berton *ventre à terre* to the left bank with barely time to destroy the roadway before the troopers were upon him; the other by the 1st King's German Legion Hussars, who would have won half-a-dozen Victoria Crosses in our own day.

The bridge of Montaudron, beyond the French right, had been strongly barricaded with barrels filled with earth, and the 22nd Chasseurs-à-cheval lined the barrier with loaded carbines, shouting derisively as the Hanoverians rode up.

The squadron halted; several men swung out of their saddles and walked up to the bridge; the carbines whistled, but the dismounted men paid no heed, and in a few minutes had torn down casks enough to let Poten in at the head of the others. When the squadron came back again their sabres were dripping, and the bridge was ours!

Meantime, Beresford's three columns had pursued its deadly march along the foot of the heights until its rear had passed the Lavaur road,

which led between the platforms to the suburbs of Toulouse, and then, in accordance with Wellington's orders, the two divisions wheeled into line to attack St. Sypière. What says our journal?

"Having arrived at their right (the French right), we were wheel-

ing into line when a column of cavalry came down towards us and would most likely have charged us, but our rockets dispersed them.

"The second rocket thrown went through the body of a horse, and left two men on the road! Just as they retired, a column of infantry came' down another road near to us, beating their drums and seeming very determined; but on our again wheeling up into line they halted and commenced a running fire, by which no harm was done.

"Colonel Henderson was shot through the coat. We returned the salute by a regular volley: as soon as the smoke cleared away, and while the men were loading, I could see the French commander's horse lying down in the road and six or eight men carrying the unfortunate colonel's body off. They put about immediately, and we, having given them five or six rounds as they were going, followed them up the hill in three lines, ourselves in the front, the Portuguese in the second, and left Brigade the third.

"The hill was so steep, and the road running through it over which we had to pass, that I was glad to lay hold of a sergeant's pike to help me up. They kept up a smart fire upon us. The right-hand man of my company was shot through the breast, and fell at my feet (he recovered and joined in about six weeks afterwards). When we had cleared the hill (for the enemy flew before us), we came in sight of their whole army and of the town of Toulouse, a noble sight."

So much for the present for the 4th Division. Their comrades of the 6th, upon whom more brunt of fighting fell, found a mass of infantry about to descend from the hill, while a strong body of horse trotted down the Lavaur road to intercept any retreat.

The whole of Beresford's command—which at the outset had not mustered 13,000, and which had suffered severely on its march—was hemmed in in a narrow difficult position, the enemy strongly entrenched above them, an unfordable river in their rear, Berton menacing the left flank and Vial the right!

Soult, up on the rocky hill, had brought Taupin and D'Armagnac up to reinforce the rest—the latter general himself a native of Toulouse—and, after some stirring words to Taupin, ordered them to descend with fury! Unfortunately for themselves, they waited and gave Beresford time to wheel into line, were met with Congreve rockets as they came shouting down, and, part of the 6th Division repulsing Vial in square while the 4th Division behaved as already narrated, the tables were completely turned, and instead of an utter annihilation of the little red mass below, that mass followed up its first successes by mounting the hill, drove the French before it, and half the formidable heights were ours.

"Their infantry ran in the greatest disorder, and cavalry in armour protected them. We kept advancing in line till, drawing near them, a regiment of their cavalry rode up towards us. We then wheeled back

by divisions and formed the solid square in double quick time; at the same time the rockets commenced again and did great damage, obliging them to withdraw. They left their guns at the end of the town to play on us, and we could see their baggage and many troops hurrying out of the other end. We had to halt here for the 6th Division, which was warmly engaged at a redoubt, and we were shortly afterwards ordered to lie down."

The town mentioned by the captain was evidently the suburb of Guillemerie, immediately below the heights, where a bridge crosses the canal to the suburb of St. Etienne, and about this time, the 18th Hussars and the 1st King's German Legion coming round the south end of St. Sypière to menace another bridge, known as the Demoiselles, Soult's position grew critical.

Beresford's artillery, which had been expending its fire against the Calvinet platform, was brought up through the marshes about two o'clock, the Horse Artillery having arrived earlier but without tumbrils and only seven or eight rounds of ammunition; and about half an hour later the 6th Division made a furious attack.

Sheltered from the fire under the hill, Pack's Scotch Brigade and Douglas's Portuguese swarmed up the steep banks, wheeled to their left by wings as they got out of the hollow road, and charged so successfully, in spite of a storm of shot and shell at close quarters, that the Black Watch and 79th Highlanders were masters of all the breastworks and in possession of the Colombette and Calvinet redoubts in a few minutes!

Then gallant Harispe led a mighty stream back upon the intruders; it burst with overwhelming force of numbers upon the Highlanders, slew or wounded four-fifths of the Black Watch, and cleared the captured works.

An eyewitness has left us an account, which though often quoted will well bear repetition, of how the French came down like a torrent, darkening the whole hill-top, officers riding in front waving their men on with hat in hand "amidst shouts of the multitude resembling the roar of the ocean."

Then in that moment of mad suspense, half in defiance, half in admiration, their voices hoarse with the lust of slaughter, the Highlanders took off their feather bonnets, giving three British cheers as they waved the ostrich-plumes in the sunlight! And, when the redoubt was retaken—for we *did* retake it, helped by the 11th and 91st—there were only ninety of the Black Watch left out of five hundred who went into action! With dogged resolve our men stuck to the summit of the hill, a weak line facing terrible odds, and yet it was the kind of conflict they had learned to love in that war whose last battle they were then fighting!

They kept the Calvinet, and later on the Cameron Highlanders—there were only sixty-three of the name in the regiment, strangely enough—retook the Colombette. Harispe was down, and about four o'clock the enemy withdrew; Soult retiring behind the canal somewhere about five, beaten, yet still full of resource and ready to renew the combat.

Happily for human life, he thought better of it, retreating in admirable order on the night of the nth, further hostilities being suspended a few days later by news of Napoleon's abdication. Had it arrived before, five generals and 3,000 men on the French side, and four generals with close on 5,000 men on ours would have been spared to their respective countries.

Dr. Jenks of the 10th Hussars, who died in 1882 at a very advanced age, was one of the last survivors of Toulouse.

The sortie from Bayonne on the 14th, by the French garrison who disbelieved in Napoleon's fall, caused more unnecessary bloodshed; it was the last actual conflict before our army sailed, and with it the greatest war we have ever seen came to a sudden and most glorious termination.

June 16, 1815
The Battle of Ligny

Archibald Forbes

Having quitted Elba, the place of his temporary exile, on February 26th, 1815, Napoleon landed in the Gulf of St. Juan on March 1st; and on the following day he began his march on Paris at the head of a single weak battalion, General Cambronne, with forty grenadiers, moving as an advance-guard. After the week immediately following his debarkation, his march was an ever-swelling triumph, and he entered Paris on March 21st, only a few hours after Louis XVIII. had hurriedly quitted the Tuileries. With characteristic energy he at once set about the stupendous task of the reorganisation of the French army, the strength and character of which had been greatly impaired in his later campaigns, as well as during the short period of the first Restoration of the Bourbons. Such was the marvellous vigour and capacity of this extraordinary man that by June 1st he had organised forces amounting in all to about 560,000 men, capable of taking active part in the national defence against the openly declared determination of the allied Powers of Europe to combine all their efforts towards the accomplishment of the complete overthrow of the resuscitated military strength of Napoleon, with whom they had resolved to enter into neither truce nor treaty. Of this number, the effective strength of the troops of the line reached a total of about 217,000 men, of whom there were available for an immediate campaign in Belgium an estimated grand total of 122,400 men, consisting of 84,235 infantry, 21,665 cavalry, 10,900 artillerymen and 5,600 train and engineers.

Some French and many English historians of the campaign of Waterloo have described Napoleon's army as being "the finest he had

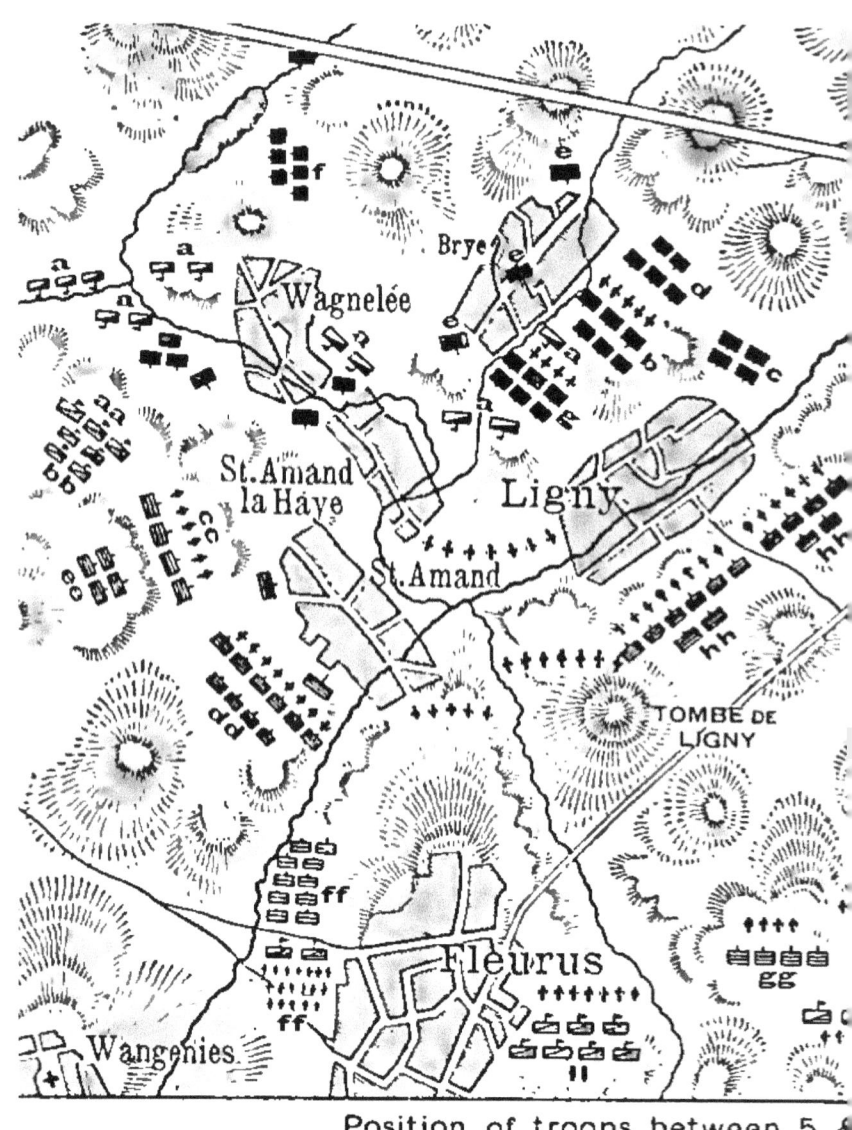

Position of troops between 5 &

French Army	
aa	Cavalry Domont.
bb	,, of Guard.
cc	Division Gérard (2nd. Corps)
dd	Corps Vandamme (3rd. Corps).
ce	Division of young Guards.
ff	Imperial Guards.
gg	6th. Corps.

hh	Division Gérard (4th C
ii	French Cavalry.
kk	,, Infantry.
ll	3rd. Cavalry (Milhaud)

Prussian Army.
a Cavalry
b 8th. Brigade.
c 4th.   ,,

✝✝✝✝ Artillery of both armi

Scale of Yards
0   500   1000

d 1st. Brigade.
e Three bat. of 1st. Brigade.
f 7th. Brigade.
g 12th.   "
h 9th.   "
i 11th.   "
k 10th.   "
l Cavalry of Landwehr.

ever commanded." This assertion is quite unwarranted, except as regarded the stature and endurance of the old soldiers who had returned in 1814 from captivity in foreign lands. They, it is true, were grand fighting-men; but they formed only a part of Napoleon's forces, among whom were many young and immature men. Sir Evelyn Wood has calculated that about one-half of the line troops were raw recruits, and that of the Imperial Guard, 18,500 strong, between 4,000 and 5,000 were untrained men. But it was not only the rank and file who were less efficient than of yore; the losses in previous campaigns had enabled many men to become company and battalion commanders who were unfitted for such posts; and thus regiments could not be successfully employed when fighting outside of the scope of the supervision of superior officers. Many of the senior officers, again, although still in middle age, had become gross in body, sluggish in enterprise, and incapable of hard and prolonged exertion; and Napoleon had to realise, though when too late, that he should have entrusted the more important commands to the hands of younger and more ardent men. Sir Evelyn Wood remarks that this slackness on the part of the senior officers had become apparent during the later campaigns in Germany; as an instance of which, at Leipzig, Napoleon observed through his field-glass one of his marshals riding up to join his troops for the first time, after they had been engaged for several hours. Napoleon had adjured every man "*to conquer or die;*" and this spirit doubtless animated the great majority of the old soldiers in the ranks. But the same exalted sentiment was not by any means universal among the generals, several of whom, though young in years, were prematurely aged in *esprit* and physique, and had lost that confident daring which had won for France so many victories under the Republic and the Empire. Unfortunately for Napoleon, most of them no longer believed that the emperor could succeed; and there were indications that his own confidence in his star was not altogether unimpaired.

The appointment of Marshal Soult to the position of chief of the staff has been generally regarded as an unfortunate selection; but now that Berthier had gone so tragically, Napoleon had but a circumscribed scope of choice; and Soult was a man of very considerable capacity, although it is obvious that after having held independent command during more than one campaign, he must have found it difficult to be content in an inferior capacity. There was not a little of intestine ill-feeling in the higher commands of Napoleon's army. Excelmans and Vandamme were not on speaking terms with Soult. Soult omitted to inform Vandamme that he was to pass under the command of Grouchy, and when Grouchy demanded his services, Vandamme, with his usual flow of expletives, refused to take orders from him. An illustration of the slackness of duty even in the higher ranks of the army is given by Sir Evelyn Wood in his admirable work on the Cavalry in the Waterloo Campaign. On the evening of the 14th June an officer was sent with an order for Vandamme to advance at three o'clock on the following morning. That general could not be found: he had gone off to a house at some distance from his corps, and had not left word where he was sleeping. The officer wandered about during the night ill a futile search of Vandamme, and eventually fell from his horse and broke his leg. He lay helpless for some time, and the order thus never reached Vandamme, who started only at seven a.m. on the 15th instead of at three, with the result of a serious dislocation of Napoleon's dispositions.

The troops constituting the Grand Army with which the emperor resolved on taking the field against the allied forces in Belgium consisted of five army corps: the 1st, commanded by General Count d'Erlon, containing four infantry divisions and Jaquinot's light cavalry division; the 2nd, commanded by General Count Reille, made up of four infantry divisions and Piré's light cavalry division; the 3rd, commanded by General Count Vandamme, comprising three infantry divisions and Domont's light cavalry division; the 4th, commanded by General Count Gérard, consisting of three infantry divisions, and

Morin's light cavalry division; and the 6th, commanded by General Count Lobau, containing three infantry divisions. The command of the Imperial Guards had been given to Marshal Mortier, in which position he would have fought at Waterloo but for a sudden attack of sciatica at Maubeuge, where, oddly enough, he had already been wounded in 1793. His presence in the battle would have prevented the over-reckless use made by Ney of the cavalry of the Guard. Of the infantry of that force, the 1st division, consisting of four regiments of grenadiers, was commanded by General Friant; the 2nd, consisting of four regiments of chasseurs, by General Morand; and the Young Guard, two regiments of *voltigeurs* and two of *tirailleurs*, by General Duhesme. The cavalry of the Guard consisted of the 1st division, under General Guyot—two heavy regiments; and of the 2nd, under General Lefebvre-Desnouettes—three light regiments. The reserve cavalry, commanded by Marshal Grouchy, was made up of four corps, each of two divisions; the 1st corps commanded by General Pajol, the 2nd by General Excelmans, the 3rd by General Kellermann, and the 4th by General Milhaud. The reserve cavalry mustered 12,800 men with 48 guns.

The junction of the several corps on the same day (June the 13th), and almost at the same hour, was a triumph of Napoleon's skill in the combination of movements. The emperor himself, who had quitted Paris at three o'clock on the morning of the 12th and had passed the following night in Laon, was now with the army. On the 14th, the French army was concentrated at Solre-sur-Sambre, Beaumont, and Philippeville. In all those three positions the troops bivouacked under cover of low hills within a short distance behind the frontier, so dexterously hidden that the enemy remained unaware of the proximity of the large masses of troops almost within striking distance. The headquarters were at Beaumont, in the centre of the army, the force there consisting of the corps of Vandamme and Lobau, the Imperial Guard, and the reserve cavalry, amounting altogether to about 66,000 men. The left, consisting of D'Erlon's and Reille's Corps (1st and 2nd), aggregating about 44,000 men, was in position on the right bank of the Sambre at Solre-sur-Sambre. The right, composed of Gérard's corps and a division of heavy cavalry, amounting to about 16,000 men, was in front of Philippeville. On the evening of the 14th the army received from its chief the following spirit-stirring appeal:

"Soldiers! this day is the anniversary of Marengo and of Friedland, which twice decided the destiny of Europe. Then, as after Austerlitz,

as after Wagram, we were too generous! We believed in the protestations and in the oaths of princes, whom we left on their thrones. Now, however, leagued together, they aim at the independence and the most sacred rights of France. They have commenced the most unjust of aggressions. Let us, then, march to meet them. Are they and we no longer the same men? Soldiers! we have forced marches to make, battles to fight, dangers to encounter; but, with firmness, victory will be ours. To every Frenchman who has a heart, the moment has now arrived to conquer or to die!"

The Prussian army which Napoleon was to fight and defeat at Ligny on the 16th was commanded by the gallant old warrior Prince Blücher. Its total strength amounted to about 117,000 men, and was composed of 99,715 infantry, 11,879 cavalry, 5,300 artillerymen, train, and engineers, with 312 guns. It was divided into four army corps. The 1st corps, commanded by General Zieten, had its headquarters at Charleroi, its right extending along the left, bank of the Sambre as far west as Thuin, with brigades at Marchiennes, at Châtelet, Fleurus, and Moustier; the reserve cavalry at Sombref, and the reserve artillery at Gembloux. The 2nd corps, commanded by General Pirch II., had its headquarters at Namur, where the Meuse and Sambre unite; the mass of the corps in rear. The 3rd corps, commanded by General Thielemann, had its headquarters at Ciney, behind the Meuse, and rearward to Huy. The headquarters of the 4th corps were at Liege, the most rearward position of all. Prince Blücher had his headquarters at Namur. His four corps were so disposed that each could be concentrated at its own headquarters within twelve hours; and it was possible to effect the concentration of the whole army at any one of those points within twenty-four hours. Blücher had decided, in the probable event of Napoleon's advance across the Sambre at and about Charleroi, to concentrate his army in a position in front of Sombref, a point on the high road between Namur and Nivelles, about fourteen miles from the former place, and about eight miles from Quatre Bras, the point of intersection of that road with the *chaussée* leading direct from Charleroi to Brussels.

Napoleon's project was to cross the Sambre at, and to east and west of, Charleroi; then to bend rightward towards Fleurus with the mass of his army, fight and defeat the Prussian army in the position which he was aware it was taking up in front of Sombref; and this accomplished, to attack Wellington's army before it should be collected in sufficient strength to prevent his further progress towards Brussels. In accordance with the emperor's orders, Pajol's cavalry corps, at 2.30 a.m. of the 15th, began the advance on Charleroi. Vandamme, with the 3rd army corps, should have followed close behind Pajol; but owing to the *contretemps* already referred to he did not start until four hours later, delaying also the Imperial Guard, which was to follow the same road. The left column advanced from Solre-sur-Sambre by Thuin, heading for the bridge of Marchiennes, and the right column from Philippeville through Gerpinnes upon Châtelet. Zieten was fully on the alert; and his vigilance on the morning of the 15th, and the arrangements made by Blücher during that night, afford a complete refutation of the charge so frequently made against the Prussian commanders, that the French attack took them by surprise. Everywhere Zieten made a good and stubborn fight against overwhelming numbers, and fell back steadily and with resolute coolness. So far out as Ham-sur-Heure a Prussian battalion had barricaded that village, and made a stout stand against one of Pajol's brigades. Attacked by the advance-guard of the left French column, a Westphalian *Landwehr* battalion defended the village of Thuin with great obstinacy. Another battalion maintained the barricaded bridge of Marchiennes against several attacks, and finally retired in good order. But nevertheless, the French by eleven o'clock were in full possession of Charleroi, and Reille's corps was effecting its passage over the river. Gérard's column of the right, having had a longer distance to travel, had not as yet reached its destined point at Châtelet.

In the early morning there had occurred in Gérard's command an unhappy and ominous occurrence. The commander of one of his divisions was a certain General Bourmont. Although a distinguished soldier, his career had not been without stain; and Napoleon, suspecting his loyalty, consented to employ him only when Gérard promised to be personally responsible for him. His return for this kindness was an act of abominable baseness. On the early morning of the 15th, Bourmont rode ahead of his division accompanied by two officers of his staff, and he and they deserted to the enemy. When the traitor was presented to Blücher, the latter could not refrain from evincing his scorn for the faithless soldier; and when an attempt was made to ingratiate him with Blücher by directing his attention to, the white cockade which Bourmont conspicuously displayed, the blunt old marshal bluntly remarked, "It matters nothing what a fellow sticks in his hat—a scoundrel always remains a scoundrel." Old "*Vorwärts*" never minced his meaning. The French soldiers were furious at the desertion of Bourmont, and they suspected many other generals of Napoleon's army as being capable of similar conduct. There is no doubt that in the Waterloo campaign the soldiers disbelieved everything which was not confirmed by their own eyesight; nor was

this difficult of explanation, since the emperor had never hesitated to give such colouring to his statements and reports as he thought would best effect the object he had in view.

Owing to the absence of infantry at the heads of the French columns, two Prussian brigades were able to retard the French advance for several hours. Reille's advance-guard, having crossed the Sambre at Marchiennes, was moving by the Charleroi-Brussels road on Gosselies. But Steinmetz with the 1st Prussian brigade stoutly held that place for a considerable time, supported by Lützow's gallant dragoons; and it was not until the main body of Reille's corps, followed at some distance by the head of D'Erlon's column, had come up, that the Prussians moved aside to Heppignies, and left the Charleroi-Brussels road open to Reille and D'Erlon. When, in conformity with Zieten's orders, Pirch I. found it necessary to abandon Charleroi, he retired up the gradual rising ground with his brigade (the 2nd), and soon after two o'clock Zieten took up a defensive position behind Gilly, along a ridge in rear of a rivulet. About three, Napoleon reached Gilly, where he found Grouchy and Vandamme halted, in the belief that there was a large force in their front. Napoleon promptly recognised that the Prussians were in no great strength, and directed on them a heavy cannonade, after which the French columns moved to the attack. Zieten did not await the attack; but Napoleon, angry that the enemy should escape him, ordered General Letort, his *aide-de-camp*, with some squadrons of the Imperial escort, to cut off the retreat of the Prussians, and at the same time Pajol sent part of his cavalry to seize a defile in the woods of Fleurus. The Prussian infantry withstood repeated attacks of the French cavalry, and aided by the devoted exertions of a dragoon regiment, succeeded in gaining the wood of Fleurus. A fusilier battalion, however, was broken by the French cavalry. It had been or-

dered to withdraw into the wood, but in the course of the attempt it had been overtaken by the enemy's cavalry, by which it was furiously assailed and suffered a loss of two-thirds of its strength. Another regiment, in square, was attacked by the French cavalry. Letort and the escort squadrons crashed home into it and it was broken with the loss of half its numbers, but the rest escaped through the wood. This success, however, was attained at the cost of the life of the gallant Letort, who fell mortally wounded in the moment of victory. Meanwhile, Excelmans' dragoons had deployed on the far side of the wood, and successfully charged the enemy when retreating across the plateau in the direction of Fleurus.

While the emperor was still at Gilly about five o'clock, before the end of the combat just described, Marshal Ney, who had just overtaken the army on the march, came to Napoleon, having ridden over from Charleroi, and received from him the command of the 1st and 2nd corps with Piré's cavalry of the 2nd corps, and the division of Bachelu—troops with which, the same evening, he drove from Frasnes the allied brigade commanded by Prince Bernard of Saxe-Weimar. The old cordial relations between Napoleon and Ney existed no longer. The emperor was aware that Ney, when Napoleon was marching on Paris after his return from Elba, had pledged himself to the Bourbons that "he would bring Napoleon back in an iron cage." Subsequently, and it as little wonder, he had kept so aloof from the emperor that when he appeared on the *Champs-de-Mai* the latter affected surprise, saying that he thought Ney "had emigrated." Ney had no intention of making the campaign. But when Mortier fell ill and an urgent summons came to him from his old master, the fighting spirit revived in him, and he hurried forward, buying at Maubeuge Mortier's horses—presumably the ill-fated animals which one after another were to be killed under him at Waterloo. He reached the army just in time to be given the command of the left wing; with which henceforth this article, treating as it does almost solely of the Battle of Ligny, has scarcely any further concern.

Late in the afternoon of the 15th, Napoleon left Gilly before the conclusion of the fighting about that place, and went back wearily to Charleroi, where he spent the night. Before quitting the front at Gilly he had decided on altering the organisation of the forces with which he intended to fight the Prussians on the morrow. Grouchy, who until now had been in command of the reserve cavalry, was given the more important command of the 3rd corps (Vandamme) and of the 4th

corps (Gérard); the emperor taking into his own hand the command of the Imperial Guard, the reserve cavalry, and the 6th corps (Lobau). As the emperor rode off he ordered Grouchy to push forward as far as possible towards Sombref, and the cavalry of Pajol and Excelmans continued to advance in that direction. When, however, Grouchy ordered Vandamme to follow the cavalry in support, that rugged commander strenuously refused to obey, no intimation having reached him that he was to come under Grouchy's command; and he ordered his corps to bivouac where it stood.

Napoleon had expected that all his troops would have been across the Sambre before noon of the 15th, but the staff arrangements were faulty, and at nightfall of that day the whole of the 6th corps, half of the 4th corps, half the cavalry of the Guard, and two corps of the reserve cavalry were still south of the river. The tardiness of the French rearward columns was in marked contrast to the alert activity of the Prussian soldiers of Zieten's corps, who from early morning had been constantly under arms, in continual motion, and almost as constantly engaged, pursued and assailed by an overwhelming superiority of hostile force. It was not until near midnight that the corps effected its concentration in position between Ligny and St. Amand, at a distance varying from fifteen to twenty miles in rear of its original line of outposts, after having gallantly fulfilled the arduous task of gaining sufficient time for the concentration on the following day of the main body of Marshal Blücher's army. The loss sustained on the 15th by Zieten's corps reached a total of 1,200 men, and two of its battalions were reduced to mere skeletons.

Late on the 14th, Zieten had ascertained that strong French columns were assembling in his front, and that everything portended an attack on the following morning. This intelligence reached Blücher at Namur at ten o'clock on the night of the 14th; and an hour later simultaneous orders were despatched for the march of Bülow's corps (4th) from Liège to Hannut, of Pirch's (2nd) from Namur upon Sombref, and for Thielemann's (3rd) from Ciney to Namur. The orders to Bülow miscarried, and eventually he did not reach Gembloux, within a few miles of the field of Ligny, until after the battle was over, although in time to be of service to the other three corps retreating from Ligny. By the afternoon of the 15th the 2nd corps had taken up a position in the immediate vicinity of Sombref; the 1st corps, as has been mentioned, was concentrated by midnight of the 15th between Ligny and Amand; and the 3rd corps arrived at Sombref on the morning of the 16th. Blücher had established his headquarters in that village on the previous evening.

The result of the operations of the 15th had been highly favourable to Napoleon. He had effected the passage of the Sambre with slight loss; he was operating with the main portion of his forces directly on Blücher's preconcerted point of concentration; and he was already in the immediate front of his adversary's chosen position before that concentration could be completed. No doubt, after their exertions of the previous day, his troops were fatigued and widely scattered. Siborne, the historian of the campaign, argues that because Lobau's corps and the Guard were halted in rear at Charleroi, and part of Gérard's corps at Châtelet in the early morning of the 16th, there was a laxity of dispositions indicating the absence of that energetic perseverance and restless activity which had characterised Napoleon's operations in his previous wars. But it may be argued that every hour of rest was of value to his troops; while, on the other hand, the whole strength of his adversary was not yet visible. It was all-important to Napoleon that he should gain a crushing and decisive victory over the Prussians. To assail them prematurely would not bring about this result; and it was sound wisdom on his part to wait patiently with the whole of his own strength until the moment should arrive when he might hope to wreck and destroy his opponent's forces to the last company and the uttermost squadron, prior to turning to rend the British ally of that shattered opponent.

Prince Blücher, supported by the advice of General Gneisenau, his able chief-of-staff, resolved on accepting battle in the Sombref-Brye position confronting the higher ground of Fleurus—a position previously chosen in the event of the enemy's adoption of that line of operations to which that enemy had now distinctly committed himself. This position (*vide* map)comprised the heights of Brye, Sombref, and Tongrines, contiguous to the high road between Namur and Nivelles. These heights are bounded on the west and south-west, the right of the position, by a shallow ravine, through which winds a petty rivulet skirting the villages of Wagnelée, St. Amand la Haye, and St. Amand. Near the lower end of the last-named village, this streamlet unites with the greater rivulet of the Ligny, which flows through a deeper valley along the whole of the south or main front of the position. In this valley, partly bordering the stream itself, partly built on the gentle acclivities of the northern slope, lie the villages of Ligny, Pont Potriaux, Tongrenelle and Boignée.

From a tactical point of view, the Prussian position was unquestionably defective. Nearly the whole of the terrain between the line of villages of Ligny, St. Amand and Wagnelée, and the great Namur *chaussée*, was in full exposure to the view of the enemy: and as there was a virtual certainty of protracted village-fighting along the front of the position, the supports and reserves required to feed a struggle of that character would obviously be subjected to the full play of the batteries on the opposite more commanding heights. Upon the sloping ground of the Prussian position every movement could be discerned from the French side; on which, on the contrary, the undulations admitted of the concealment of considerable bodies. It was this defect which chiefly caused Wellington—who had ridden over from Quatre Bras to consult with Blücher at the windmill at Bussy before the battle of Ligny began—to regard Blücher's dispositions for battle as objectionable. "If old *Vorwärts* fights here," was his comment to Hardinge, "he will get most damnably licked!" The same defect was strikingly manifested later, by the fact that the gradual weakening of the Prussian centre and left for the purpose of reinforcing the right was closely observed by Napoleon, who took advantage of the insight thus attained into his adversary's designs by collecting the force with which, when he discerned that the Prussian reserves were expended, he so suddenly assailed and broke the centre of Blücher's lines.

There has been any amount of controversy regarding the strengths of the armies which fought at Ligny. In attributing to Blücher a force 97,000 strong for the three corps engaged, Sir Evelyn Wood, generally so correct, is manifestly in error. Thiers and Dorsey Gardner, both good authorities, are at one in stating the Prussian strength at 84,000, and the French at 60,000, after deduction of Lobau's 11,000, who were not engaged. Those also are approximately Siborne's figures. But counting heads is not always a correct method of computation. There was a large leaven of green youngsters in the Prussian ranks; and probably the two armies were of about equal fighting value, although Wellington always held that Napoleon in a battle was equal to 40,000 men.

The preliminaries of the battle began about noon, when the French light artillery cannonaded the Prussian cavalry posts. Von Röder, as soon as he saw the advancing French array, ordered the retreat of his cavalry to the further side of the stream, remaining himself until withdrawn with two regiments near the Tombe de Ligny. Meantime the main body of the French army advanced imposingly in columns of corps. Vandamme, with Girard's division attached, moved forward against St. Amand, the most salient point of the Prussian position. While deploying, the corps was fiercely cannonaded by the Prussian batteries behind the village. Girard prolonged Vandamme's corps to the left, and Domont's light cavalry division took post beyond Girard. The centre column, under Gérard, moved out along the Fleurus highroad, and presently manned the heights fronting the village of Ligny, its left near the Tombe de Ligny, its right resting on a knoll south of Mont Potriaux. The right column, comprising Pajol's and Excelmans' cavalry corps, took post on Gérard's flank along with Morin's light cavalry of the 4th corps, the whole showing a front to the eastward against the villages of Tongrines, Tongrenelle, Boignée, and Balatre, to watch any hostile movements on their left and to divert their attention from the centre.

Gérard, during the deployment, had an awkward adventure. Ordering his men to fall out—the actual fighting had not yet begun—

the general himself went forward to reconnoitre the enemy's position, accompanied by his staff-officers and a few hussars as escort. When near the Prussian line of front a body of Prussian cavalry advanced rapidly against him, and Gérard and his escort retreated at full gallop. During the flight the general's horse fell into a ditch which was hidden from view by the high-standing wheat crops, and the whole of the escort, seeing that their chief was down, turned back to defend him. His *aide-de-camp*, Lafontaine, having killed two Prussian lancers and broken his sword on the head of a third, was struck in the side by a bullet fired from a pistol close to his body. The chief-of-staff, Saint Remi, was dangerously wounded by seven lance-thrusts. Another *aide-de-camp*, Captain Duperron, dismounted and tried to put Count Gérard up into the saddle, but in the hand-to-hand fighting then being waged this became impossible, and the general must have been killed or taken prisoner had not a cavalry regiment, led by the son of General Grouchy, who was attracted by the firing, galloped up and driven off the Prussian horsemen.

Soon after three o'clock Napoleon gave the signal for his troops to advance to the attack; and for the next five and a half hours a continuous and desperate struggle was carried on in and about the villages bordering the ravine. There remained out of action in the earlier phases of the fighting, the Imperial Guard and Milhaud's *cuirassiers* halted in reserve, the former on the left, the latter on the right of Fleurus. Those troops were held back for the final stroke, which Napoleon himself was intending to administer. Lobau had not yet come up, and his command never fired a shot.

When his assailants came on, Blücher was quite ready for them. He had marshalled his forces betimes. Zieten with the 1st corps occupied the right and centre, that portion of the position included in the villages of Brye, St. Amand la Haye, St. Amand, and Ligny. The brigades of this corps had been greatly mixed during the night when occupying those villages, and the battalions were distributed rather promiscuously during the battle. Its main body was drawn up on the slope between Brye and Ligny, near the farm and windmill of Bussy, the highest point of the whole position. Seven battalions stood in rear of it, two more linking Bussy and Ligny, and four battalions were specially charged with the defence of Ligny itself. Three battalions were posted in the vicinity of the village of Brye; and several companies were distributed in the intersected ground between that village and St. Amand la Haye. Four battalions were posted on the high ground in rear of St. Amand, their right resting on St. Amand la Haye, and the defence of St. Amand itself was entrusted to three battalions of the 3rd brigade. The remaining six battalions of this brigade were posted in reserve northward of Ligny. The 2nd army corps, commanded by General Pirch I., was formed up in reserve to Zieten; and to the 3rd corps (Thielemann) was assigned the left, in that part of the field lying between Sombref and Balatre.

The actual battle was begun by an attack on St. Amand on the part of a division of Vandamme's corps. Made in three columns with great vigour, it proved successful, and after a stubborn resistance the Prussians were driven from the village. But when the French attempted to debouch from it, they were met by showers of grape and canister from the Prussian guns; the Prussian infantrymen hurled themselves forward strenuously, and, as the result of a prolonged and bloody *mêlée*, regained possession of the village, and held it for a while. This, however, was but a prelude, bloody though it was. St. Amand was a place of great importance, constituting as it did the strength of the Prussian right, and, from the intersection of gardens and hedges, was very capable of defence although so much in advance of the rest of the Prussian position. Continued desperate fighting for two hours had the result that the French were in possession only of half the village. But Vandamme was not content with this half-success. Before the furious onset he now made the Prussian troops, who had lost most of their officers, gave way with a loss of 2,500 men, and withdrew into position between Brye and Sombref, while loud shouts of "*Vive l'Empereur!*" proclaimed the triumph of the French infantry.

The village of Ligny was long and stubbornly held by the Prussians. Its defenders sheltered by stone walls, hollow ways, and banked-up hedges, remained quiescent under the hurricane of French shot and shell; but as the French infantry were visible descending the slope, they quitted their concealment, sent forward their skirmishers, and once and again threw into disorder with their fire the advancing adversaries. Column after column forced its way into the village, only to be hurled back. Gérard himself headed one of the French attacks, and almost penetrated within the precincts of the old castle in the upper part of the village; but he was repulsed again and again with great slaughter by the four Prussian battalions of Henkel's brigade, which gallantly maintained the post of Ligny. As the discomfited French troops withdrew, their batteries played with redoubled energy on the village, and fresh columns prepared for another assault. That presently came, and a desperate struggle

ensued. Mingled with the din of musketry-fire throughout the whole extent of the village rose from the French fierce shouts of "*En avant!*" and "*Vive l'Empereur!*" responded to by the Prussians with counter-cries of "*Vorwärts!*" and the wild "*Hourra!*" whilst the batteries on the heights poured destruction into the masses descending either slope to join in the desperate struggle in the valley, out of which arose from the old castle volumes of thick dark smoke with occasional flashes of lurid flames. Once again the Prussian defenders succeeded in clearing the village of the French, who in retreating abandoned two guns; and four fresh Prussian battalions were thrown into shattered and bloodstained Ligny, whose streets and gardens were heaped with the slain.

Vandamme, on the French left, held possession of St. Amand, but was unable to debouch from it. Napoleon then ordered General Girard, on the extreme left, to carry the village of St. Amand la Haye, which he accomplished after a bitter struggle. Blücher then ordered General Pirch II. to retake the place; but his brigade, closely pressed by the French occupants, and having got into great contusion, was forced to withdraw its scattered remnants and to re-form. In this combat Girard, whose division had so gallantly held the village, fell mortally wounded. Blücher resolved on a renewed attack; and when the preparations therefore were accomplished, aware how much depended on the result, he galloped to the head of his column, and addressed some rough, stirring words to his young soldiers. "Now, lads!" he shouted, "behave well! Don't let the *grande nation* get the better of us again! Forward—in God's name— Forward!" Pirch's battalions dashed into the village at a charging pace, sweeping the enemy completely before them. Sallying forth on the other side, they pursued the enemy with an impetuosity which the officers had difficulty in restraining; and many plunged into the very midst of the French reserves. The cavalry caught the enthusiasm of their brethren of the infantry, and supported the attack on the village by a headlong charge on the enemy's cavalry. Almost simultaneously the adjacent village of Wagnelée was assailed by the Prussians; but the attempt, although sustained with vigour, ultimately failed. For hours a constant struggle was maintained until darkness, on the Prussian right flank, every village taken and retaken with immense slaughter.

Meanwhile the village-fighting in Ligny was at its hottest. The place was utterly congested with combatants ablaze with excitement, and its streets and enclosures were choked with dead, dying, and wounded. Every house that was not in flames was the scene of a hand-to-hand contest. Order had long been lost, and men fought furiously in little groups; the bayonet, and even the butt, being freely used in adding to the dreadful carnage. A dense pall of smoke overhung the whole village and settled on it with a darkness almost of night; but the incessant din of musketry, the crashing of burning timbers, the smashing of doors and gateways, the yells and imprecations of the combatants, gave dread indication to the reserves on the slopes beyond the gloom of the savage and ruthless character of the bloody struggle being waged under the overhanging darkness. Long did this desperate strife continue without material results on either side. Then fresh Prussian batteries from the rear came into action; as did also a reinforcement, on the French side, from, the artillery of the Imperial Guard. The earth trembled under the tremendous cannonade; and as the flames from the burning houses shot upwards

through the volumes of smoke, the spectacle seemed some violent convulsion of nature, rather than a conflict between man and man.

Neither in the villages on the right nor in the key of the centre at Ligny did the contest slacken for a moment during this long afternoon of blood and death. Fresh and eager masses from both sides poured into the blazing villages as soon as the diminished strength and utter exhaustion of the combatants required relief. So equally balanced were the courage, energy, and devotion of either side that the obstinate struggle seemed likely to desist only when the utter exhaustion of the one should yield to the greater command of reserves possessed by the other. Napoleon's eagle eye discerned that the Prussian reserves were nearly exhausted; and he considered that the time to end the sanguinary fighting along the chain of villages, and to bring the battle to an issue by breaking in upon the centre of the Prussian front with the Imperial Guard and Milhaud's corps of *cuirassiers* in support. Soon after 5.30, these troops were in march towards Ligny, when they were suddenly halted by an order from the emperor. At two o'clock Soult had despatched an officer to Ney at Frasnes, carrying the order that the 1st corps (D'Erlon) should join Napoleon in the Ligny position. The messenger on his way to Ney had already given the order to the head of the column to wheel to its right; and the new direction had been taken up by D'Erlon about 4.30. Several officers about an hour later had reported to the emperor the appearance of a column of about 25,000 men, marching apparently in the direction of Fleurus. It did not seem to have occurred to anyone about Napoleon that this distant body might be D'Erlon's corps; and the suspicion arose, confirmed by the reports of several of Vandamme's officers, that the column was English. The Imperial Guard and Milhaud's corps were therefore kept

in hand, and several staff-officers were sent off at a gallop in the direction of the unknown army corps. According to Sir Evelyn Wood their intelligence was simply that "the column had disappeared;" whereas Siborne states that the emperor's *aide-de-camp*, returning from his reconnaissance, reported that the column which had caused uneasiness proved to be D'Erlon's corps.

The strange adventures of D'Erlon's corps on the afternoon of Ligny are narrated by Sir Evelyn Wood. Having first got on the wrong road, D'Erlon eventually took up a position in rear of Brye, so near to the Prussians that the men at the head of the column could read distinctly the numbers painted on the backs of the Prussian soldiers' knapsacks. D'Erlon's artillery came into action and was just about to open fire, when General D'Elcambre, Ney's chief-of-staff, arrived with a positive order from Ney to D'Erlon to bring his corps back immediately to Quatre Bras. Had D'Erlon disobeyed and fallen on Blücher's rear while Napoleon was attacking him in front, nothing could have saved the right wing of the Prussian army.

As the twilight was gathering on the lurid scene, the fortune of the battle was gradually becoming adverse to the Prussians. It was only by dint of extraordinary exertions that the defenders of Ligny were holding out against an adversary who was continually throwing in fresh reinforcements. In reply to their appeal came Gneisenau's stern reply, that at whatever sacrifice the village must be held for half an hour longer. Then came tidings to Blücher that the brigade in St.

Amand la Haye had expended the whole of its ammunition, and that even from the pouches of the slain the last cartridge had been taken. Blücher curtly answered that the brigade must not only maintain the post, but take the offensive with the bayonet. But there is a limit even to the most resolute endurance. Officers and men, overcome by long exertion, were falling from sheer exhaustion. The protracted struggle in the villages took on a yet more savage and relentless character. The animosity and exasperation of the combatants were uncontrollable. Every house, every court, every wall was the scene of bitter fighting. An ungovernable rage had seized on the soldiers of both sides—a strife in which every man sought an opponent in whose slaughter he might glut the hatred and revenge which were maddening him. Quarter was neither begged nor granted.

At about eight o'clock Napoleon arrived near the lower extremity of Ligny with eight battalions of the Imperial Guard, the regiment of the Grenadiers à Cheval of the Guard, and Milhaud's eight regiments of *cuirassiers*—a force perfectly fresh, having hitherto been in reserve. When the emperor noted the comparatively bare space in rear of Ligny, he remarked to Gérard, "They are lost: they have no reserve remaining!" The defenders of Ligny saw, on the French right of the village, a massive column issuing from under the smoke of the batteries which had opened on them, and whose fire was tearing lanes through their ranks; and as the mass rapidly descended the southern slope they could not fail to realise by its order and solidity, as well as by the dark lofty front of bearskins, that this new adversary was the redoubted Imperial Guard. Ligny was turned; and it only remained for its defenders to effect an orderly retreat from the bloodstained ruins which they had held so long and so staunchly. But their courage was not daunted, notwithstanding their exhausted condition and their knowledge that a body of fresh and chosen troops was advancing against them. The battlefield would soon be in darkness; hence they needed but a brief term of perseverance to secure the means of effecting a retreat unattended with the disastrous consequences which an utter defeat in the light of day would have entailed on them.

The Prussian infantry, compelled to evacuate Ligny, effected its withdrawal in squares with perfect order although surrounded by the enemy, stoutly repelling the hostile attacks made in repeated but vain attempts to scatter it in confusion. One battalion withstood the assault of Milhaud's cuirassiers, which had crossed the stream on the other side of the village. Blücher, panting to stem the

further advance of the enemy, called to him the three cavalry regiments immediately at hand—the 6th Uhlans, the 1st West Prussian Dragoons, and the 2nd Kurmark Landwehr Cavalry. General von Röder sped the Uhlans to make the first charge. It was led by Colonel von Lützow, the chief of the famous "night-riders" of the War

of the Liberation. As his squadrons were galloping down the slope against the French infantry, they encountered a hollow way hidden by the standing corn. The formation was broken up, and during the check caused by this obstacle the colonel, eleven officers, and some seventy men were shot down. A second volley completely repulsed the attack, and as the regiment went to the rear it was followed up by the French *cuirassiers*, and Lützow was captured. Another attack made by the Prussian dragoons and *Landwehr* cavalry was on the point of penetrating a battalion of French infantry, when the Prussian regiments were suddenly struck in flank by Milhaud's cuirassiers and completely dispersed. Later a mass of twenty-four squadrons was collected, but the attack which this body made was without success. Blücher, realising that the only hope depended on the possibility of his cavalry still succeeding before the darkness in hurling the French columns back into the valley, rallied his troopers, and, placing himself at their head charged in his old hussar style *ventre à terre*. The French stood fast and the charge failed, Blücher and his horsemen hotly pursued by the French cuirassiers. His charger, a fine grey—a present from the Prince Regent of Great Britain—was mortally wounded and began to falter in his stride. Looking back at the pursuing *cuirassiers* Blücher exclaimed to Nostitz, his staff-officer: "Now I am done for!" Presently the gallant horse went down and rolled over on its rider. Nostitz promptly alighted and with drawn sword stood over his revered chief. As the struggling masses surged backwards and forwards in the *mêlée*, Blücher was several times trampled on by galloping horses. Nostitz threw a cloak over his master, who lay half-stunned for nearly a quarter of an hour, when the devoted staff-officer, with the help of some dragoons, pulled aside the carcase of the grey, and eventually in the darkness got Blücher up on another horse and led him out of the focus of the strife.

Meanwhile Excelmans and Pajol rode through St. Amand and fell on the flank of the Prussian infantry while simultaneously attacked in front by Vandamme's regiments. Spent by long fighting, there was little resistance left in them; and by 9.30 the Prussians were everywhere in retreat and resistance ceased in the open country, although Brye, Sombref, and Point du Jour were occupied by rear-guards until after midnight. The French did not push a pursuit—they did not even cross the Namur-Nivelle *chaussée*; and by daybreak of the 17th the Prussian army was several miles away from the battlefield on which it had fought gallantly if unsuccessfully. The Prussian losses in the Battle of Ligny were over 12,000; those of the French about 8,000.

Blücher was carried to Gentinnes, a village about six miles in rear of Ligny. As soon as his fall was known, Gneisenau—the energetic chief-of-staff—undertook the direction of affairs, and promptly issued his orders for a retreat on Wavre. Blücher was himself again on the day after the battle, having dosed himself with his favourite nostrum of gin and sulphur. He kissed Colonel Hardinge, the British Commissioner with his army, remarking apologetically in his blunt way, "*Ich stinke etwas;*" and the tough old warrior was in the saddle on the day of Waterloo, and headed the pursuit of the French army on the evening of that day, having previously kissed Wellington on horseback, not at Belle Alliance but at Rosomme.

January 8-15, 1815
Campaign of New Orleans
C. Stein

At the western end of Jamaica is Negril Bay, a wide, safe, and convenient anchorage. There, on the 24th of November, 1814, was assembled one of the most imposing and efficient combined naval and military forces that Great Britain has ever sent across the Atlantic. More than fifty ships were there, most of them men-of-war, and the remainder transports. The men-of-war included many vessels of the largest size, and their commanders numbered amongst them the most renowned and trusted officers of England's navy. Sir Alexander Cochrane's flag was hoisted on the 80-gun *Tonnant*, and he had with him Rear-Admiral Malcolm in the 74, *Royal Oak*. Sir Thomas Hardy—Nelson's Hardy—was in the *Ramilies*, and Sir Thomas Trowbridge was in the *Armide*. Many others there were, scarcely less well known to fame and fresh from the great deeds which had given to England the un- disputed sovereignty of the seas. The decks of the fleet were crowded with soldiers. The 4th, 44th, 85th, and 21st Regiments, with a proportion of artillery and sappers, had come from North America, where they had fought the battle of Bladensburg, burned the public buildings of Washington, and lost in action their general—the gallant Ross—during the past summer. These had just been joined by the 93rd Highlanders, six companies of the 95th Rifles, two West India Regiments, two squadrons of the 14th Dragoons (dismounted), with detachments of artillery and engineers, and recruits for the regiments which had been already campaigning in America. The whole probably formed an army of about 6,000 men, though of them it could not be said that above 4,400 were troops on which a general could thor-

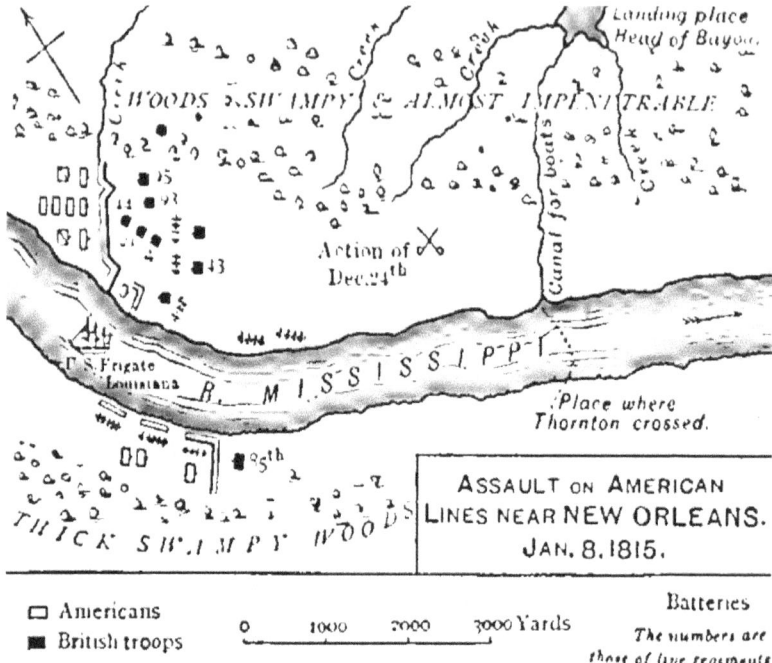

oughly depend, as the two West India Regiments, being composed of negroes, were not completely trustworthy, particularly if they were to be called upon to endure much exposure to cold in coming service. Their leader was Major-General Keane, a young and dashing officer, who had been sent out from England to be second in command to General Ross, and who did not know till he reached Madeira on his voyage that, by Ross's lamented death, he had no senior. Other forces were also on their way, which would eventually join the great armament now in Negril Bay. A fleet from Bordeaux was still on the ocean, the naval squadron of Captain Percy was to effect a junction from Pensacola, and more ships were to come from England conveying a commander- in-chief.

 The object with which so much warlike power had been collected had long been studiously kept secret, but at last it was known that a descent on Louisiana was intended, and that the first operation would be the capture of New Orleans. It was thought that the government of the United States would be taken by surprise, that little or no resistance would be met with, and that the charges of the expedition would be more than covered by the large booty in cotton, sugar, and other products which had not been able to leave the country during the course of the war while the seas were watched by English cruisers.

There was no long delay at the place of rendezvous, and the great fleet got under weigh on the 26th November. Confidence was in every heart, and no forebodings of disaster clouded the anticipations of success which, as by second nature, came to soldiers and sailors accustomed to victory.

New Orleans is built on the east bank of the Mississippi, the "father of waters," about eighty miles from its mouth. In 1814 its inhabitants numbered from 20,000 to 30,000, of whom the majority were French Creoles, while the remainder were Spaniards and Americans, besides a floating multitude of merchants, sailors, and others who had been detained in the city and debarred from their usual avocations by the war. It was doubtful whether this population was loyal to the American Republic, of which it had only for a few years formed a part, and, indeed, if the defence of the town had fallen into less vigorous hands than it did, it is more than likely that serious disaffection might have showed itself. The mighty flood of the Mississippi, bearing down with it a vast accumulation of detritus, had formed a great delta, and the waters themselves found their way to the Gulf of Mexico through many channels. Its main outlet was, however, the only one navigable for ships of any size, and this had at its mouth a constantly shifting bar, which was impassable for any craft drawing over sixteen or seventeen feet of water. Besides the natural difficulties of the entrance to the river, it was further defended by a fort, strong in itself and almost impregnable by its position in the midst of impervious swamps. Even supposing that an enemy should be able to pass the bar and the first fort, he would find that when he had ascended the river about sixty miles two other strong forts presented themselves, whose cross fire swept the channel, at a point, too, where the river makes a bend, and the sailing ships of the day had to wait for a change of wind to ensure their further progress.

The banks of the river were composed of slimy morasses, rank with semi-tropical vegetation and intersected by bayous, or creeks, utterly impracticable for landing or for the march and manoeuvring of troops. To the east of the swampy delta formed by the great river, a shallow- sheet of open water stretched inland from the Gulf of Mexico, and was only divided from the Mississippi at its further extremity by a narrow neck of comparatively firm land, and on this neck was situated the town of New Orleans. The open water near the gulf was known as Lake Borgne, and, where it widened out eastward of the city, as Lake Pontchartrain. The entire width of the neck of land between Lake Pontchartrain and the river might vary from eight to ten miles, but of this about two-thirds was reed-grown morass, while the remainder was occupied by cotton and sugar plantations, separated by strong railings and drained by numerous deep ditches or canals. The whole at certain seasons of the year was below the level of the river, and was protected from inundation by high artificial dykes, or ramparts, called in Louisiana *levées*. When the designs of the British armament became apparent, Major-General Jackson, of the United States army, an officer who had greatly distinguished himself in Indian wars, was entrusted with supreme command at the threatened point, and arrived at New Orleans on the 2nd December. As a man who made his mark in history, and who served his country well at a great crisis in her fortunes, his personal description is of peculiar interest:

"A tall, gaunt man, of very erect carriage, with a countenance full of stern decision and fearless energy, but furrowed with care and anxiety. His complexion was sallow and unhealthy, his hair was iron grey, and his body thin and emaciated, like that of one who had just recovered from a lingering and painful illness. But the fierce glare of his bright and hawk-like eye betrayed a soul and spirit which triumphed over all the infirmities of the body. His dress was simple and nearly threadbare. A small leather cap protected his head, and a short Spanish blue cloak his body, whilst his feet and legs were encased in high dragoon boots, long ignorant of polish or blacking, which reached to the knees. In age he appeared to have passed about forty-five winters."

Immediately on his arrival at New Orleans, General Jackson began making every arrangement for the defence of the town, inspecting and improving the river forts, reconnoitring the shores of Lake Borgne and Lake Pontchartrain, fortifying and obstructing the bayous which gave a waterway to the near neighbourhood of the town, and stimulating and encouraging the people. In truth he had apparently no easy task before him. We have seen how mighty was the force arrayed against him, which was even now lying off the coast ready to advance in a wave of invasion. To oppose it he had at his immediate disposal only two newly raised regiments of regular troops, a battalion of uniformed volunteers, two badly- equipped and imperfectly-disciplined regiments of State militia—some of whose privates were armed with rifles, some with muskets, some with fowling-pieces, some not armed at all—and a battalion of free men of colour, the whole amounting to between 2,000 and 3,000 fighting-men. Two small vessels of war lay in the river, but these were, so far, unmanned. There were

also six gunboats on Lake Pontchartrain. Commodore Patterson was the senior naval officer, and he had few subordinates. Reinforcements were, however, on their way, and were strenuously pushing forward in defiance of the inclement season, swollen streams, nearly impassable roads, and scant supply of food and forage. General Coffee, with nearly 3,000 men, was coming from Pensacola. General Carroll was bringing a volunteer force from Tennessee, and Generals Thomas and Adair, at the head of 2,000 Kentuckians, were also on their way down the Mississippi to join in the defence of Kentucky's sister State. Such an army as—even when all should be assembled—General Jackson was to command would, to all seeming, have little chance in a ranged field against the highly-disciplined soldiery of England; but it had, for its greatest and most reliable advantage, the occupation of a position in the highest degree difficult of approach, and, when reached, capable by its nature of. effectual resistance.

On the 8th December the leading ships of the English fleet, which had left Negril Bay on the 26th November, anchored off the Chandeleur Islands, which stud the gulf opposite to the entrance of Lake Borgne; and by the 12th the whole of the men-of-war and troop-ships had arrived. It had been recognised that to advance against New Orleans by the channel of the Mississippi was a task too difficult to be attempted, and Sir Alexander Cochrane and General Keane had determined to effect a landing on the shore of Lake Pontchartrain, and hoped, by pushing on at once, to be able to take possession of the town before effectual preparation could be made for its defence. It has been said that Lake Borgne and Lake Pontchartrain were shallow; indeed, their depth varied from six to twelve feet. The troops were, therefore, transferred from the larger into the lighter vessels, and on the 13th were prepared to enter upon the transit of the land-locked waters. They had not proceeded far, however, when it became apparent that the American gunboats which occupied the lake were prepared to offer resistance to the movement, and, until that resistance could be removed, no disembarkation could be attempted. The gunboats, with their light draught of water, could bid defiance to even the lightest vessels of the English fleet, which could not float where they sailed. They could only be reached by ships' launches and barges rowed by seamen, and a flotilla combined under Captain Lockier of the navy was at once prepared for the enterprise. The boats pushed off, and by noon came in sight of the foe, who would willingly have retreated and given their attackers long and weary toil in their approach, but that, the morning breeze having died away, they were

compelled perforce to fight at anchor in line moored fore and aft. Captain Lockier resolved to refresh his men before he commenced the action, and, dropping his grapnels just out of reach of the enemy's guns, allowed his crews to eat their dinner. After an hour's repose the boats again got ready to advance, and, with a hearty cheer, they moved on steadily in a long line. Then began one of those brilliant boat actions in which some of the best qualities of the English sailors so often showed themselves. The American guns opened, and a hail of balls was showered upon Captain Lockier's flotilla. One or two boats were sunk, others disabled, and many men were killed and wounded. But the English carronades returned the fire, and, as the determined, stalwart rowers gradually closed with the Americans, the marines were able to open a deadly discharge of musketry. A last powerful effort, the gunboats were reached, and, cutlass in hand, the bluejackets sprang up their sides. The resistance was stern and unyielding, worthy of the American Republic. Captain Lockier received several severe wounds, but, fighting from stem to stern, the boarders at length over- powered their enemy, the "Stars and Stripes" was hauled down, and on every vessel the English flag was hoisted in its place.

On the waterway of the lakes there was now no longer any resistance, and again the light vessels, to which the troops had been transferred, essayed to pass over it. But the depth beneath the keels became less and less, and even the lightest craft one after another stuck fast. The boats were of necessity hoisted out, and the soldiers, packed tightly in them, cramped in one position, began a miserable transit of thirty miles to Pine Island—a barren spot where all were to be concentrated before further operations were attempted. No boat, heavily laden as all were, could cover the long distance in less than ten hours, and, besides the discomfort to the men, inseparable from such long confinement, matters were made infinitely worse by a change in the weather. A heavy rain began, to which a cloak formed no protection, and such as is only seen in semi-tropical countries.

The operation began on the 16th, and, with all the diligence and continued exertion of which officers and men, soldiers and sailors, were capable, it was not finished till the 21st. By day and night for these days boats were being pulled from the fleet to the island, and from the island to the fleet. The strain upon the sailors was terrific, and many of them were almost without cessation at the oar. Not only had they to support hunger, fatigue, and sleepless nights, but the constant changes of temperature aggravated the hardships. Drench-

ing rain by day alternated with severe frosts by night, and tried to the uttermost the endurance of all. Nor was the army, as it landed in successive detachments on Pine Island, in a better plight. Bivouacked on a barren, swampy spot, which did not even produce fuel for camp fires, the clothes which had been saturated with rain by day congealed into hard and deadly chilling husks by night, with no supply of food but salt meat, biscuit, and a little rum provided from the fleet, soldiers have seldom been exposed to more severe trials of their fortitude. But, in spite of all, no complaints or murmurings rose from the expedition. The miseries of the present were forgotten in the high hopes of the immediate future, and this confidence did not arise alone from trust in their own strength, but deserters from the enemy related the alarm that existed in New Orleans, assured the invaders that not more than 5,000 men were in arms against them, that many of the city's inhabitants were ready to join them when they

appeared, and that conquest, speedy and bloodless, was within their grasp.

Meanwhile, in New Orleans itself. General Jackson had been meeting difficulties, working to restore confidence, and providing for the necessities of the military situation with all the energy of his nature. The news of the disaster to the American gunboats had filled the people with alarm. Rumours of treason began to spread, an insurrection of the slaves was dreaded, the armed ships in the river were still unmanned, and the expected reinforcements had not arrived. A desperate situation demanded the strongest and most unusual measures. Jackson did not hesitate to adopt them, and assumed the great responsibility of proclaiming martial law, so that he could wield the whole resources of the town, and direct them unimpaired by faction against his foe. Expresses were sent to the approaching additions to his strength, urging them to increase their efforts to push forward. The two war vessels—the *Carolina* and *Louisiana*—whose possible importance as factors in the approaching struggle was recognised, were manned and prepared for service; and even a lawless semi-piratical band of barratarian smugglers was forgiven its crimes, taken into the service of the Republic, and organised into two companies of artillerymen. So great, however, was the lack of war munitions that even the flints of these privateers' pistols were received from them as a precious prize, and were forthwith fitted to muskets.

The whole of the English field army was assembled on Pine Island on the 21st December, but having been so long on board ship, and its various corps having been gathered from many different points, it became necessary, before further advance was made, to form it in brigades, to allot to each brigade a proportion of depart mental staff—such as commissaries, medical attendants, etc.—and to establish depots of provisions and military stores. In completing these arrangements the whole of the 22nd was passed, and it was not till the morning of the 23rd that General Keane's advanced guard could start for its descent on the mainland. This advanced guard was made up of the 4th, the 85th Light Infantry, and the six companies of the 95th Rifles. To it were attached a party of rocket-men and two light three-pounder field-pieces. The whole was under command of Colonel Thornton, 85th. The main body of the force was divided into two brigades—the first, composed of the 21st, 44th, and one West India regiment, with a proportion of artillery and rockets, under Colonel Brook; and the second, containing the 93rd and the other West India regiment, under Colonel Hamilton, also provided with rockets and field-guns. The dismounted dragoons remained as a personal bodyguard to the general until they could be provided with horses.

It was intended that the descent of the army on the mainland should take place on the bank of the Bayou Bienvenu—a long creek which ran up from Lake Pontchartrain to within a short distance of New Orleans through an extensive morass. Every boat that could be sent from the fleet was to be used for the service, but not more could be provided than were sufficient to transport a third of the army at one time. The undertaking was therefore most hazardous, as, if the troops were placed in proximity to the enemy in successive divisions at long intervals a of time, each might be cut to pieces in detail. Neither leaders nor rank and file were, however, men to be deterred even by excessive risks, and, as has been said, they had the assurance of deserters that great resistance was not to be anticipated. Colonel Thornton's advanced guard was therefore embarked. Many miles had to be traversed, and again the soldiers were exposed to long hours of confinement in a cramped position; again the heavy rain of the day was succeeded at sundown by a bitter frost. Nor could they proceed after dark had set in, and, during the long weary hours of night, the boats lay in silence off their landing-place. By nine o'clock on the following morning, however, the landing was effected, and with limbs stiffened and almost powerless, with little available food to restore exhausted strength, 1,600 men stood at last upon the enemy's shore.

Wild and savage was the scene where the little band found itself A scarcely distinguishable track followed the bank of the bayou. On either side was one huge marsh, covered with tall reeds. No house or vestige of human life was to be seen, and but few trees broke the monotony of the dreary waste. Forbidding as was the spot, and ill-adapted for defence in case of attack, it might have possibly been supposed that General Keane, who accompanied the advanced guard, would have here remained in concealment till the boats, which had returned to Pine Island, had brought the remainder of his force; but he judged it best to push on into more open country, influenced by the hope of striking a swift and unexpected blow, and by his fairly well-founded doubts whether even now his enemy's scouts might not be hovering round him. The advance was formed, and, after several hours'

march, delayed by the difficulties of the marshy road, by the numerous streams and ditches that had to be crossed, and by the fetid miasma that filled the air, the track began to issue from the morass, there were wider and wider spots of firm ground, and some groves of orange trees presented themselves.

It was evident that human habitations must be near, and increased caution and regularity became necessary. At last two or three farmhouses appeared. The advanced companies rushed forward at the double and surrounded them, securing the inmates as prisoners. There was a moment of carelessness, however, and one man contrived to effect his escape. Now all further hope of secrecy had to be abandoned. General Keane knew that the rumour of his landing would spread with lightning speed, and all that was left to him was to act with determination, and make the appearance of his force as formidable as possible. The order of march was re-formed so that, moving upon a wide front, the three battalions had the semblance of twice their real strength, and the pace was quickened in order to gain a good military position before an enemy's force could show itself. Onward they pressed, till they found themselves close to the bank of the mighty Mississippi, and, wheeling to their right, they were on the main road leading to New Orleans.

They faced towards the city on a narrow plain, about a mile in width, with the river on their left, and the marsh which they had quitted on their right. A spot of comparative safety had been reached, the little column halted, piled arms, and its bivouac was formed. It was late in the afternoon before the moment of repose came, but the soldiers prepared to make the most of it: outposts were placed to secure them from surprise, foraging parties collected food, and fires were lighted.

The evening passed with one slight alarm, caused by a few horsemen who hovered near the picquets, and darkness began to set in. In the twilight a vessel was seen dropping down the current, and roused curiosity among those who had not stretched themselves by the fires to seek much-needed sleep. It was thought that she might be an English ship, which had managed to pass the forts at the mouth of the river. She showed no colours, but leisurely and silently she dropped her anchor abreast of the camp and furled her sails. To satisfy doubt she was repeatedly hailed, but no answer was returned. A feeling of uneasiness began to spread, and several musket shots were fired at her, but still reply came not from her dimly-seen bulk. Suddenly she swung her broadside toward the bank, and a commanding voice was heard to cry, "Give them this for the honour of America." The words were instantly followed by the flash and roar of guns, and a deadly shower of grape swept through the English bivouac. The light artillery which had accompanied General Keane's advanced guard was helpless against so powerful an adversary, and nothing could be done but to withdraw the exposed force behind the shelter of the high *levée*. The fires were left burning, and, in the pitch-dark night, those who were uninjured were forced to cower low while the continued storm of grape whistled over their heads, and they could hear the shrieks and groans of their wretched comrades who had been wounded by the first discharge. Thus they lay for more than an hour, when a spattering fire of musketry was heard from the picquets which had been able to hold their position. Whether this fire was only the sign of slight skirmishing at the outposts, or whether it foreboded a serious attack, was for some minutes doubtful, but a fierce yell of exultation was heard, the blackness of night was lighted by a blaze of musketry fire breaking out in semi-circle in front of the position, and the certainty came that the enemy were upon the advanced guard in overpowering numbers.

The situation seemed almost desperate. Retreat was impossible, and the only alternatives were to surrender or to beat back the assailants. General Keane and his followers were not the men to surrender, and at once assumed the bolder course. The 85th and 95th moved rapidly to support the picquets, while the 4th were formed as a reserve in the rear of the encampment. In the struggle that followed there was no opening for tactics, none for the supervision and direction of a general, or even of the colonels of battalions. The darkness was so intense that all order, all discipline were lost. Each man hurled himself direct at the flashes of musketry; if twenty or thirty united for a moment under an officer, it was only to plunge into the enemy's ranks and to engage in a hand-to-hand conflict, bayonet against bayonet, sword against sword. In the dire confusion of the bloody *mêlée* it soon became impossible to distinguish friend from foe. The British field-artillery dared not fire for fear of sweeping away Americans and Englishmen by the same discharge. Prisoners were taken on both sides, and often released at once by the sudden rush of assistance. As both armies spoke the same tongue a challenge was of no avail, and till the deadly thrust or shot came no man could be certain who stood in front of him.

In the nature of things such fighting could not be of long continuance. The Americans, astonished by the vigour of the assault, gave way, and were followed up for some distance; but the English officers

strove to rally their men, and to make them fall back to their first position; and soon all but those who had fallen were re-formed and concentrated. The Americans had been repulsed on all sides, but the fight had cost the English dearly, as, including the loss from the fire of the ship, 46 were killed and 167 wounded, besides 64 taken prisoners. The miserable night wore on, but with the morning's dawn there came a renewal of inglorious peril. The schooner whose fire had been so disastrous on the preceding evening still lay off in the river, and had now been joined by another vessel. They were the *Carolina* and *Louisiana*. Safe from any retaliation, their guns covered the shore and effectually precluded any movement of the English, who were obliged—hungry, cold, and wearied—to seek shelter under the *levée* from the shower of projectiles which swept the plain.

But meanwhile the rest of the army was landing, and hastening to join their comrades. The roar of the cannon had been heard far over the waters of Lake Pontchartrain, and had added energy to the strong arms that were pulling the boats. By nightfall on the 23rd the two brigades had both arrived on the scene of battle, and had taken up their ground between the morass and the river, but throwing back their left, so as to avoid the fire of the ships. The advanced guard could at last be extricated from the trap into which it had fallen, and the night of the 24th was passed in quiet and in disheartened speculation whether the advance could be resumed or not. The responsibility of decision was, however, removed from General Keane by the unexpected arrival on the morning of the 25th of Sir Edward Pakenham and General Gibbs, who had been sent from England as first and second in command.

Let us see what had been the course of affairs in New Orleans while the events just related were occurring. At the time that the English army was concentrating at Pine Island the defence of the city still depended alone on the small, half-organised force which General Jackson had found under his hand on his first arrival. But on the 21st the long-expected reinforcements began to pour in. General Coffee—the numbers of his following terribly reduced by the toils of an unprecedentedly rapid march—came at the head of mounted Tennessee sharpshooters, hunters and pioneers from their youth. Colonel Hinds brought the Mississippi Dragoons. On the 22nd General Carroll's flotilla arrived with a further body of Tennesseans, and, what was almost more important, a supply of muskets. The different corps were not yet, however, actually united in one body, and when the sudden report came that General Keane had actually landed, there was no military cohesion among them. If the English advanced guard had pushed at once on the city, instead of bivouacking during the afternoon of the 23rd, they might possibly have encountered no combined resistance, and have overthrown the Americans in detachments. But Keane's halt, however much it may possibly be justified, gave Jackson the opportunity he required, and enabled him to put all his men in line. The *Carolina* and *Louisiana* were sent down the river, with what result we have seen. The land troops were hurried to meet the enemy in the field, and the bitter struggle on the night of the 23rd took place.

When Sir Edward Pakenham took over the command of the English Army he found himself in as unsatisfactory a position as could well fall to the lot of any general. He found himself committed to a course of action which he had not initiated, and of which possibly he did not approve. He found his force in a cramped position, which offered no scope for the operations of highly trained and disciplined soldiers, and he learned that its advanced guard had suffered, if not a defeat, at least a very serious check. If the end of the campaign was failure, he certainly should not, be laden with all the blame. Carefully he reconnoitred the situation, and carefully he considered the state of affairs. It was evident that no advance could be made as long as the *Carolina* and *Louisiana* were able to pour forth their murderous fire, and the night

of the 25th was employed in erecting on the *levée* batteries armed with heavy ship-guns sent from the fleet. When these opened with red-hot shot on the morning of the 26th, the doom of the *Carolina* was sealed, her crew escaped in their boats, and she blew up. The *Louisiana* effected her escape while her consort was the sole object of the English artillery. Now that the river was thus cleared, and the left flank of his force was no longer exposed to destruction if it moved forward on the road to New Orleans, Pakenham made his dispositions for decisive advance. He reorganised his army, dividing it into two columns. That on the right—consisting of the 4th, 21st, 44th, and one West India Regiment—he placed under command of General Gibbs; the other—comprising the 95th, 85th, 93rd, and the other West India regiment, with all the available field-artillery, now increased to ten guns—remained under General Keane, and was to take the left of the line, while the dragoons, few of whom were yet mounted, furnished the guards to hospitals and stores.

But there was still much to do. Heavy guns, stores, and ammunition had to be brought from the distant fleet, the wounded had to be disposed of, and the numberless requirements of provision and protection for an army in the field had to be attended to. For two days the English lay perforce inactive, though their outposts were exposed to constant harassing and deadly attack from the American sharpshooters and partisans. In European war, by tacit convention, picquets and sentries confined themselves to the duties of watchfulness alone; but the riflemen of America saw in every enemy's soldier a man to be killed at any time, and they stalked individuals as they would have stalked deer in their own backwoods, slaying and wounding many, and causing anxiety by the never-ceasing straggling fire.

At length all was ready for the long-delayed advance, and on the bright, frosty morning of the 28th the army began its march. Confidence in a new commander of high reputation had restored spirits to the men; cold, wet, hunger, and broken rest were forgotten, and as the enemy's advanced corps fell back before them, hopes of conquest were renewed. Four or five miles were traversed without opposition. On the dead flat of the plain nothing could be seen far in advance of the columns, and they had no cavalry to scout in front and say what lay in their path. Suddenly, where a few houses stood at a turning in the road, the leading files came in view of the foe's position. In their front was a canal, extending from the morass on their left towards the river on their right. Formidable breastworks had been thrown up, powerful batteries erected, while the *Louisiana* and some gunboats moored in the Mississippi flanked their right. Sudden and tremendous was the cannonade, withering the musketry fire that burst upon the English column and mowed down their ranks. Red-hot shot set fire to the houses which were near to them. Scorched by flame, stifled with smoke, shattered by the close discharge, the infantry were, for the time, powerless, and had to be withdrawn to either side of the line of attack, and the artillery were hurried forward to reply to the American guns. To no purpose. The contest was too unequal. The heavy guns in the batteries and the broadsides of the *Louisiana* destroyed the light English field-pieces almost before they could come into action. The infantry again pressed forward, only to find themselves hopelessly checked by the canal. Staggered, shaken, and disordered, the English columns reeled under the blows which they had received. A halt was ordered, and then, slowly, sullenly, with sorrow, the whole force fell back. Again Sir Edward Pakenham found himself obliged to bivouac by the river side instead of occupying New Orleans, again he had to consider how the determined American resistance was to be overcome. The English bivouac was formed two miles from the American lines. A sorry place of rest it was. Once more the outposts were exposed to the stealthy attacks of an ever-vigilant, cunning, and active foe. Even the main body was hardly secure, for, by giving their guns a great elevation, the Americans were occasionally able to pitch their shot among the camp fires.

The possibility of turning the enemy's left by penetrating the morass which protected it was contemplated, but the idea had to be abandoned as soon as conceived. In the meanwhile General Jackson was vigorously at work in strengthening his already strong position. Numerous parties could be seen labouring upon his lines, and daily reinforcements came in to swell the numbers of their defenders. By the suggestion of Commodore Patterson, a strong field-work was constructed on the opposite bank of the river, and armed with heavy ship-guns, from which a flanking fire could be poured on all the space over which the English must attack. In view of the many difficulties which presented themselves, General Pakenham called a council of war, which was attended by all the English naval and military leaders. It was impossible to carry the American lines by assault, for their powerful artillery would deal certain destruction to infantry columns. To turn them was impossible, and their defenders could not be induced by any manoeuvring to leave their protection. The council decided on the only other possible alternative—to treat them as a regular fortification, and, by breaching batteries, to try to silence some of their guns, and to make in them a practicable gap, through which an entrance might be effected.

To give effect to this resolution the 29th, 30th and 31st December were employed in bringing up heavy cannon, accumulating a supply of ammunition, and making preparations as for a regular siege. When these arrangements were complete—arrangements which demanded the most strenuous and unremitting toil from everyone, from the general in command to the humblest private soldier—hesitation had no place and delay was at an end. Under cover of night, on the 31st, half of the army stole silently to the front, passing the picquets, and halted within 300 yards of the American lines. Here a chain of works was rapidly marked out, the greater part of the detachment piled their fire-locks, and addressed themselves vigorously to work with pick and shovel, while the remainder stood by armed and ready for their defence. So silently and to such good purpose was the work performed, that before the day dawned six batteries were completed, in which were mounted thirty pieces of heavy ordnance.

The morning of the 1st January, 1815, broke dark and gloomy. A thick mist obscured the sun, and, even at a short distance, no objects could be seen distinctly. The English gunners stood anxiously by their pieces, and the whole of the infantry were formed hard by, ready to rush into the breach which they hoped to see made. Slowly, very

slowly, the mist at length rolled away, and the American camp was fully exposed to view. As yet unconscious of the near presence of the thirty muzzles which were ready to belch forth their contents, the Americans were seen on parade. Bands were playing, colours flying, and there was no preparation for immediate deadly struggle. Suddenly the English batteries opened, and the scene was changed. There was a moment of dire confusion, a dissolution of the ordered masses which stood ready for review by their general. The batteries were unmanned, the pieces silent. But, though the English salvo was unexpected, there was no real unreadiness to resist and to reply to its stern challenge. The American corps fell quickly into their positions in the line of defence, their artillery, after brief delay, opened with rapidity and precision, the furious cannonade on both sides rent the air with its thunder, and battery answered battery with storm of shot and shell. Heavy as was the attackers' fire, however, it produced comparatively little effect on the solid earthworks of the defence, while the numerous guns which Jackson had mounted, aided by the flanking fire from the works on the opposite bank of the river, were crushing in their power. Hour after hour the duel continued, and yet no advantage was gained which would warrant Pakenham in hurling his infantry at the fortifications that stood in their front. The English ammunition began to fail and their fire slackened, while that of the Americans redoubled in vigour; and towards evening it became evident that another check had been suffered, and that again the invading army must fall back.

Dire was the mortification in the English ranks, bitter the murmurs that spread from man to man. The army had endured hardships with cheerfulness, they had undertaken severest toil with alacrity, but they had thought that victory was their due, and still they encountered repeated defeat. Now their encampment was open to the enemy's unremitting fire, and advance or retreat seemed equally impossible. But Pakenham had some, at least, of the best qualities of a leader. He refused to lose heart, and adopted a plan which well merited success by its boldness, and whose ultimate failure was in no way to be credited to any laxity on his part. He had recognised that the enemy's flanking battery on the right bank of the Mississippi was his greatest obstacle, and he conceived the idea of sending a strong force across the river, which should carry this battery by assault and turn its guns against the Americans themselves, while a simultaneous attack should be delivered directly upon the entrenchments. To do this, however, a sufficient number of boats must be provided, and it was necessary to cut a canal

from the Bayou Bienvenu wide and deep enough to float the ships' launches now in the lake. Upon this arduous undertaking the whole of the force was at once set to work. Day and night the labour was carried on; relay after relay of soldiers took up the task, and by January 6th it was accomplished. No better means could have been taken to restore the spirits of the men than the imposing of work, however hard, which seemed to promise a definitely favourable influence on their fortunes. Discouragement and forebodings were still further dissipated by the unexpected arrival of Major-General Lambert with the 7th and 43rd, two fine battalions, each mustering 800 effective men. Further reinforcements of marines and seamen also joined, bringing the English fighting strength up to nearly 6,000. At the same date, General Jackson had probably about 12,000 under his command.

It has been said that the canal from the bayou to the river was finished on the 6th, and no time was lost in carrying out the plan of which it was so great a factor. Boats were ordered up for the conveyance of 1,400 men, and Colonel Thornton, with the 85th, the marines, and a party of sailors, was appointed to cross the river. But ill-fortune still dogged the English general, still it seemed fated that his best-laid plans should be frustrated by accident. The soil through which the canal was dug being soft, part of the bank gave way, choking the channel and frustrating the passage of the heaviest boats. These, in turn, impeded others, and, instead of a numerous flotilla, only sufficient for about 350 men reached their destination, and even these did not arrive at the time appointed.

It was intended that Colonel Thornton's force should cross the Mississippi immediately after dark on the evening of the 7th. They were to carry the enemy's battery and point the guns on Jackson's lines before daybreak on the 8th. The discharge of a rocket was to give them the signal to commence firing, and also was to let loose the rest of the army in a direct attack.

The disposition for this direct attack was as follows:—General Keane, with the 95th, the light companies of the 21st, 4th, and 44th, and the two West India regiments, was to make a demonstration on the enemy's right; General Gibbs, with the 4th, 21st, 44th, and 93rd should force their left; whilst General Lambert, with the 7th and 43rd, remained in reserve. Scaling ladders and fascines were provided to fill the ditch and mount the wall; and the honourable duty of carrying them to the point of attack was allotted to the 44th, as being the regiment most experienced in American war. It was hoped that the fate of New Orleans would be sealed on the 8th January.

While the rest of the army laid down to sleep on the night of the 7th, Colonel Thornton, with 1,400 men, moved to the river's brink But the boats had not arrived. Hour after hour passed before any came, and then so few were they that only the 85th, with about 50 seamen—in all 340 men—could be embarked. The duty admitted of no hesitation or delay, and Colonel Thornton, with his force thus sadly weakened, pushed off. The loss of time was irreparable. It was nearly dawn ere they quitted the canal, and they should have been on the opposite bank six hours earlier. In vain they made good their landing without opposition; day had broken, the signal rocket was seen in the air, and they were still four miles from the battery which ought long before to have been in their hands.

Before daylight the main body was formed in advance of the picquets, ready for the concerted attack. Eagerly they listened for the expected sound of firing, which should show that Thornton was doing his work; but they listened in vain. Nor did Pakenham's plan fail him in this respect alone. The army, in its stern array, was ready for the assault, but not a ladder or a fascine was in the field. The 44th, who had been appointed to bring them, had misunderstood or disobeyed their orders, and were now at the head of the column without the means of crossing the enemy's ditch or mounting his parapet. Naturally incensed beyond measure, the general galloped to Colonel Mullens, who led the 44th, and bade him return with his regiment for the ladders; but the opportunity for using them was lost, and when they were at last brought up they were scattered useless over the field by the demoralised bearers.

The order to advance had been given, and, leaving the 44th behind them, the other regiments rushed to the assault. On the left a portion of the 21st, under the gallant Rennie, carried a battery, but, unsupported and attacked in turn by overpowering numbers of the enemy, they were driven back with terrible loss. The rest of the 21st, with the 4th, supported by the 93rd, pushed with desperate bravery into the ditch, and, in default of the ladders, strove to scale the rampart by mounting on each other's shoulders—and some, indeed, actually effected an entrance into the enemy's works. But, all too few for the task, they were quickly overpowered and slain, or taken prisoners. The withering fire that swept the glacis mowed down the attacking columns by companies. Vainly was the most desperate courage displayed. Unseen themselves, the defenders of the entrenchments fired at a distance of a few yards into the throng that stood helplessly exposed, while the guns on the other side of the river—yet unmenaced—kept up a deadly cannonade. Never have English soldiers died to so little profit, never has so heavy a loss been so little avenged.

Sir Edward Pakenham saw his troops in confusion, and the wavering in effort which ever preludes hopeless flight. All that a gallant leader could do was done by him. The 44th had come up, but in so great disorder that little could be hoped from such a battalion. Riding to their head, he called for Colonel Mullens[1] to lead them forward, but he was not to be found at his post. Placing himself at their head, the general prepared to lead them in person; but his horse was struck by a musket-ball, which also gave him a slight wound. He mounted another horse, and again essayed to lead the 44th, when again he was hit. Death took him before he had tasted the full bitterness of defeat, and he fell into the arms of his *aide-de-camp*. Nor did General Gibbs and General Keane fail to do their duty as English soldiers. Riding through the ranks, they strove to restore order and

---

1. Colonel Mullens was subsequently tried by court-martial and cashiered.

to encourage the failing energy of the attack, till both were wounded and were borne from the field. Their leaders gone, and ignorant of what should be done, small wonder if the troops first halted, then began slowly to retire, and then betook themselves to disordered flight. Great as was the disaster, its results might have been even more crushing than they were but that the 7th and 43rd, presenting an unbroken, steadfast front, prevented an attempt on the part of the enemy to quit the shelter of their lines in pursuit.

We left Colonel Thornton and his 340 men on the right bank of the Mississippi, and four miles from the battery which they had been detailed to take, and whose power was so severely felt by the main body of the English army.

They had seen the signal-rocket which told that their comrades were about to attack, and late though they were, they pressed forward to do their share of the day's operations. A strong American outpost was encountered, but it could not withstand the rush of the 85th, and fled in confusion. The position where the battery was mounted was reached, and to less daring men than Colonel Thornton and his little following might have seemed impregnable. Like their countrymen on the other side, the Americans, 1,500 in number, were strongly entrenched, a ditch and thick parapet covering their front. Two field-pieces commanded the road, and flanking fire swept the ground over which any attack must be made. The assailants had no artillery, and no fascines or ladders by means of which to pass the entrenchment. But, unappalled by superior numbers, undeterred by threatening obstacles, the English formed for immediate assault. The 85th extended across the whole line; the seamen, armed with cutlasses as for boarding, prepared to storm the battery, and the few marines remained in reserve. The bugle sounded the advance. The sailors gave the wild cheer that has so often told the spirit and determination of their noble service, and rushed forward. They were met and momentarily checked by a shower of grape and canister, but again they pressed on. The 85th dashed forward to their aid in the face of a heavy fire of musketry, and threatened the parapet at all points. From both sides came an unremitting discharge; but the English, eager to be at close quarters, began to mount the parapet. The Americans, seized with sudden panic, turned and fled in hopeless rout, and the entrenchment, with eighteen pieces of cannon, was taken. Too late! These very guns had been able already to take their part in dealing destruction to Sir Edward Pakenham's morn-

ing attack, and if they were now taken—if their defenders were dispersed—they had done all that they were wanted to do. Even yet, if the disaster to the British main body had not been so complete and demoralising, they might have been turned upon Jackson's lines and covered a second assault; but this was not to be. General Lambert, on whom had fallen the command of all that remained of the army, resolved—perhaps, under the circumstances, with wisdom—to make no further attempts on New Orleans. To withdraw his army was, in any case, difficult; another defeat would have rendered it impossible; and, as the Americans had gained confidence in proportion as the English had lost it, defeat was only too probable. In the last fatal action nearly 1,500 officers and men had fallen, including two generals, for General Gibbs had only survived his wound for a few hours. The English dead lay in piles upon the plain—a sacrifice to faulty generalship, and even more to a course of relentless ill-fortune. Of the Americans who had so gallantly defended their country, eight only were killed and fourteen wounded.

Alas! that electricity did not then exist to prevent so great a sacrifice of honour and life; for the preliminaries of peace between England and the United States had been signed in Europe before the campaign of New Orleans was begun.

June 18, 1815
Waterloo

D. H. Parry

The great Imperial Eagle of France had been caught and caged at Elba, and after close on twenty-five years of storm and tumult, Europe was at peace. The armies which had driven the Eagle out of France had marched home again, robbing the Eagle's nest of many ill-gotten trophies and leaving in his place a horde of vultures who claimed the nest as theirs.

As is the manner of vultures, there was much gorging: Louis XVIII., the man "who had learned nothing, and *forgotten* nothing," brought back in his train a host of hungry folk, princes of the blood royal, dukes, and noble dames; and France soon found that it would be made to suffer for its Revolution and its Republic, and that the victories of its emperor were like to cost it dear. Royalists filled the high places in Church and State. Shameless rapacity and mean reprisals were seen on every side; and in the army the most scandalous injustices were unblushingly practised.

People began to look with regret towards the Mediterranean isle where the Eagle plumed his ruffled feathers moodily.

There were mysterious nods and glances, and allusions to a certain flower which a certain "little corporal" was known to have loved.

"He will return again with the violet," they said in whispers.

Ladies affected violet-coloured silks, and rings of the same hue became fashionable, bearing the motto "It will reappear in Spring."

Nor were they wrong, for on the 1st March, 1815, at five o'clock in the afternoon, Napoleon the Great, with a hundred dismounted Lancers of the Guard, some veteran Grenadiers and a few officers, landed in the Gulf of San Juan, and began that triumphal progress which ended at *Waterloo*.

His advance is curiously recorded in the papers of the day: I quote from the *Moniteur*:—

"The cannibal has left his den."

"The Corsican wolf has landed in the Bay of San Juan."

"The tiger has arrived at Gay."

"The wretch spent the night at Grenoble."

"The tyrant has arrived at Lyons."

"The usurper has been seen within fifty miles of Paris."

"Bonaparte is advancing with great rapidity, but he will not set his foot inside the walls of Paris."

"Tomorrow Napoleon will be at our gates!"

"The emperor has arrived at Fontainebleau."

"His Imperial Majesty Napoleon entered Paris yesterday, surrounded by his loyal subjects."

At midnight on the 19th March, Louis the Gross got into his carriage by torchlight, and was driven off to Lille; the Comte d'Artois and the Court followed an hour later, and the good citizens found when they rose next morning, two notices fastened to the railings of the Place Carrousel—

"Palace to let, well furnished, except the kitchen utensils, which have been carried away by the late proprietor."

And the other—

"A large fat hog to be sold for one Napoleon."

At eight o'clock that evening the emperor was carried up the grand staircase of the Tuileries on the shoulders of his officers, and from that moment until the 12th June the master-mind was wrestling with a task vast enough to have discouraged twenty brains!

Out of chaos he produced order; a new government was formed, a new army created; five days after his entry the Allied sovereigns declared him an outlaw; on the 1st June he distributed Eagles to his troops, and took an oath of allegiance to the new Constitution. But Europe had meanwhile flown to arms, and 300,000 Austrians were to enter France by Switzerland and the Rhine; 200,000 Russians were marching on Alsace; Prussia had 236,000, half of whom were ready for action, so that, including our English 80,000, the Netherland contingent and the minor States of Germany, he had to face the onslaught

of more than 1,000,000 men, with only 214,000 at his immediate command. England and Prussia were the first to arrive; it would be July before the others could reach the frontier, so. Napoleon, leaving armies of observation at various points, marched against Belgium, hoping to defeat Wellington and Blücher in time to turn about and face the storm clouds gathering in the east.

******

It was the month of June, and the weather was intensely warm. An army under Wellington, some 100,000 strong, including British, King's German Legion, Hanoverian, Brunswick, Dutch, Belgian, and Nassau troops, was distributed in cantonments from the Scheldt to the Charleroi *chaussée*. It was a heterogeneous force, hastily got together, and a large proportion of it by no means to be depended upon.

Of the British regiments, many were formed of weak second and third battalions which had never been under fire, and nearly 800 militiamen fought in the ranks of the 3rd Guards and 42nd Highlanders, those in the Guards actually wearing their Surrey jackets.

Blücher's force, seasoned veterans for the most part, lay in four separate corps on the frontier south of Brussels, and so masterly were Napoleon's movements, that until the lights of his bivouac fires were suddenly seen glowing redly in the darkness beyond Charleroi, no one knew exactly where he was.

******

Brussels swarmed with fashionable folk, and the families of officers who were with the army.

The Duchess of Richmond gave a ball on the night of the 15th June, the list of invited guests being curious, and not a little melancholy. Among the two hundred odd names we read those of Wellington, Uxbridge, and Hussey Vivian; two Ponsonbys, one of whom was to die three days later; Hay, the handsome lad who had won a sweepstake at Grammont the Tuesday before, and whose young life ebbed out on the Friday at Quatre Bras; Cameron, of Fassifern, who also fell there; Dick of the 42nd, killed at Sobraon in '46; and *aide-de-camp* Cathcart, who lived till Inkerman, where a ball and three bayonet thrusts closed his strange career. These and many others of more or less note danced in the long, low-roofed, barn-like room which His Grace of Richmond had hired for the occasion from his neighbour. Van Asch, the coachbuilder.

About midnight Wellington, having already learned that the outposts had been engaged, went to the ball, where he found the Prince of Orange. Now, the Prince of Orange, who seemed fated to cause the useless sacrifice of valuable life, ought to have been at his post at Binche, and thither the duke promptly sent him, after first inquiring if there were any news.

"No, nothing, but that the French have crossed the Sambre, and had a brush with the Prussians!" Müffling had previously brought the intelligence, which should have arrived much sooner, the duke afterwards saying to Napier: "I cannot tell the world that Blücher picked the fattest man in his army to ride with an express to me, and that he took thirty hours to go thirty miles."

Far from being surprised (as some writers have it), the duke's orders were despatched *before* he went to that now historic entertainment, and the dancing continued long after he and his officers had left.

At two o'clock, while it was yet dark, strange sounds were heard under the trees—the shuffling of men's feet, the ringing of musket-butts on the ground, short words of command, and the running ripple of the roll-call along the ranks. People opened their windows and looked out; carriages returning from the ball drew up and waited: it was Picton's Division off to the front.

At four o'clock Pack's Highlanders, in kilt and feather bonnet, swung across the Place Royale and passed through the Namur Gate—the rising sun glinting on their accoutrements, their bagpipes waking the sleeping streets. "Come to me and I will give you flesh," was the weird pibroch of the Black Watch, and many a Highland laddie heard it that morning for the last time.

Some of the officers marched in silk stockings and dancing-pumps. Lingering too long at the ball, they had not had time—or perhaps, as the, night was warm, they had not troubled— to change them; and there were not, a few who never found time again.

Out in the early morning along the great highway they went, past lonely farms and clustering villages, through the grey-green gloom of the beech woods of Soigne to Mont St. Jean, where they halted for breakfast, and where about eight the duke passed them with his staff, leaving strict orders to keep the road clear; and at noon the troops were on the march again for Quatre Bras, which was the fiery prelude to the greatest battle fought in modern times.

The heat was so intense that one man of the 95th Rifles went mad, and fell dead in the road; but the others pushed on, and were soon afterwards under fire. If you take a map of Belgium, placing your finger on Brussels, and pass it down the great road running south, you will find, some twelve miles from the capital, the village of Mont St. Jean; a little beyond which place a crossroad from Wavre intersects the *chaussée*, and at that point move your finger at right angles, right and left, for a mile or so each way, and you have, roughly, the English position on the 18th June.

Continuing again, still southward, you will pass La Belle Alliance and Genappe, and nine miles from the crossroads before Mont St. Jean is Quatre Bras. Rolling ridges of waving grain, some woods in all their summer beauty, a gabled farmhouse, and a few cottages where four ways meet— that is one's impression of Quatre Bras, which Ney had orders to take, and drive out Perponcher's Dutch Belgians posted there; but we arrived to their assistance, corps after corps, at intervals, and forming up in line and square, repulsed the *cuirassiers* and lancers who charged through the tall rye.

The crops were so high that the gallant French cavalry had to resort to a curious device in singling out our regiments. A horseman would dash forward, find out the position, plant a lance in the ground, and disappear; then, in a few moments, guided by the fluttering pennon, his comrades would burst upon us—invisible until within a few horse-lengths.

Waterloo has put Quatre Bras into the shade, but few conflicts have been more brilliant.

Our 69th—thanks to Orange, who interfered with its formation just as the 8th Cuirassiers came through the corn—lost its only colour, taken by Trooper Lami, although Volunteer Clarke received twenty-three wounds and lost the use of an arm in its defence. The 69th's other colour had been captured at Bergen-op-Zoom, and was hung in the Invalides.

By four o'clock the 44th had upwards of 16 officers and 200 men killed and wounded.

A grey-headed French lancer drove his point into Ensign Christie's left eye, down through his face, piercing his tongue and entering the jaw: but in that shocking condition he still stuck manfully to the colour-pole, until, finding himself overpowered, he threw the colour down and lay upon it, and some privates of the regiment closing round the Frenchman, lifted him out of his saddle on their bayonet points!

The 92nd Highlanders—the old Gordons of Peninsular fame—were the last of Picton's men to reach the field, and were formed up in line. "Ninety-second, don't fire till I tell you!" cried Wellington, as a mass of *cuirassiers* charged them in his presence; and the word was not given until the dashing horsemen were within twenty yards.

A little later, the duke said again: "Now, 92nd, you must charge these two columns of infantry;" and charge they did, over a ditch, driving the French before them, but their beloved colonel, Cameron, received a death-wound from the upper windows of a house.

His horse turned and bolted with him, back along the road, until he came to his master's groom holding a second mount, when, stopping suddenly, the dying man was pitched on his head on to the stone causeway. But he had been terribly avenged; for the kilted Highland men burst into the house with a roar and put every soul inside to the bayonet.

"Where is the rest of the regiment?" asked Picton in the evening. Alas! upwards of half the "gay Gordons" had perished in the fray.

Through the broiling heat of that summer day our infantry stood firm, growing stronger as regiment after regiment arrived, and fresh batteries unlimbered in the trampled corn, until at night Ney fell back, leaving us in possession; our cavalry came up, jaded by their long marches; and we bivouacked on the battlefield, cooking our suppers in the *cuirasses* of the slain.

******

Meanwhile, Napoleon had beaten Blücher a few miles away at Ligny, but had neglected, in most un-Napoleonic fashion, to follow up his advantage, and the wily old hussar—he was over seventy-three—slipped off in the dark and retreated on Wavre.

When Wellington learned this next morning, he said to Captain Bowles: "Old Blücher has had a good licking, and has gone back to Wavre. As he has gone back, we must go too. I suppose in England they will say we have been licked. I can't help that." So back we went, along the Brussels road, our cavalry covering the retreat until we reached the stronger position before Mont St. Jean, where we halted and faced about,

and glued ourselves on the ridge across the causeway in such a manner that all the magnificent chivalry of France could never move us.

During the retreat from Quatre Bras on the 17th, all went well until the middle of the day. The wounded had been collected; the

columns fled off along the road; one of the regiments even found time to halt and flog a marauder: when, the enemy's cavalry pressing our rearguard too closely, some Horse Artillery-guns opened fire, and the discharge seemed to burst the heavy rainclouds.

It poured down in torrents; roads were turned into watercourses, the fields and hollows became swamps; we had a smart brush with some Lancers at Genappe, where our 7th Hussars and 1st Life Guards charged several times; the 10th Hussars had also occasion to dismount some men and line a hedgerow with their carbines; but the main feature of the retreat was a weary tramp in a deluge of rain. The cavalry had their cloaks, it is true, but the greatcoats of the foot-soldiers had been sent back to England. Soaked to the skin, we arrived at the ridge above La Haye Sainte, and prepared to pass the night without covering of any kind. The French advanced almost up to us, and Captain Mercer was giving them a few rounds from his 9-pounders when a man in a shabby old drab overcoat and rusty round hat strolled towards him and began a conversation. Mercer, who thought him one of the numerous *amateurs* with whom Brussels was swarming, answered curtly enough, and the stranger went away.

That shabby man was General Picton, who fell next day on the very spot where he received this unmerited snubbing. He fought at Quatre Bras in plain clothes, having joined the army hurriedly in advance of his baggage, and there is good reason to believe that he wore the same dress at Waterloo.

Now commenced preparations for a dismal bivouac. The French fell back and did not disturb us again, they too suffering from the drenching rain, which beat with a melancholy hissing on the cornfields, the clover, the potato patches and ploughed land which formed both positions.

Some of our officers found shelter in neighbouring cottages; Lord Uxbridge, afterwards Marquis of Anglesey, crept into a piggery and sipped tea with Waymouth of the 2nd Life Guards; but most of them cowered with their men round wretched fires which here and there were coaxed into burning.

One of Mercer's lieutenants had an umbrella, which had caused much merriment during the march, but he and his captain found it a haven of refuge under the lee of a hedge that night.

The cavalry stood to their horses, cloaked, with one flap over the saddle; some few were luck)' enough to get a bundle of straw or peasticks to sit down upon, and all looked anxiously for the dawn—fated to prove the last to thousands of them. With morning the rain gradually declined to a drizzle, which finally ceased; fires sprang up, arms were cleaned, and a buzz of voices rose along the line as tall Lifeguardsmen went down behind La Haye Sainte to dig potatoes, where, a few hours later, they were charging knee to knee, and everyone made shift to get what he could—with most it was only a hard biscuit—and to dry himself, which was a still more difficult matter.

Wet to the skin, splashed from head to foot in mud and mire, cold, shivering, unshaven (the foundation laid of acute rheumatism, to which a pension of five pence a day, in some cases ten pence, was applied by a grateful country, to its indelible disgrace), such was the condition of those brave hearts who were about to make the name of "Waterloo-man" a household word for all the ages.

****

The Brussels road runs across a shallow valley, three-quarters of a mile in width, all green and golden with the ripening grain, dipping sharply into it by the white-walled, blue-roofed farmstead of La Haye Sainte, and rising gently out again at the cabaret of La Belle Alliance on its way to the frontier beyond Charleroi.

The valley is bounded by two ridges: on the northern one along the cross road which runs nearly the whole length of the position, our army was posted in the form of a thin crescent; on the southern ridge and the slopes leading down into the valley the French forces were afterwards distributed, also, to some extent, in crescent shape.

These crescents had their tips advanced towards each other, and enclosed in the oval thus formed were two important strongholds—La Haye Sainte, in advance of our left centre, and the *château* of Hougoumont, some distance in front of our right wing; while away to the extreme left, the white buildings of Papelotte partly concealed Ter La Haye farm and the red-tiled hamlet of Smohain, the end of our line in that direction.

The crossroad which I have mentioned as lying along our position, and which was the celebrated "sunken road of Ohain," runs in some places between banks, at others on the level; it is paved down its centre, like most Belgian roads, with irregular stones, terrible to traverse for any distance, and it undulates gently, as the ridge rises and falls, until it joins the Nivelle *chaussée* beyond Hougoumont. Hougoumont, surrounded by a quadrangle of tall trees, lies in a hollow in front of our ridge, perhaps halfway between it and the enemy's line. A Flemish *château* with a garden laid out in the French style, and a smaller garden full of currant bushes; barns and quaint outbuildings clustering round the *château*, a brick wall about the height of a tall man, built on lower courses of grey stone, enclosing

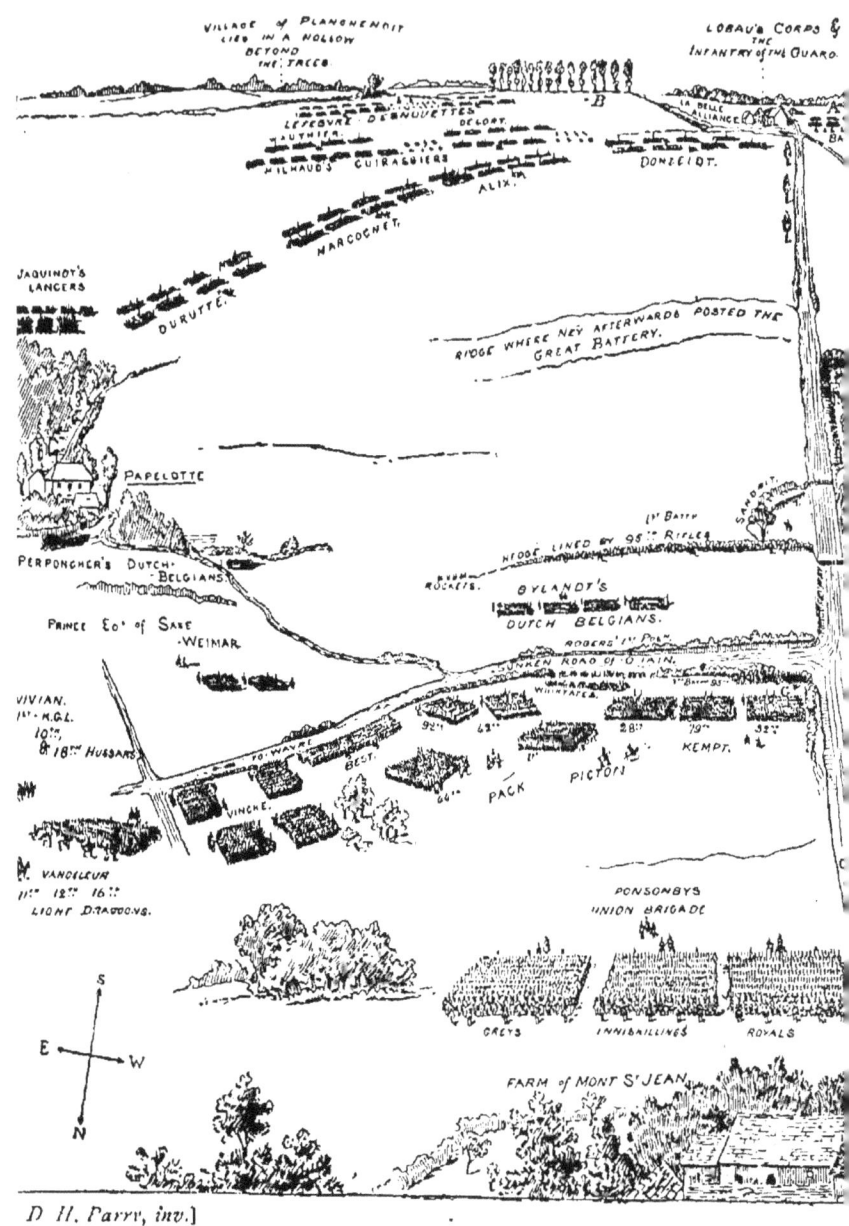

THE FIELD OF WATERLOO ON THE M

A and B, Napoleon's first and second positions; C, Napoleon's last position, from which he sa
stood when he ordered the whole line to advance; F, Mercer's post when he repulsed thre
H, only the 23rd Regiment, of Mitchell's Brigade, is shown, behind Byng, the others are
Mont St. Jean farm, a little to the left, and raised above the field.

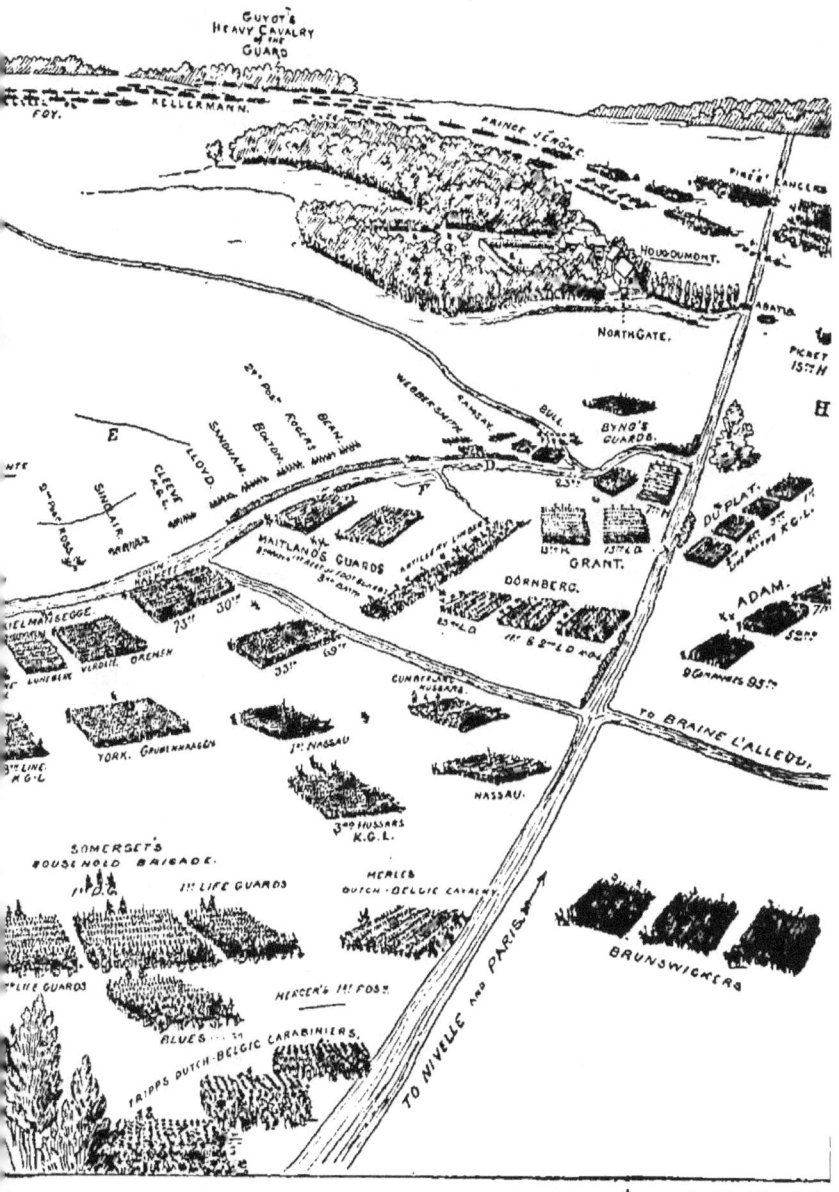

F THE BATTLE, SUNDAY, JUNE 18, 1815.

f the Imperial Guard; D, Wellington's position when the battle began; E, where Wellington
the Guard; G, post of 27th Regiment when Lambert's Brigade came into the front line;
H, except company of 51st keeping the *abattis*. The spectator is supposed to be behind

the garden, and at the east end of it a large open orchard; from the north-west corner, an avenue of ancient poplars winding into the Nivelle road with an *abattis* of tree trunks there, held by a company of the 51st Light Infantry; between the south wall and the French, a beech wood, through which one could see the corn-clad slopes beyond: and that was Hougoumont on the day of the battle.

The beech wood has been cut down, the apple-trees are sparse and scanty now, the *château* was burned by the French shells, and the garden is a grassy paddock; but the rest remains, loopholed and pock-marked with balls, a monument to the gallantry of two brave nations. The light companies of the Foot Guards occupied it on the 17th, and all night long they were busy, boring walls, barricading the gateways and erecting platforms from which to pour their fire.

On the high ground behind Hougoumont on our side the 2nd Brigade of British Guards was posted, having Maitland's Guards on its left; beyond Maitland was Alten's Infantry and Kielmansegge's Hano-verians, flanked in their turn by the gallant King's German Legion, in the pay of England, whose left rested on the Brussels *chaussée*, behind La Haye Sainte. On the other side of the *chaussée* was Kempt, then Pack's Highlanders, the Royal Scots, and 44th Regiment, some more Hanoverians, under Best, the 5th Hanoverians of Vincke, Vandeleur's Light Dragoons, and Vivian's Hussar Brigade.

The 2nd Rifles of the German Legion held La Haye Sainte, three companies of our 95th occupying a knoll and sandpit on the other side of the road, and Papelotte was garrisoned by Dutch Belgians, who behaved with the greatest gallantry.

Along the front of this, our first fighting line, the artillery was posted at intervals, and sufficient justice has not been done to the brave gunners, the duke always being unfairly severe on that arm of the service. Our heavy cavalry stood, in hollows behind the line, right and left or the great road in front of the farm of Mont St. Jean, already full of the Quatre Bras wounded. Other troops were in reserve out of sight of the enemy, behind our ridge, ready to advance and fill up any gaps, and we had a strong force in and about Braine l'Alleud, two miles to our right, in case the French should try to turn us there.

Crops, as at Quatre Bras, covered the valley and ridges, and the whole plain undulated in every direction. The battlefield today is full of surprises. Sudden dips occur where the land seems flat from a little distance; tongues of ground and barley-covered hillocks rise unexpect-edly as you approach them; and it is possible to lose sight of the entire

field by a few yards of walking in some directions; so that, flat as Belgium is generally considered, it is not astonishing that the survivors of Waterloo could only speak to events in their own immediate vicinity.

Between nine and ten there was loud cheering, as the Duke of Wellington rode along the line with his staff. He wore a blue frock coat, white cravat, and buckskin breeches, with tasselled Hessian boots; a short blue cloak with a white lining, and a low cocked hat with the British black cockade, and three smaller ones for Spain, Portugal, and the Netherlands. He was mounted on his favourite chestnut, Copenhagen, a grandson of Eclipse, and carried a long field-telescope drawn out for use.

At nine o'clock there was a movement on the opposite side of the valley; columns debouched into the fields right and left of the *chausée* and took up their positions as orderly as if upon parade; glittering files of armoured *cuirassiers* trotted through the corn, and formed behind the infantry, lance-pennons fluttered on each flank, and by half-past ten 61,000 French soldiers were drawn up in battle array, their right opposite Papelotte, their centre at La Belle Alliance, their left wing somewhat beyond Hougoumont.

The two greatest living commanders were about to measure swords for the first and only time; and as Napoleon galloped along his line, the music of the French bands was distinctly heard; helmets and weapons were brandished in the air, and a shout of "*Vive l'Empereur!*" rolled across the field.

Blue-coated infantry formed their first ranks, with batteries of brass cannon dotted here and there; behind stood the heavy cavalry with more guns, supported, on their right, by the gay light horse of the Guard, on the left by the heavy cavalry of the Imperial *cohort*, and in rear of the centre about the farm of Rossomme, stood the invincible infantry of the Guard, the most renowned body of warriors in Europe.

*****

Napoleon was unwell. At two in the morning he had been reconnoitring, and his horses were ordered for seven; at ten he still sat in an upper room in an attitude of bodily and mental suffering.

A little later he came down the steep ladder, and as his page, Gudin, was helping him into the saddle he lifted the Imperial elbow too suddenly, and Napoleon pitched over on the offside, nearly coming to the ground.

"*Allez*," he hissed, "*a tous les diables!*" and away he started in a great rage. The page stood watching the *cortége* with tearful eyes, but when it had gone some hundred yards the ranks of the staff opened, and Napoleon came riding back alone.

With one hand placed tenderly on the lad's shoulder he said, very softly, "My child, when you assist a man of my girth to mount, it is necessary to proceed more carefully." Yet it was of this man that Wellington could say, in after years, "The fellow was no gentleman!"

The page became a general, and fell in a sortie from Paris during the Franco-Prussian war.

******

There was a lull before the storm, and the duke went to have a final look at Hougoumont, where, in addition to the Guards, he had posted, in the woods and grounds, some Nassauers, Hanoverians, and Luneberg riflemen. These foreigners were dissatisfied at their position, and as Wellington rode away *several bullets came whistling after him!* "How can they expect me to win a battle with troops like those?" was his only comment. About half-past eleven came the *First Attack!*

One booming cannon echoed dully in the misty Sabbath morning, and a cloud of dark-blue skirmishers ran forward against Hougoumont, firing briskly into the wood. Puffs of white smoke issued from the trees; here and there a blue-coat turned a somersault and lay still; but the cloud increased, and a loud rattle of musketry was kept up on both sides, which lasted, with short intervals, the whole day. Our men fell back upon the buildings through the open beech-trees, and in twenty minutes the French supporting columns were pouring up the hill towards the *château* grounds.

Cleeve's German battery opened on them, and his first shot killed seventeen men, the guns checking the advance and sending the column, broken and bleeding, down the ridge again. Our batteries on the right now began; the French artillery replied; Kellermann's horse

batteries joined in, and the infernal concert was in full blast. The green Lunebergers and the yellow knapsacks of the Hanoverians came helter-skelter back across the orchard, but the Foot Guards went forward at a run and drove the enemy off.

Bull's howitzers sent a shower of 5½-inch shells over the *château* into the wood, and as often as the death-dealing globes fell crashing through the branches, so often did the enemy retire in confusion, until Jérôme Bonaparte, ex-king of Westphalia, who was in command at Hougoumont, brought up Foy's Division to help the attack.

Bravely led by their officers, the tall shakoes and square white coat-facings of the line regiments, the dark-blue and black gaiters of the light infantry, pressed through the wood until they reached a stiff quickset hedge, separated by a thin strip of apple orchard from the long south wall, over which peeped the head gear of our Guardsmen, and in the confusion of smoke and skirmish the bright-red brick-work was mistaken for a line of British—you can see today where the French balls crumbled that barrier. But soon discovering their error, the brave fellows struggled through the hedge and rushed forward.

A line of loopholes perforated the wall about three feet from the ground, crossed bayonets protruded viciously from the openings, and a hail of bullets poured forth with such ghastly effect that in half-an-hour there were *fifteen hundred* of God's creatures dead and dying on the green grass in the orchard, and still the others came on.

Some got as far as the loopholes, and seized the bayonets; others struck with their gunbutts at the men, who, on platforms behind the wall, fired down over the top, piling up the dead in dreadful heaps—privates and officers, conscripts and veterans.

From time to time our Foot Guards charged over the large orchard at the east end of the enclosed garden, and also at the south-west angle of the farm buildings, where a haystack helped to cover them until the French burned it; and this repulse and attack went on, time and again, until the evening, the enemy gaining no advantage but the beech wood for all their desperate valour.

The rest of our line had remained passive listeners to the firing, except for a little skirmishing here and there, but a hurricane was brewing and about to burst against our left and centre.

******

La Haye Sainte was a farm, lying like Hougoumont in a hollow; it was on the Brussels road, and was built with barn and stabling round three sides of an oblong yard, the fourth side being a high white wall, with a gate and a piggery alongside the roadway.

Towards the French position stretched a long orchard, a small garden lay behind the house, and a large double door opened from

the yard into the fields on the Hougoumont side, half of which door had been burned for bivouac fires the night previous. The 2nd Rifles of the German Legion, dressed like our own in green with slate-coloured pantaloons, held the post, and held it like the heroes of old, three companies in the orchard, two in the building, and one in the garden. Major Baring, who had two horses shot under him, being in command.

The post was not as strong as Hougoumont, all the pioneers having been sent to fortify the latter place, and the "Green Germans" had a very insufficient supply of ammunition; Wellington afterwards admitting that he had neglected to make the most of the position there.

At 1.30 p.m. Marshal Ney had gathered seventy-four guns, mostly 12-pounders, on a ridge very near to La Haye Sainte on the French *right* of the road, and this was known as the "Great Battery."

Behind the guns the whole of D'Erlon's Corps, together with Bachelu's Division, was massed in columns for the attack twenty regiments, Bachelu being in reserve. Ney sent to the emperor to tell him all was ready, and with an appalling cannonade on our left and centre, they commenced the *Second Attack*.

When the smoke which hung about the guns had drifted slowly

away across the slopes we could see four massive columns, led by the brave Ney, pouring steadily forward straight for our ridge.

The firing became general as we opened on the advance: men had to shout to be audible to their neighbours; long lanes were ploughed through Picton's Division, and the balls went tearing through our cavalry in reserve, many of them striking the hospital farm, and some even travelling into the village beyond.

Bylandt's Dutch Belgians, posted in front of the crossroad, forgot their gallantry at Quatre Bras, and bolted, almost running over the grenadiers of our 28th, who were restrained with difficulty from firing into them. One ball cut a tall tree into half at the hedgerow above the sandpit, bringing the feathery top down and half-smothering two doctors of the 95th, who had stationed themselves beneath it.

Nearly 24,000 men advanced, with loud cries and the hoarse rolling of drums, in four masses: Durutte against Papelotte, Alix and Marcognet in front of Kempt and Pack, Donzelot upon the devoted Rifles in La Haye Sainte, the shock taking place about two o'clock, and lasting for more than an hour.

Durutte took Papelotte, but was driven out again; Alix and Marcognet breasted the rise, and gained the ridge under a murderous discharge; the smell or trampled corn mingling with the powder smoke as the Great Battery ceased firing lest it should kill its comrades, and with shouts of "*Vive l'Empereur!*" the two columns hurled themselves against the steel barrier of bayonets on the hedge-lined bank above them.

Hand to hand, no quarter asked or given, veteran and conscript came on yelling like mad, Picton's Division meeting them in line.

Some of Marcognet's fellows crossed the Wavre road and blazed into the 92nd; but our men advanced, after a withering volley, and, jumping into the cross-road, went at them with a will. Cameron Highlanders, 32nd and 28th, Scots Royals, and Black Watch, Gordons and 44th, with colours waving and courage high, over the causeway they rushed, into the wheat and barley.

"Charge, charge! Hurrah!" cried Picton, his little black eyes sparkling, his florid complexion redder with excitement—a ball struck his right temple, he fell dead from his horse, and his men passed over him driving the foe down hill.

A mounted French officer had his horse shot, and getting to his feet seized the regimental colour of the 32nd, which was nearly new. Belcher, who carried it, grasped the silk and the Frenchman groped for his sabre hilt, but Colour-sergeant Switzer thrust a pike at his

breast. "Save the brave fellow!" was the cry, but it came too late; a private, named Lacy, fired point blank into him, and he fell lifeless.

Ney stood in the road beyond La Haye Sainte watching Donzelot's attack on the farm, where the "Green Germans" were forced, after a

struggle, out of the long orchard into the buildings, and simultaneously a mass of *cuirassiers* tore past the Hougoumont side and rode at the ridge.

Our Household Cavalry and Ponsonby's Heavies had walked on

foot to the height overlooking the struggle; the trumpets rang out "Mount," and swinging into their saddles they swooped down into the thick of it. With a clatter across the causeway, and the muffled thunder of hoofs on the ground beyond it, the scarlet-coated Life Guards, wearing no armour then, and mounted on black horses, dashed past the Wellington tree into the potato field, with the Blues and King's Dragoon Guards, swinging, slashing, stirrup to stirrup, to meet Kellermann's troopers and Ordener's Cuirassiers. There was the snort of eager horses, the creaking of leather, the clash of sword on steel *cuirass*, the yell of passion and the scream of agony; a seething mass of fighting-men and steeds, glinting and gleaming, swaying this way and that way, but always onward, jostling down the hill.

The 1st Lifes got jammed in the road beyond the farm with a body of *cuirassiers*, on the spot where Ney had just before been standing, *voltigeurs* firing into them, on friend and foe alike! Their Colonel, Ferrier, led eleven charges although badly wounded by sabre and lance.

The King's Dragoons jumped their horses over a barrier of trees which our Rifles had built across the causeway and went thundering along that way, while the Blues were reaping a harvest of glory in another direction, and the 2nd Life Guards charged to the left for a great distance beyond the sandpit alongside the farm, where Corporal Shaw met his fate after slaying nine of the enemy single-handed.

After the battle men remembered this mighty swordsman, and told in solemn voices his deeds of derring-do. One *cuirassier* sat, out of the *mêlée*, coolly loading his carbine and picking off our troopers, and it is believed he gave Shaw his mortal hurt. A survivor narrated how, exhausted at nightfall, he had lain down on a dung-heap, when Shaw crawled beside him, bleeding from many wounds. In the morning the life-guardsman was still there, his head resting on his arm as if asleep, but it was the sleep which knows no waking.

Ponsonby's Union Brigade was meanwhile making its immortal onslaught, more towards Papelotte, the ground they went over being billowy, and the troops before them infantry of the line.

The Royals gave a ringing cheer; "Scotland for ever!" was the war-cry of the Greys; and the Inniskillings went in with an Irish howl.

As they passed the 92nd, many of the Highlanders caught hold of their stirrup-leathers and charged down with them; the very ground seemed trembling under the iron hoofs; Marcognet and Alix were broken and trampled, and in three minutes more than 2,000 prisoners were wending their disconsolate way to the rear.

"Those beautiful grey horses!" said Napoleon, as he watched the charge. Did he see that struggle round the Eagle of his 45th, I wonder—that famous "Battle for the Standard" which Ansdell has painted so well? What says Sergeant Ewart, the hero of the incident? "It was in the charge I took the Eagle from the enemy. He and I had a hard contest for it. He made a thrust at my groin; I parried it off, and cut him down through the head. After this a lancer came at me; I threw the lance off by my right side, and cut him through the chin and upwards through the teeth. Next a foot-soldier fired at me, and then charged me with his bayonet, which I also had the good luck to parry, and then I cut him down through the head. Thus ended the contest."

Captain Clarke and Corporal Styles, of the Royals, took an Eagle from the 105th between them—a glorious gilded thing, embroidered with the names of Jena, Eylau, Eckmühl, Essling, and Wagram—the gallant captain losing the tip of his nose in the struggle.

A man of the Inniskillings named Penfold claimed to have taken that colour; but his story is vague, and I incline to think that a blue silk camp-colour of the 105th, now at Abbotsford, was the one that Penfold seized and afterwards lost in the fray.

Sir William Ponsonby led the charge on a restive bay hack, and was killed; while some of the Greys got as far as the Great Battery, disabling many of the guns, and getting slain in the end.

Part of the 28th lost its head, and charged with the brigade; Lieutenant Deares of that regiment being taken prisoner, stripped of his clothes, rejoining at night in nothing but shirt and trousers.

Tathwell, of the Blues, tore off a colour, but his horse was shot and he lost it; and the greater part of the two brigades rode along the battery until heavy bodies of *cuirassiers* and lancers came to drive them back.

Vandeleur charged to their relief with his Light Dragoons—the 12th with bright yellow lancer facings, the 16th with scarlet, the buff nth remaining in reserve.

"Squadrons, right half-wheel! Charge!" and the sabres of our light horsemen were soon busy in the valley below. The ground was very soft, for a month after the battle some of the holes made by horses' feet were measured, and found to be *eighteen* inches deep, and in speaking of artillery movements it must be remembered that the guns were at times up to the axle in clay.

The heavy cavalry regained our position; but so much had they suffered that, later in the day, when they were drawn up in line to show a bold front, there were only fifty of them; Somerset, who led

the "Households," losing his hat, and wearing the helmet of a life-guardsman, with its red and blue worsted crest, until nightfall.

The attack had failed, and there was a long pause, broken only by the firing at Hougoumont and some feeble attempts on La Haye Sainte; but it was now the turn of our troops in the centre, from the *chaussée* to the back of the *château*; and a terrible time they had! A renewal of the cannonade—a forming of our regiments into squares and oblongs—and then the

grandest cavalry affair in history, as forty squadrons of *cuirassiers* and dragoons crossed from the French right in beautiful order, wheeled up until they almost filled the space from Hougoumont to La Haye Sainte, and, about four o'clock, put spurs to their horses and began the Third Attack! A forest of sword-blades, an undulating sea of helmets, a roar of mighty shouting as they came through the yet untrampled grain.

Wave after wave, far as the eye could scan, now glinting with thousands of bright points as the sullen sun shone for a moment upon them, now grey and sombre as the clouds closed together again. Nearer! nearer! nearer! Men clutched their muskets tighter and breathed hard; gunners rammed home and hastened to reload before the smoke had drifted from the cannon.

Suddenly they left their guns, and ran to the infantry for protection as the sea burst upon us, and our ridge became alive with furious horsemen, surging and foaming round and round the squares. There were many who thought that all was over, but the little clumps of scarlet fringed with steel were impenetrable.

In vain the moustached troopers cut desperately at the bayonets; in vain they rode up and fired their pistols into the faces of our lads. For three-quarters of an hour they expended their strength in a hopeless task; and when our fresh cavalry from Dörnberg's and Grant's Brigades charged them, they went down the slope again, leaving the ground dotted with dead and dying. A moment's respite to re-form in the hollows below, and back they came once more, in the face of a fearful fire from our artillery, whose guns were double-shotted—some loaded with scattering grape and canister. Lanes, sickening to behold, were torn through the squadrons; but Milhaud's men were not to be daunted, and the same strange scene was repeated many times.

A small body of *cuirassiers* that had surrendered was being escorted to the rear by a weak party of the 7th Hussars, when they made a bold dash for liberty along the Nivelle road, stampeding, *ventre à terre*, until they reached the *abattis* at the end of the Hougoumont avenue.

Here they met Ross's company of the 51st, who killed eight men and twelve horses, the rest— about sixty—surrendering again.

One artilleryman was seen, under his gun, dodging a French trooper, who tried to reach him with his long sword.

After some moments the *cuirassier's* horse was shot, and the gunner, sallying out, hit him over the head with his rammer, and packed him off to the rear with a parting kick.

The ridge was once more cleared, and Mercer's battery brought into the front line. The whole field was now littered with corpses and accoutrements. Gaily-dressed trumpeters, and officers on whose breasts hung crosses of the Legion of Honour, lay bleeding in the barley among hundreds of dead and wounded horses. Here a lancer in green and light blue, there a heap of cuirassiers of the 1st Regiment, mown down by grape shot; yonder a *chasseur-à-cheval*, propped against his charger, while swords and *cuirasses* were almost as numerous as the stalks of corn.

All the slope was torn and trampled; flies were busy in the now loathsome hollows; there was constant firing still at Hougoumont and La Haye Sainte, when the trumpets sounded again, and with seventy-seven squadrons, including the cavalry of the Guard, France returned to the charge. Every arm of the mounted service was represented in this attack, the beauty and brilliancy of the uniforms baffling description. *Carabiniers*, white-coated, with brass *cuirasses* and red-crested helmets; Lancers, dragoons, and *chasseurs* in green, with facings of every hue; the Red Lancers of the Guard, clad in scarlet from head to heel, and Napoleon's own favourite *Chasseurs-à-cheval*, with hussar caps and red pelisses, richly braided with orange lace; tall bear-skinned Horse Grenadiers, with white facings to their blue coats; the cuirassiers, dark and sombre looking; the high felt *shakoes* of the Hussars—it was as though a flower garden in all its summer dress were moving at a slow trot upon us, heralded by the thunder of hell from the batteries behind it.

When the thunder stopped, which it always did as the leading files reached the crest of the ridge, our men could hear in the momentary intervals of their own firing the jingling of bits and scabbards, and the heavy breathing of the horses. Mounted skirmishers came close to the batteries and commenced firing at the gunners, who were literally dripping with perspiration from the exertions they made. One fellow took several pot-shots at Captain Mercer, who was coolly walking his horse backwards and forwards along a bank to set an example to his men. He missed each time, and grinned grimly as he reloaded, but as the head of the squadrons closed up the skirmishers vanished and were succeeded by the rush which threatened death to every soul on the plateau. Wellington's orders were to retire into the squares and leave the batteries, but Mercer's men stuck to their guns, repulsing three charges of the Horse Grenadiers, and dealing such slaughter that the position of "G Troop" was known next day by the enormous heap of slain lying before it, visible from a considerable distance.

The carnage on the slope was shocking—the oldest soldiers had seen nothing like it: men and horses lay piled one on another, five and six in a heap, every fresh discharge adding to the ghastly pyramid. The 1st Cuirassiers numbered 300 of the Legion of Honour in its ranks—it lost 117, including two lieutenants and the brave Captain Poinsot, page to the emperor in 1807, wounded at Moscow and Brienne. One officer, finding the fire from a particular gun playing havoc with his men, rode straight at it and was blown to atoms.

The horses during the battle suffered cruelly, and some of the details are heartrending: the charger of a very stout officer with the duke's staff, probably Müffling, was seen to rear for some time without the rider being able to bring it down—its front legs had been both shot off. Another trooper's horse was seen next morning sitting on its tail, its hind legs gone; and one poor beast ran for sympathy to six guns in succession, and was driven off from each with exclamations of horror until it reached "G Troop," where they mercifully killed it: the whole of its face below the great brown pleading eyes had been carried away by a round shot!

After a repulse and a re-attack, the remnant of the seventy-seven squadrons reeled back to their own lines: the cavalry of France, magnificent, irresistible, brave as lions, and nobly led, had shattered itself without result, and *the third great attempt had failed!*

*****

All the afternoon there had been great doings at Hougoumont. About one o'clock Colonel Hepburn had relieved Saltoun in the large orchard with a battalion of the 3rd—now the Scots Guards—and the combat on that side became a long succession of advances with the bayonet to the front hedge and retirings into a green dry ditch, which is known to us as the "friendly hollow-way." When our men fell back, a terrific fire from the short east wall would stagger the foe, and the Scots, having formed again, would scramble out of the hollow and clear the orchard of all but the dead. Along the terrible south wall a staff-officer, who had been through all the Peninsula battles, afterwards said that the slain lay thicker than he had ever seen them elsewhere.

The *château* and barns were now burning furiously, fired by Haxo's howitzers at Napoleon's orders, and many of our wounded perished in the flames; some officers' horses tore out of the barn, galloped madly round the yard, and rushed into the fire again to be destroyed.

Twice the enemy got in: once by a little door in the west wall, through which they never got out alive; and the second time, when our Guardsmen had sallied out into the lane to drive off a body of infantry, about fifty French entered on their heels through the north gate. Then, by main strength of arm, Colonel Macdonell, Sergeant Graham, and three or four more, shut and barred the wooden gate in the faces of the others, and those inside were all shot down.

A brave fellow climbed on to the beam that crossed the gateway; but Graham fired, and he dropped with a scream on to the heads of his comrades outside the wall.

The fire stopped at the door of the *château* chapel, which was full of wounded, and a wooden figure of our Saviour had the feet nibbled by the flames, at which the superstitious marvel greatly to this day.

Columns of smoke hung over everything. A gallant artillery driver rushed his horses to the wall, and flung a barrel of welcome cartridges over into the yard. At the corner, before the gardener's house, Baron de Cubières lay wounded under his horse; afterwards, when Governor of Ancona, he expressed himself very grateful that we had not fired on him! Crawford of the 3rd Guards was killed in the kitchen garden,

Blackman of the Coldstreams died in the orchard; but the attack and repulse grew gradually weaker, as both sides tired of the hideous slaughter. Meanwhile, a serious trouble which had been menacing" the emperor on his right flank for some time at last grew terribly imminent.

The Prussians were coming in spite of Grouchy, who had been sent in their pursuit.

They should have arrived about one o'clock; but, thanks to the bad roads, a fire in the town of Wavre, which had to be extinguished before the ammunition-waggons could be got through, and some hesitation on the part of Gneisenau, Blücher's Chief of Staff, who doubted Wellington's good faith, it was half-past four when part of Billow's corps came out of the woods at St. Lambert and confirmed Napoleon's previously awakened fears.

In the hazy weather they thought it was Grouchy, and a false report was afterwards sent through the French army to cheer the wearied men; but the emperor and Soult knew otherwise, and the line of battle was weakened by a strong force being detached to meet the new arrivals.

There was no time to be lost; drums rolled and trumpets sounded again, and the last remnants of the cavalry had not regained their position when the Fourth Grand Attack began with a fury that even exceeded the others.

While fresh bodies of horse and foot advanced up the ridge, a most determined rush was made on La Haye Sainte. Baring had been reinforced, it is true; but, although he sent time after time for more ammunition, not a single cartridge was forthcoming!

A feeble excuse has been made that there were no means of getting it into the building; but a large door and several windows faced our line at the back of the house then, as now. They may still be seen by the visitor to Waterloo.

A horde of French infantry flung themselves on the buildings, setting the barn on fire, and besieging the broken gateway.

While the brave Germans filled their camp-kettles from the pond and extinguished the flames, others, with their bayonets only, kept the door leading into the field. Seventeen corpses they piled up there in a few minutes, one gallant fellow defending a breach with a brick torn from the wall! The individual acts of heroism on authentic record would fill many pages: but, without ammunition, they were at a fearful disadvantage.

The *voltigeurs* climbed on to the roof of the stable, and shot them down at their ease: the half barn-door is preserved to the present day, with eighty bullet-holes in it! Alten sent the brave Christian Ompteda to their aid, if practicable, with the 5th Battalion. He pointed to an overwhelming force; but the irrepressible Orange repeated Alten's suggestion in a tone that brooked no delay, and Ompteda went down with his 5th Battalion, and they died, almost to a man!

Baring dismounted to pick up his cap, knocked off by a shot; four balls had lodged in the cloak rolled on his saddle-bow, and a fifth then pierced the saddle itself, while the Scotch Lieutenant Graeme, sitting on the rafters of the piggery, in which a calf was lowing, raised his *shako* to cheer his men, and his right hand was taken off at the wrist. He was only eighteen.

It was hopeless. "If I receive no cartridges," said Baring in his last appeal, "I not only must, but *will* abandon the post!" And very soon those neglected heroes retreated slowly through the house and out through the garden beyond, the French, bursting into the yard, chasing the remnant round and round and bayoneting them on the dungheaps.

A roar of cheering rang above the battle. At last they were victorious, and the French had taken La Haye Sainte.

Without a moment's hesitation their conquest was turned to the best possible advantage. Smart red-braided Horse Artillery galloped down the causeway, dragging their guns to the knoll above the sandpit, from which our 95th had been driven, and, unlimbering, opened fire at *sixty yards range* on to our line. Skirmishers filled the hedgerows and the farm buildings. The Great Battery renewed its work of death, and in a few moments there was a serious gap in the centre of our position. Lambert's brigade had been brought up before this, and suffered terribly. The 27th, which had lain down and slept soundly behind Mont St. Jean until after three o'clock, lost 478 out of 698 in its new quarters; and the 40th thirteen officers and 180 rank and file, one round shot taking off the head of Captain Fisher and killing twenty-five men.

Ompteda's brigade mustered a mere handful, Kielmansegge was almost destroyed, Halkett had two weak squares, one of his regiments being very shaky indeed, and, altogether, things were unpleasant when the duke came up with reinforcements to patch our front as best he could. Far off on our right Chassé's Dutch Belgians had arrived, shouting and singing, from Braine l'Alleud, *very drunk*, narrowly escaping a volley from us, as they wore the French uniform; and at this time, by reason of the bolting of Hake's Cumberland Hussars and some of our supports, with the enormous losses from the six hours of carnage, the British affairs were in bad case.

Halkett's 30th and 73rd in square had been charged no less than eleven times: the duke pointed to a scarlet mass in front through the smoke, and inquired what regiment it was. It was the dead and wounded of those two corps, huddled together where they had fallen.

The green-faced 73rd was at one time commanded by Lieutenant Stewart, all the other officers having been killed or wounded; and at half-past seven the colours of both regiments were sent to the rear.

The 2nd Line Battalion of the German Legion went into action with 300 men, but mustered only six officers and thirty-six privates after the battle; but Blücher was now nearing the French right rear with nearly 52,000 troops and 104 guns, and the emperor was obliged to send General Duhesme with eight battalions of the young Guard down into the straggling village of Planchenoit to help to check them.

He had been at La Belle Alliance all day, and Prussian shot were now falling about him.

Marshal Ney sent for more infantry to renew the attack. *"Ou voulez vous que j'en prenne: voulez vous que j'en fasse?"* was the emperor's impatient reply—"Where can I get them: do you wish me to make them?"

The long June day was drawing into evening, and shadows began to lengthen across the fields! Wellington, who had always been seen where the fire was hottest, rode with a calm, inscrutable face, followed by a sadly diminished staff,, his eagle eye taking note of the strength and weakness of our line.

The hussars had been moved in rear of the centre; and Adams' Brigade took position immediately behind the ridge. In front of the clover field where the 52nd stood in square, a pretty little tortoiseshell kitten, which had been frightened out of Hougoumont by the firing, lay dead—a strange feature in the scene of destruction.

The men were growing accustomed to the hideous sights and sounds around them, and became impatient at the inactivity which doomed them to endure without reprisal. Suddenly the brass guns blazed forth once more upon us; the *pas de charge* was rolling from a thousand drums; a serried line was seen advancing along our entire front, and, led by the emperor himself, on his grey charger Marie, his famous *redingote gris* open and showing the well-known dark-green *chasseur* coat, the grenadiers of the Guard marched in solid columns into the valley.

Two winding serpents of determined men; ten battalions in tall black bearskins, white facings and dark-blue pantaloons—that was their dress at Waterloo—with Friant and Morand, Petit, whom Napoleon had kissed at Fontainebleau, Poret de Morvan, and old Cambronne. The *élite* of the French army, the grenadiers and *chasseurs* of the Old and Middle Guard, marching sternly to victory or death. Marcognet, Alix, and Donzelot, with their remnants, against our reeling left; Reille, Foy, and Jérôme renewing on Hougoumont—cavalry in the gaps and spaces—a simultaneous, mighty last attack!

The yet unbroken Imperial Guard set their faces towards the spot where Maitland's, Adams' and Byng's red-coats looked to their priming and closed their ranks: had Napoleon hurled them against the crossroad behind. La Haye Sainte, the story of Waterloo had been written differently.

He missed his chance; he threw away his final hope. The greatest of his many mistakes was committed, and, handing over the leadership to Ney, he remained on a hillock above the farm, and watched the downfall of France and the death-blow of his empire! For the last time in this world their emperor addressed them, pointing towards the heights with a gesture all could understand.

"*Déployez les aigles. En avant! Vive l'Empereur!*" and with a great shout they quickened their pace, passing proudly, unheeding, over the bodies of those comrades who had gone before.

Red tongues of flame burst from the smoke of our guns; *whiz* came

the fiery rockets, darting into their ranks, scorching, blinding, and burning in their course; humming shells dropped among them with terrible destruction; but the Old Guard pressed on, and began to mount the ridge.

Ney's horse fell—the *fifth* killed under him that day, and the "bravest of the brave," went forward on foot. Alas, would that it had been to death!

Our Guards were lying down to avoid the hurricane from the French artillery. A shell dropped in one of the squares, and Colonel Colquitt, picking it up, fizzing and fuming, walked to the edge and flung it outside to burst harmlessly. Another officer, mortally wounded, said faintly:

"I should like to see the colours of the regiment again before I quit them for ever": they were brought and waved round his body, and with a smile, he was carried away, to die. It was men like those that the oncoming columns had to face, and batteries as famous as those of Bull and Bolton, of Norman Ramsay, Whinyates, and Webber Smith, with guns double shotted and served as on parade; no need to sight so carefully, for the moving target is a wide one, and they hit in every time! Now the skirmishers run out, shouting and firing as before, and when they have said their say, they fall back leaving all clear for the others; but the columns seem to get no nearer, though they are marching steadily; front rank after front rank is blown to shreds—*that is why they appear stationary!*

The gunners have done their work; the guns recoil, and are left there: it is the turn of the infantry now, and the time has come for that historic signal, "*Up, Guards, and at 'em!*" which in reality was never said.

But whatever the word was, they *do* "up," and they *do* "at 'em"; and again it is bayonet to baronet, and man to man.

One Welsh giant, named Hughes, six feet seven inches in height, is seen to knock over a dozen of the Old Guard single handed; the redcoats and the blue-coats mingle for a moment and the blue-coats melt away. The second column, a little behind the other, is in good order: it has suffered less from the cannonade, and is full of fire and fury; but' so also are our 52nd lads, who advance down the slope with three tremendous cheers. Colborne is leading, and when they get abreast of the column he cries—"Halt! Mark time!"

The men touch in to their left, and regain their dressing; Colborne's horse is shot, and he comes forward wiping his mouth with a white handkerchief, still wearing Ensign Leeke's blue boat-cloak.

"Right shoulders forward" The regiment swings round, and, four deep, faces the column's flank two hundred yards away.

"Forward, 52nd—charge!" and the Foot Guards, who are back on the ridge again, behold a noble spectacle.

The crash is terrific; the Imperial *phalanx* is taken in flank. The contest is fierce, but it is soon over. Brave Michel, in response to our officers, replies with glorious *esprit de corps*, "The Guard dies, and never surrenders!" his words instantly fulfilled, as he falls lifeless, sword in hand, while Cambronne, grown old in the service (to whom these words have been falsely attributed), gives up his weapon to William Halkett.

Halkett's horse is shot, and Cambronne hastens away, but his captor is too quick for him, and seizing his gold aiguillette, hands him to a sergeant to be taken care of.

On presses the 52nd, driving the broken Guard before it: it is a sight probably never repeated in history—one regiment traversing the field alone, in sight of the army; sending the foe like sheep into the hollow; dispersing and pushing them relentlessly back, until they turn and fly, and other corps make haste to join in that glorious progress.

There is a movement along the ridge as the setting sun shines out in a burst of sinking splendour, and the duke, with cocked hat raised above his head, gives the magic word, "The whole line will advance!" and then spurs down after the 52nd.

On the rising ground near La Haye Sainte, Napoleon sits on horseback, close to a small battalion which has formed square.

Jérôme, his brother, bleeding and exhausted, is with him, with honest old Drouot in his artillery uniform, in the pocket of which is a well-worn Bible; Soult and Gourgaud, Bertrand and brave young La Bédoyère are there, too: but the English Hussars are coming on at a fast trot. All day long the waves of valour have been rolling northward, and breaking against an ironbound shore; now the tide has turned, and rushes madly south again.

Nothing but confusion meets the eye: everywhere the French are in full retreat—solitary men, groups of three and four, ruined regiments, and the skeletons of squadrons.

Jérôme rides close to his brother, and says in a meaning tone—"It were well for all who bear the name of Bonaparte to perish here!"

Napoleon orders some guns to open on the Hussars, and one shot hits Lord Uxbridge on the right knee as, mounted on a troop horse belonging to a sergeant-major of the 23rd Light Dragoons, he is leading the pursuit.

"Here we must die on the field of battle," exclaims the emperor, preparing to head the weak column; but Soult seizes his bridle, saying, "They will not kill you: you will be taken prisoner"; and, held up in the saddle by two faithful officers, for he is worn out, Napoleon is galloped away in the gathering darkness.

On the left of the Brussels road some Prussian guns had come up and fired *on our men*.

They were the sole representatives of Blücher's force present before Mont St. Jean until *after* the retreat had begun; and they had been far better absent, as their pounding was cruelly felt by Mercer's battery and several of our regiments.

They were induced, after some time, to change the direction of their range, and then all went well. The 52nd still pursued its march, halting for a moment near La Haye Sainte to face and charge some rallying squares, where a Belgian soldier was seen killing a wounded Frenchman, and was run through by an officer of the regiment.

Leeke, who carried the King's colour, found a foot and a half of the pole wet with blood; Holman, the brother of the blind traveller, had three musket balls through his sword blade, and wore it for many years; Colborne and Major Rowan, being both dismounted, jumped on to two horses attached to an abandoned gun, calling to their men to cut the harness; but the advance continuing, they had to dismount with a hearty laugh and march on again on foot.

It was getting dark, and our hussars were clearing the field in splendid style, the 10th. whose sabres were soon red as their scarlet cuffs, engaging with some strong remnants of the Old Guard and losing two officers.

Major Murray, of the dashing 18th, met a gun going at full speed, and leaped his charger over the traces, between the leaders and wheelers, while his men proceeded to cut the gunners down.

Colquhoun Grant, who had lost five horses and was then mounted on a magnificent chestnut, sent the gallant remains of his brigade at the retreating foe; and until it was impossible any longer to pick one's way among the vast heaps of dead, disabled cannon, and miserable wounded—in short, the absolute wreck of an army—our light cavalry went wheeling and slashing right and left, hurrying on the veteran, the conscript, the artillery driver and the officer alike, all the French accounts doing justice to these light horsemen. It is only in private letters, hardly in the official documents, that England can learn the heroism of her hussars at Waterloo.

Meanwhile the 52nd had crossed to the left of the road and scattered a column debouching from Planchenoit, behind the buildings of La Belle Alliance, in front of which a mass of guns had been left to their fate. The regiment passed on, and on its return found them marked with the numbers of other corps that had succeeded them.

All the causeway was crammed with flying troops: a terrible struggle for liberty took place, in which discipline gave way to terror. General officer and baggage waggon fled side by side; rifles and accoutre-

ments were thrown away that their owners might hurry faster. The fields, the by-lanes, the woods, were all filled with fugitives—even the emperor had to turn aside in order to get past.

Marshal Ney was one of the last to go. He had joined the army on the 15th, without money, without horses, almost without a uniform. He was to be found everywhere on that dreadful 18th, planting batteries, heading charges, rallying, raging, facing death at every stride, and when it was over he tottered exhausted away on foot, leaning on the shoulder of a compassionate corporal.

Now the Prussians have arrived in force. Planchenoit, its churchyard and crooked street. Its orchards and barnyards, are full of French and Prussian slain.

The young Guard fought well, but they were outnumbered, and Blücher rides into the *chaussée* at La Belle Alliance.

A Uhlan band plays "God Save the King," and farther along the road they meet the duke returning on his way in the dark to write his despatches announcing the victory.

The two soldiers embrace, and sit talking for ten minutes while the stream goes hurrying by. Then the fiery old German follows up the retreat with a fury that is incredible. At Genappe the Silesians have taken the emperor's baggage; Gneisenau mounts a drummer on one of the cream-coloured carriage horses, and away they go into the darkness after the fugitives, driving them from seven bivouacs, slaving, hacking, giving no rest, until the land is strewn for leagues with dead men, fallen under the Prussian steel.

Merciless it may seem to us, looking back with fourscore years between us, (as at time of first publication), and that moonlit night; but such was the vitality of the French that the most drastic steps were necessary to prevent their army mustering again.

······

What can I say of the battlefield, after the pursuit had rolled away, and it was left to the searcher and the plunderer?

If I could re-create one tithe of the horror those slopes and roads revealed you would sicken and turn away in disgust.

Prussian, Belgian, *and* British, there were, out on the plain that night, bent on no errand of mercy; stragglers and camp-followers creeping from group to group, tearing the rings from the fingers, and the teeth from the jaws!

Many a life was foully taken that tender nursing might have saved;

but there were some groups who sought for a lost comrade or a favourite officer, and women there were, with woman's gentle sympathy, soothing and tending as only they can soothe.

The bulk of the British force had gone to bivouac beyond and about Rosomme, which was behind the French position; but some detached portions remained where they had fought, too weary to advance with the others.

Mercer was one of these, and creeping under the cover of a waggon, worn out with slaughter, he slept—waking to find a dead man stark and stiff beneath him! His men came to him in the morning, and asked permission to bury one of their comrades.

"Why him in particular? "asked the captain, for many a bearskin-crested helmet was empty in "G Troop."

Then they showed him the horror of it.

The whole of the man's head had been carried away, leaving the fleshy mask of what had been a face, from which the eyes were still staring wildly.

"We have not slept a wink, sir," they said. "Those eyes have haunted us all night!"

With daybreak men stood aghast at the spectacle of that battle-ground.

The losses have never been satisfactorily reckoned; but I have seen it stated, curiously, that of the red-coats 9,999 were actually killed there. The French loss for the four days' campaign has been counted as 50,000; and you can tell off the survivors of both armies today, perhaps, on the fingers of *one* hand.

Every house in the neighbourhood was full of wounded. For three days, the doctors tell us, they were being brought in by the search parties, a sharp frost having congealed the wounds of many and so saved them, and lines of carts jolted the shrieking wretches over that dreadful causeway to Brussels in endless succession.

At Hougoumont, where the orange-trees were in blossom, they flung three hundred bodies down a well: it was a simple method, saving time and trouble; but a dark tradition lingers that voices were heard afterwards, faintly imploring, from the cavernous depths.

Wild strawberries hung their red clusters, and the little, blue forget-me-not peeped in the woods; birds of prey came croaking on the wing; and within twenty four hours ten thousand horses had been flayed by the Flemish peasants, many of whom made fortunes by plunder!

Men gathered jewelled decorations and crosses by handfuls: it was impossible to take three strides without treading on a sword, a broken musket, a carbine, or a corpse!

Near La Haye Sainte they found a pretty French girl in hussar uniform, and the farm itself was encrusted with blood; tufts of hair

adhered to the doorways, the yard presenting a sight never to be forgotten. A pole to which a scrap of torn silk clung was picked up under the body of Ensign Nettles: it was the King's colour.

The remains of three French brothers named Angelet were among the slain, and the history of one was most romantic. Wounded in some of the Napoleonic wars, where he had lost a leg, he was taunted by a lady with the fact that he could only talk of what he *had* done for France—that he could *do* no more. The brave fellow seized his crutches, limped after the army, and met his fate at Waterloo.

Picton's body—wounded at Quatre Bras, though none but his valet knew it—was taken to England, and by a strange coincidence was laid, at the Fountain Inn, Canterbury, on the very table at which he had dined, a fortnight before, on his way to join the army.

Byng of the Guards said to Sir John Colborne in Paris: "How do your fellows like our getting the credit of what you did at Waterloo? I could not advance because our ammunition was all done."

The Foot Guards got their bearskins as a well-merited reward, only the grenadier companies wearing them during the battle. The 52nd, for their great share in the closing scene, received—*nothing!* and the duke, when approached on the subject of that glaring injustice, said, "Oh, I know nothing of the services of particular regiments. There was glory enough for all!"

******

They are nearly all gathered to the "land o' the leal" now. The last of Hougoumont's defenders—Von Trovich of the Nassauers—died in 1882; Albemarle, who fought with the 14th Foot, passed away quite recently, (as at time of first publication); while the Guards turned out to bury a veteran not long since who paraded for the last time in Caterham workhouse! In 1894 John Stacey aged *ninety-six*, of the German Legion, *walked* from Yorkshire to London to see if his *tenpence a day* might not be increased.

For thirty years you could mark, by the deeper colour of the corn, where they had buried the dead in greatest numbers: they still find buttons in the plough-land after rain, with bullets cut in half against our sword-blades, and sometimes bones! Ten thousand people, on an average, visit the field each year; and, though the land lies dozing under its wealth of crops, and the lark trills his requiem where the guns once thundered, and the herdboy's song rises in place of "*Vive l'Empereur!*"—never will the nations forget that fearful Sunday or the names of *Wellington* and *Waterloo*.

ALSO FROM LEONAUR
AVAILABLE IN SOFTCOVER OR HARDCOVER WITH DUST JACKET

A HISTORY OF THE FRENCH & INDIAN WAR *by Arthur G. Bradley*—The Seven Years War as it was fought in the New World has always fascinated students of military history—here is the story of that confrontation.

WASHINGTON'S EARLY CAMPAIGNS *by James Hadden*—The French Post Expedition, Great Meadows and Braddock's Defeat—including Braddock's Orderly Books.

BOUQUET & THE OHIO INDIAN WAR *by Cyrus Cort & William Smith*—Two Accounts of the Campaigns of 1763-1764: Bouquet's Campaigns by Cyrus Cort & The History of Bouquet's Expeditions by William Smith.

NARRATIVES OF THE FRENCH & INDIAN WAR: 2 *by David Holden, Samuel Jenks, Lemuel Lyon, Mary Cochrane Rogers & Henry T. Blake*—Contains The Diary of Sergeant David Holden, Captain Samuel Jenks' Journal, The Journal of Lemuel Lyon, Journal of a French Officer at the Siege of Quebec, A Battle Fought on Snowshoes & The Battle of Lake George.

NARRATIVES OF THE FRENCH & INDIAN WAR *by Brown, Eastburn, Hawks & Putnam*—Ranger Brown's Narrative, The Adventures of Robert Eastburn, The Journal of Rufus Putnam—Provincial Infantry & Orderly Book and Journal of Major John Hawks on the Ticonderoga-Crown Point Campaign.

THE 7TH (QUEEN'S OWN) HUSSARS: Volume 1—1688-1792 *by C. R. B. Barrett*—As Dragoons During the Flanders Campaign, War of the Austrian Succession and the Seven Years War.

INDIA'S FREE LANCES *by H. G. Keene*—European Mercenary Commanders in Hindustan 1770-1820.

THE BENGAL EUROPEAN REGIMENT *by P. R. Innes*—An Elite Regiment of the Honourable East India Company 1756-1858.

MUSKET & TOMAHAWK *by Francis Parkman*—A Military History of the French & Indian War, 1753-1760.

THE BLACK WATCH AT TICONDEROGA *by Frederick B. Richards*—Campaigns in the French & Indian War.

QUEEN'S RANGERS *by Frederick B. Richards*—John Simcoe and his Rangers During the Revolutionary War for America.

AVAILABLE ONLINE AT **www.leonaur.com**
AND FROM ALL GOOD BOOK STORES

ALSO FROM LEONAUR
AVAILABLE IN SOFTCOVER OR HARDCOVER WITH DUST JACKET

JOURNALS OF ROBERT ROGERS OF THE RANGERS *by Robert Rogers*—The exploits of Rogers & the Rangers in his own words during 1755-1761 in the French & Indian War.

GALLOPING GUNS *by James Young*—The Experiences of an Officer of the Bengal Horse Artillery During the Second Maratha War 1804-1805.

GORDON *by Demetrius Charles Boulger*—The Career of Gordon of Khartoum.

THE BATTLE OF NEW ORLEANS *by Zachary F. Smith*—The final major engagement of the War of 1812.

THE TWO WARS OF MRS DUBERLY *by Frances Isabella Duberly*—An Intrepid Victorian Lady's Experience of the Crimea and Indian Mutiny.

WITH THE GUARDS' BRIGADE DURING THE BOER WAR *by Edward P. Lowry*—On Campaign from Bloemfontein to Koomati Poort and Back.

THE REBELLIOUS DUCHESS *by Paul F. S. Dermoncourt*—The Adventures of the Duchess of Berri and Her Attempt to Overthrow French Monarchy.

MEN OF THE MUTINY *by John Tulloch Nash & Henry Metcalfe*—Two Accounts of the Great Indian Mutiny of 1857: Fighting with the Bengal Yeomanry Cavalry & Private Metcalfe at Lucknow.

CAMPAIGN IN THE CRIMEA *by George Shuldham Peard*—The Recollections of an Officer of the 20th Regiment of Foot.

WITHIN SEBASTOPOL *by K. Hodasevich*—A Narrative of the Campaign in the Crimea, and of the Events of the Siege.

WITH THE CAVALRY TO AFGHANISTAN *by William Taylor*—The Experiences of a Trooper of H. M. 4th Light Dragoons During the First Afghan War.

THE CAWNPORE MAN *by Mowbray Thompson*—A First Hand Account of the Siege and Massacre During the Indian Mutiny By One of Four Survivors.

BRIGADE COMMANDER: AFGHANISTAN *by Henry Brooke*—The Journal of the Commander of the 2nd Infantry Brigade, Kandahar Field Force During the Second Afghan War.

BANCROFT OF THE BENGAL HORSE ARTILLERY *by N. W. Bancroft*—An Account of the First Sikh War 1845-1846.

AVAILABLE ONLINE AT **www.leonaur.com**
AND FROM ALL GOOD BOOK STORES

ALSO FROM LEONAUR
AVAILABLE IN SOFTCOVER OR HARDCOVER WITH DUST JACKET

AFGHANISTAN: THE BELEAGUERED BRIGADE *by G. R. Gleig*—An Account of Sale's Brigade During the First Afghan War.

IN THE RANKS OF THE C. I. V *by Erskine Childers*—With the City Imperial Volunteer Battery (Honourable Artillery Company) in the Second Boer War.

THE BENGAL NATIVE ARMY *by F. G. Cardew*—An Invaluable Reference Resource.

THE 7TH (QUEEN'S OWN) HUSSARS: Volume 4—1688-1914 *by C. R. B. Barrett*—Uniforms, Equipment, Weapons, Traditions, the Services of Notable Officers and Men & the Appendices to All Volumes—Volume 4: 1688-1914.

THE SWORD OF THE CROWN *by Eric W. Sheppard*—A History of the British Army to 1914.

THE 7TH (QUEEN'S OWN) HUSSARS: Volume 3—**1818-1914** *by C. R. B. Barrett*—On Campaign During the Canadian Rebellion, the Indian Mutiny, the Sudan, Matabeleland, Mashonaland and the Boer War Volume 3: 1818-1914.

THE KHARTOUM CAMPAIGN *by Bennet Burleigh*—A Special Correspondent's View of the Reconquest of the Sudan by British and Egyptian Forces under Kitchener—1898.

EL PUCHERO *by Richard McSherry*—The Letters of a Surgeon of Volunteers During Scott's Campaign of the American-Mexican War 1847-1848.

RIFLEMAN SAHIB *by E. Maude*—The Recollections of an Officer of the Bombay Rifles During the Southern Mahratta Campaign, Second Sikh War, Persian Campaign and Indian Mutiny.

THE KING'S HUSSAR *by Edwin Mole*—The Recollections of a 14th (King's) Hussar During the Victorian Era.

JOHN COMPANY'S CAVALRYMAN *by William Johnson*—The Experiences of a British Soldier in the Crimea, the Persian Campaign and the Indian Mutiny.

COLENSO & DURNFORD'S ZULU WAR *by Frances E. Colenso & Edward Durnford*—The first and possibly the most important history of the Zulu War.

U. S. DRAGOON *by Samuel E. Chamberlain*—Experiences in the Mexican War 1846-48 and on the South Western Frontier.

AVAILABLE ONLINE AT **www.leonaur.com**
AND FROM ALL GOOD BOOK STORES

ALSO FROM LEONAUR
AVAILABLE IN SOFTCOVER OR HARDCOVER WITH DUST JACKET

THE 2ND MAORI WAR: 1860-1861 by *Robert Carey*—The Second Maori War, or First Taranaki War, one more bloody instalment of the conflicts between European settlers and the indigenous Maori people.

A JOURNAL OF THE SECOND SIKH WAR by *Daniel A. Sandford*—The Experiences of an Ensign of the 2nd Bengal European Regiment During the Campaign in the Punjab, India, 1848-49.

THE LIGHT INFANTRY OFFICER by *John H. Cooke*—The Experiences of an Officer of the 43rd Light Infantry in America During the War of 1812.

BUSHVELDT CARBINEERS by *George Witton*—The War Against the Boers in South Africa and the 'Breaker' Morant Incident.

LAKE'S CAMPAIGNS IN INDIA by *Hugh Pearse*—The Second Anglo Maratha War, 1803-1807.

BRITAIN IN AFGHANISTAN 1: THE FIRST AFGHAN WAR 1839-42 by *Archibald Forbes*—From invasion to destruction-a British military disaster.

BRITAIN IN AFGHANISTAN 2: THE SECOND AFGHAN WAR 1878-80 by *Archibald Forbes*—This is the history of the Second Afghan War-another episode of British military history typified by savagery, massacre, siege and battles.

UP AMONG THE PANDIES by *Vivian Dering Majendie*—Experiences of a British Officer on Campaign During the Indian Mutiny, 1857-1858.

MUTINY: 1857 by *James Humphries*—Authentic Voices from the Indian Mutiny-First Hand Accounts of Battles, Sieges and Personal Hardships.

BLOW THE BUGLE, DRAW THE SWORD by *W. H. G. Kingston*—The Wars, Campaigns, Regiments and Soldiers of the British & Indian Armies During the Victorian Era, 1839-1898.

WAR BEYOND THE DRAGON PAGODA by *Major J. J. Snodgrass*—A Personal Narrative of the First Anglo-Burmese War 1824 - 1826.

THE HERO OF ALIWAL by *James Humphries*—The Campaigns of Sir Harry Smith in India, 1843-1846, During the Gwalior War & the First Sikh War.

ALL FOR A SHILLING A DAY by *Donald F. Featherstone*—The story of H.M. 16th, the Queen's Lancers During the first Sikh War 1845-1846.

AVAILABLE ONLINE AT **www.leonaur.com**
AND FROM ALL GOOD BOOK STORES

ALSO FROM LEONAUR
AVAILABLE IN SOFTCOVER OR HARDCOVER WITH DUST JACKET

THE FALL OF THE MOGHUL EMPIRE OF HINDUSTAN *by H. G. Keene*—By the beginning of the nineteenth century, as British and Indian armies under Lake and Wellesley dominated the scene, a little over half a century of conflict brought the Moghul Empire to its knees.

LADY SALE'S AFGHANISTAN *by Florentia Sale*—An Indomitable Victorian Lady's Account of the Retreat from Kabul During the First Afghan War.

THE CAMPAIGN OF MAGENTA AND SOLFERINO 1859 *by Harold Carmichael Wylly*—The Decisive Conflict for the Unification of Italy.

FRENCH'S CAVALRY CAMPAIGN *by J. G. Maydon*—A Special Correspondent's View of British Army Mounted Troops During the Boer War.

CAVALRY AT WATERLOO *by Sir Evelyn Wood*—British Mounted Troops During the Campaign of 1815.

THE SUBALTERN *by George Robert Gleig*—The Experiences of an Officer of the 85th Light Infantry During the Peninsular War.

NAPOLEON AT BAY, 1814 *by F. Loraine Petre*—The Campaigns to the Fall of the First Empire.

NAPOLEON AND THE CAMPAIGN OF 1806 *by Colonel Vachée*—The Napoleonic Method of Organisation and Command to the Battles of Jena & Auerstädt.

THE COMPLETE ADVENTURES IN THE CONNAUGHT RANGERS *by William Grattan*—The 88th Regiment during the Napoleonic Wars by a Serving Officer.

BUGLER AND OFFICER OF THE RIFLES *by William Green & Harry Smith*—With the 95th (Rifles) during the Peninsular & Waterloo Campaigns of the Napoleonic Wars.

NAPOLEONIC WAR STORIES *by Sir Arthur Quiller-Couch*—Tales of soldiers, spies, battles & sieges from the Peninsular & Waterloo campaingns.

CAPTAIN OF THE 95TH (RIFLES) *by Jonathan Leach*—An officer of Wellington's sharpshooters during the Peninsular, South of France and Waterloo campaigns of the Napoleonic wars.

RIFLEMAN COSTELLO *by Edward Costello*—The adventures of a soldier of the 95th (Rifles) in the Peninsular & Waterloo Campaigns of the Napoleonic wars.

AVAILABLE ONLINE AT **www.leonaur.com**
AND FROM ALL GOOD BOOK STORES

ALSO FROM LEONAUR
AVAILABLE IN SOFTCOVER OR HARDCOVER WITH DUST JACKET

AT THEM WITH THE BAYONET by Donald F. Featherstone—The first Anglo-Sikh War 1845-1846.

STEPHEN CRANE'S BATTLES by Stephen Crane—Nine Decisive Battles Recounted by the Author of 'The Red Badge of Courage'.

THE GURKHA WAR by H. T. Prinsep—The Anglo-Nepalese Conflict in North East India 1814-1816.

FIRE & BLOOD by G. R. Gleig—The burning of Washington & the battle of New Orleans, 1814, through the eyes of a young British soldier.

SOUND ADVANCE! by Joseph Anderson—Experiences of an officer of HM 50th regiment in Australia, Burma & the Gwalior war.

THE CAMPAIGN OF THE INDUS by Thomas Holdsworth—Experiences of a British Officer of the 2nd (Queen's Royal) Regiment in the Campaign to Place Shah Shuja on the Throne of Afghanistan 1838 - 1840.

WITH THE MADRAS EUROPEAN REGIMENT IN BURMA by John Butler—The Experiences of an Officer of the Honourable East India Company's Army During the First Anglo-Burmese War 1824 - 1826.

IN ZULULAND WITH THE BRITISH ARMY by Charles L. Norris-Newman—The Anglo-Zulu war of 1879 through the first-hand experiences of a special correspondent.

BESIEGED IN LUCKNOW by Martin Richard Gubbins—The first Anglo-Sikh War 1845-1846.

A TIGER ON HORSEBACK by L. March Phillips—The Experiences of a Trooper & Officer of Rimington's Guides - The Tigers - during the Anglo-Boer war 1899 - 1902.

SEPOYS, SIEGE & STORM by Charles John Griffiths—The Experiences of a young officer of H.M.'s 61st Regiment at Ferozepore, Delhi ridge and at the fall of Delhi during the Indian mutiny 1857.

CAMPAIGNING IN ZULULAND by W. E. Montague—Experiences on campaign during the Zulu war of 1879 with the 94th Regiment.

THE STORY OF THE GUIDES by G.J. Younghusband—The Exploits of the Soldiers of the famous Indian Army Regiment from the northwest frontier 1847 - 1900.

AVAILABLE ONLINE AT **www.leonaur.com**
AND FROM ALL GOOD BOOK STORES

ALSO FROM LEONAUR
AVAILABLE IN SOFTCOVER OR HARDCOVER WITH DUST JACKET

ZULU:1879 *by D.C.F. Moodie & the Leonaur Editors*—The Anglo-Zulu War of 1879 from contemporary sources: First Hand Accounts, Interviews, Dispatches, Official Documents & Newspaper Reports.

THE RED DRAGOON *by W.J. Adams*—With the 7th Dragoon Guards in the Cape of Good Hope against the Boers & the Kaffir tribes during the 'war of the axe' 1843-48'.

THE RECOLLECTIONS OF SKINNER OF SKINNER'S HORSE *by James Skinner*—James Skinner and his 'Yellow Boys' Irregular cavalry in the wars of India between the British, Mahratta, Rajput, Mogul, Sikh & Pindarree Forces.

A CAVALRY OFFICER DURING THE SEPOY REVOLT *by A. R. D. Mackenzie*—Experiences with the 3rd Bengal Light Cavalry, the Guides and Sikh Irregular Cavalry from the outbreak to Delhi and Lucknow.

A NORFOLK SOLDIER IN THE FIRST SIKH WAR *by J W Baldwin*—Experiences of a private of H.M. 9th Regiment of Foot in the battles for the Punjab, India 1845-6.

TOMMY ATKINS' WAR STORIES: 14 FIRST HAND ACCOUNTS—Fourteen first hand accounts from the ranks of the British Army during Queen Victoria's Empire.

THE WATERLOO LETTERS *by H. T. Siborne*—Accounts of the Battle by British Officers for its Foremost Historian.

NEY: GENERAL OF CAVALRY VOLUME 1—1769-1799 *by Antoine Bulos*—The Early Career of a Marshal of the First Empire.

NEY: MARSHAL OF FRANCE VOLUME 2—1799-1805 *by Antoine Bulos*—The Early Career of a Marshal of the First Empire.

AIDE-DE-CAMP TO NAPOLEON *by Philippe-Paul de Ségur*—For anyone interested in the Napoleonic Wars this book, written by one who was intimate with the strategies and machinations of the Emperor, will be essential reading.

TWILIGHT OF EMPIRE *by Sir Thomas Ussher & Sir George Cockburn*—Two accounts of Napoleon's Journeys in Exile to Elba and St. Helena: Narrative of Events by Sir Thomas Ussher & Napoleon's Last Voyage: Extract of a diary by Sir George Cockburn.

PRIVATE WHEELER *by William Wheeler*—The letters of a soldier of the 51st Light Infantry during the Peninsular War & at Waterloo.

AVAILABLE ONLINE AT **www.leonaur.com**
AND FROM ALL GOOD BOOK STORES

ALSO FROM LEONAUR
AVAILABLE IN SOFTCOVER OR HARDCOVER WITH DUST JACKET

OFFICERS & GENTLEMEN *by Peter Hawker & William Graham*—Two Accounts of British Officers During the Peninsula War: Officer of Light Dragoons by Peter Hawker & Campaign in Portugal and Spain by William Graham .

THE WALCHEREN EXPEDITION *by Anonymous*—The Experiences of a British Officer of the 81st Regt. During the Campaign in the Low Countries of 1809.

LADIES OF WATERLOO *by Charlotte A. Eaton, Magdalene de Lancey & Juana Smith*—The Experiences of Three Women During the Campaign of 1815: Waterloo Days by Charlotte A. Eaton, A Week at Waterloo by Magdalene de Lancey & Juana's Story by Juana Smith.

JOURNAL OF AN OFFICER IN THE KING'S GERMAN LEGION *by John Frederick Hering*—Recollections of Campaigning During the Napoleonic Wars.

JOURNAL OF AN ARMY SURGEON IN THE PENINSULAR WAR *by Charles Boutflower*—The Recollections of a British Army Medical Man on Campaign During the Napoleonic Wars.

ON CAMPAIGN WITH MOORE AND WELLINGTON *by Anthony Hamilton*—The Experiences of a Soldier of the 43rd Regiment During the Peninsular War.

THE ROAD TO AUSTERLITZ *by R. G. Burton*—Napoleon's Campaign of 1805.

SOLDIERS OF NAPOLEON *by A. J. Doisy De Villargennes & Arthur Chuquet*—The Experiences of the Men of the French First Empire: Under the Eagles by A. J. Doisy De Villargennes & Voices of 1812 by Arthur Chuquet .

INVASION OF FRANCE, 1814 *by F. W. O. Maycock*—The Final Battles of the Napoleonic First Empire.

LEIPZIG—A CONFLICT OF TITANS *by Frederic Shoberl*—A Personal Experience of the 'Battle of the Nations' During the Napoleonic Wars, October 14th-19th, 1813.

SLASHERS *by Charles Cadell*—The Campaigns of the 28th Regiment of Foot During the Napoleonic Wars by a Serving Officer.

BATTLE IMPERIAL *by Charles William Vane*—The Campaigns in Germany & France for the Defeat of Napoleon 1813-1814.

SWIFT & BOLD *by Gibbes Rigaud*—The 60th Rifles During the Peninsula War.

AVAILABLE ONLINE AT **www.leonaur.com**
AND FROM ALL GOOD BOOK STORES

ALSO FROM LEONAUR
AVAILABLE IN SOFTCOVER OR HARDCOVER WITH DUST JACKET

ADVENTURES OF A YOUNG RIFLEMAN *by Johann Christian Maempel*—The Experiences of a Saxon in the French & British Armies During the Napoleonic Wars.

THE HUSSAR *by Norbert Landsheit & G. R. Gleig*—A German Cavalryman in British Service Throughout the Napoleonic Wars.

RECOLLECTIONS OF THE PENINSULA *by Moyle Sherer*—An Officer of the 34th Regiment of Foot—'The Cumberland Gentlemen'—on Campaign Against Napoleon's French Army in Spain.

MARINE OF REVOLUTION & CONSULATE *by Moreau de Jonnès*—The Recollections of a French Soldier of the Revolutionary Wars 1791-1804.

GENTLEMEN IN RED *by John Dobbs & Robert Knowles*—Two Accounts of British Infantry Officers During the Peninsular War Recollections of an Old 52nd Man by John Dobbs An Officer of Fusiliers by Robert Knowles.

CORPORAL BROWN'S CAMPAIGNS IN THE LOW COUNTRIES *by Robert Brown*—Recollections of a Coldstream Guard in the Early Campaigns Against Revolutionary France 1793-1795.

THE 7TH (QUEENS OWN) HUSSARS: Volume 2—1793-1815 *by C. R. B. Barrett*—During the Campaigns in the Low Countries & the Peninsula and Waterloo Campaigns of the Napoleonic Wars. Volume 2: 1793-1815.

THE MARENGO CAMPAIGN 1800 *by Herbert H. Sargent*—The Victory that Completed the Austrian Defeat in Italy.

DONALDSON OF THE 94TH—SCOTS BRIGADE *by Joseph Donaldson*—The Recollections of a Soldier During the Peninsula & South of France Campaigns of the Napoleonic Wars.

A CONSCRIPT FOR EMPIRE *by Philippe as told to Johann Christian Maempel*—The Experiences of a Young German Conscript During the Napoleonic Wars.

JOURNAL OF THE CAMPAIGN OF 1815 *by Alexander Cavalié Mercer*—The Experiences of an Officer of the Royal Horse Artillery During the Waterloo Campaign.

NAPOLEON'S CAMPAIGNS IN POLAND 1806-7 *by Robert Wilson*—The campaign in Poland from the Russian side of the conflict.

AVAILABLE ONLINE AT **www.leonaur.com**
AND FROM ALL GOOD BOOK STORES

ALSO FROM LEONAUR
AVAILABLE IN SOFTCOVER OR HARDCOVER WITH DUST JACKET

OMPTEDA OF THE KING'S GERMAN LEGION *by Christian von Ompteda*—A Hanoverian Officer on Campaign Against Napoleon.

LIEUTENANT SIMMONS OF THE 95TH (RIFLES) *by George Simmons*—Recollections of the Peninsula, South of France & Waterloo Campaigns of the Napoleonic Wars.

A HORSEMAN FOR THE EMPEROR *by Jean Baptiste Gazzola*—A Cavalryman of Napoleon's Army on Campaign Throughout the Napoleonic Wars.

SERGEANT LAWRENCE *by William Lawrence*—With the 40th Regt. of Foot in South America, the Peninsular War & at Waterloo.

CAMPAIGNS WITH THE FIELD TRAIN *by Richard D. Henegan*—Experiences of a British Officer During the Peninsula and Waterloo Campaigns of the Napoleonic Wars.

CAVALRY SURGEON *by S. D. Broughton*—On Campaign Against Napoleon in the Peninsula & South of France During the Napoleonic Wars 1812-1814.

MEN OF THE RIFLES *by Thomas Knight, Henry Curling & Jonathan Leach*—The Reminiscences of Thomas Knight of the 95th (Rifles) by Thomas Knight, Henry Curling's Anecdotes by Henry Curling & The Field Services of the Rifle Brigade from its Formation to Waterloo by Jonathan Leach.

THE ULM CAMPAIGN 1805 *by F. N. Maude*—Napoleon and the Defeat of the Austrian Army During the 'War of the Third Coalition'.

SOLDIERING WITH THE 'DIVISION' *by Thomas Garrety*—The Military Experiences of an Infantryman of the 43rd Regiment During the Napoleonic Wars.

SERGEANT MORRIS OF THE 73RD FOOT *by Thomas Morris*—The Experiences of a British Infantryman During the Napoleonic Wars-Including Campaigns in Germany and at Waterloo.

A VOICE FROM WATERLOO *by Edward Cotton*—The Personal Experiences of a British Cavalryman Who Became a Battlefield Guide and Authority on the Campaign of 1815.

NAPOLEON AND HIS MARSHALS *by J. T. Headley*—The Men of the First Empire.

AVAILABLE ONLINE AT **www.leonaur.com**
AND FROM ALL GOOD BOOK STORES

ALSO FROM LEONAUR
AVAILABLE IN SOFTCOVER OR HARDCOVER WITH DUST JACKET

COLBORNE: A SINGULAR TALENT FOR WAR *by John Colborne*—The Napoleonic Wars Career of One of Wellington's Most Highly Valued Officers in Egypt, Holland, Italy, the Peninsula and at Waterloo.

NAPOLEON'S RUSSIAN CAMPAIGN *by Philippe Henri de Segur*—The Invasion, Battles and Retreat by an Aide-de-Camp on the Emperor's Staff.

WITH THE LIGHT DIVISION *by John H. Cooke*—The Experiences of an Officer of the 43rd Light Infantry in the Peninsula and South of France During the Napoleonic Wars.

WELLINGTON AND THE PYRENEES CAMPAIGN VOLUME I: FROM VITORIA TO THE BIDASSOA *by F. C. Beatson*—The final phase of the campaign in the Iberian Peninsula.

WELLINGTON AND THE INVASION OF FRANCE VOLUME II: THE BIDASSOA TO THE BATTLE OF THE NIVELLE *by F. C. Beatson*—The final phase of the campaign in the Iberian Peninsula.

WELLINGTON AND THE FALL OF FRANCE VOLUME III: THE GAVES AND THE BATTLE OF ORTHEZ *by F. C. Beatson*—The final phase of the campaign in the Iberian Peninsula.

NAPOLEON'S IMPERIAL GUARD: FROM MARENGO TO WATERLOO *by J. T. Headley*—The story of Napoleon's Imperial Guard and the men who commanded them.

BATTLES & SIEGES OF THE PENINSULAR WAR *by W. H. Fitchett*—Corunna, Busaco, Albuera, Ciudad Rodrigo, Badajos, Salamanca, San Sebastian & Others.

SERGEANT GUILLEMARD: THE MAN WHO SHOT NELSON? *by Robert Guillemard*—A Soldier of the Infantry of the French Army of Napoleon on Campaign Throughout Europe.

WITH THE GUARDS ACROSS THE PYRENEES *by Robert Batty*—The Experiences of a British Officer of Wellington's Army During the Battles for the Fall of Napoleonic France, 1813.

A STAFF OFFICER IN THE PENINSULA *by E. W. Buckham*—An Officer of the British Staff Corps Cavalry During the Peninsula Campaign of the Napoleonic Wars.

THE LEIPZIG CAMPAIGN: 1813—NAPOLEON AND THE "BATTLE OF THE NATIONS" *by F. N. Maude*—Colonel Maude's analysis of Napoleon's campaign of 1813 around Leipzig.

AVAILABLE ONLINE AT **www.leonaur.com**
AND FROM ALL GOOD BOOK STORES

ALSO FROM LEONAUR
AVAILABLE IN SOFTCOVER OR HARDCOVER WITH DUST JACKET

BUGEAUD: A PACK WITH A BATON by *Thomas Robert Bugeaud*—The Early Campaigns of a Soldier of Napoleon's Army Who Would Become a Marshal of France.

WATERLOO RECOLLECTIONS by *Frederick Llewellyn*—Rare First Hand Accounts, Letters, Reports and Retellings from the Campaign of 1815.

SERGEANT NICOL by *Daniel Nicol*—The Experiences of a Gordon Highlander During the Napoleonic Wars in Egypt, the Peninsula and France.

THE JENA CAMPAIGN: 1806 by *F. N. Maude*—The Twin Battles of Jena & Auerstadt Between Napoleon's French and the Prussian Army.

PRIVATE O'NEIL by *Charles O'Neil*—The recollections of an Irish Rogue of H. M. 28th Regt.—The Slashers—during the Peninsula & Waterloo campaigns of the Napoleonic war.

ROYAL HIGHLANDER by *James Anton*—A soldier of H.M 42nd (Royal) Highlanders during the Peninsular, South of France & Waterloo Campaigns of the Napoleonic Wars.

CAPTAIN BLAZE by *Elzéar Blaze*—Life in Napoleons Army.

LEJEUNE VOLUME 1 by *Louis-François Lejeune*—The Napoleonic Wars through the Experiences of an Officer on Berthier's Staff.

LEJEUNE VOLUME 2 by *Louis-François Lejeune*—The Napoleonic Wars through the Experiences of an Officer on Berthier's Staff.

CAPTAIN COIGNET by *Jean-Roch Coignet*—A Soldier of Napoleon's Imperial Guard from the Italian Campaign to Russia and Waterloo.

FUSILIER COOPER by *John S. Cooper*—Experiences in the 7th (Royal) Fusiliers During the Peninsular Campaign of the Napoleonic Wars and the American Campaign to New Orleans.

FIGHTING NAPOLEON'S EMPIRE by *Joseph Anderson*—The Campaigns of a British Infantryman in Italy, Egypt, the Peninsular & the West Indies During the Napoleonic Wars.

CHASSEUR BARRES by *Jean-Baptiste Barres*—The experiences of a French Infantryman of the Imperial Guard at Austerlitz, Jena, Eylau, Friedland, in the Peninsular, Lutzen, Bautzen, Zinnwald and Hanau during the Napoleonic Wars.

AVAILABLE ONLINE AT **www.leonaur.com**
AND FROM ALL GOOD BOOK STORES

ALSO FROM LEONAUR
AVAILABLE IN SOFTCOVER OR HARDCOVER WITH DUST JACKET

CAPTAIN COIGNET *by Jean-Roch Coignet*—A Soldier of Napoleon's Imperial Guard from the Italian Campaign to Russia and Waterloo.

HUSSAR ROCCA *by Albert Jean Michel de Rocca*—A French cavalry officer's experiences of the Napoleonic Wars and his views on the Peninsular Campaigns against the Spanish, British And Guerilla Armies.

MARINES TO 95TH (RIFLES) *by Thomas Fernyhough*—The military experiences of Robert Fernyhough during the Napoleonic Wars.

LIGHT BOB *by Robert Blakeney*—The experiences of a young officer in H.M 28th & 36th regiments of the British Infantry during the Peninsular Campaign of the Napoleonic Wars 1804 - 1814.

WITH WELLINGTON'S LIGHT CAVALRY *by William Tomkinson*—The Experiences of an officer of the 16th Light Dragoons in the Peninsular and Waterloo campaigns of the Napoleonic Wars.

SERGEANT BOURGOGNE *by Adrien Bourgogne*—With Napoleon's Imperial Guard in the Russian Campaign and on the Retreat from Moscow 1812 - 13.

SURTEES OF THE 95TH (RIFLES) *by William Surtees*—A Soldier of the 95th (Rifles) in the Peninsular campaign of the Napoleonic Wars.

SWORDS OF HONOUR *by Henry Newbolt & Stanley L. Wood*—The Careers of Six Outstanding Officers from the Napoleonic Wars, the Wars for India and the American Civil War.

ENSIGN BELL IN THE PENINSULAR WAR *by George Bell*—The Experiences of a young British Soldier of the 34th Regiment 'The Cumberland Gentlemen' in the Napoleonic wars.

HUSSAR IN WINTER *by Alexander Gordon*—A British Cavalry Officer during the retreat to Corunna in the Peninsular campaign of the Napoleonic Wars.

THE COMPLEAT RIFLEMAN HARRIS *by Benjamin Harris as told to and transcribed by Captain Henry Curling, 52nd Regt. of Foot*—The adventures of a soldier of the 95th (Rifles) during the Peninsular Campaign of the Napoleonic Wars.

THE ADVENTURES OF A LIGHT DRAGOON *by George Farmer & G.R. Gleig*—A cavalryman during the Peninsular & Waterloo Campaigns, in captivity & at the siege of Bhurtpore, India.

AVAILABLE ONLINE AT www.leonaur.com
AND FROM ALL GOOD BOOK STORES

ALSO FROM LEONAUR
AVAILABLE IN SOFTCOVER OR HARDCOVER WITH DUST JACKET

THE LIFE OF THE REAL BRIGADIER GERARD VOLUME 1—THE YOUNG HUSSAR 1782-1807 *by Jean-Baptiste De Marbot*—A French Cavalryman Of the Napoleonic Wars at Marengo, Austerlitz, Jena, Eylau & Friedland.

THE LIFE OF THE REAL BRIGADIER GERARD VOLUME 2—IMPERIAL AIDE-DE-CAMP 1807-1811 *by Jean-Baptiste De Marbot*—A French Cavalryman of the Napoleonic Wars at Saragossa, Landshut, Eckmuhl, Ratisbon, Aspern-Essling, Wagram, Busaco & Torres Vedras.

THE LIFE OF THE REAL BRIGADIER GERARD VOLUME 3—COLONEL OF CHASSEURS 1811-1815 *by Jean-Baptiste De Marbot*—A French Cavalryman in the retreat from Moscow, Lutzen, Bautzen, Katzbach, Leipzig, Hanau & Waterloo.

THE INDIAN WAR OF 1864 *by Eugene Ware*—The Experiences of a Young Officer of the 7th Iowa Cavalry on the Western Frontier During the Civil War.

THE MARCH OF DESTINY *by Charles E. Young & V. Devinny*—Dangers of the Trail in 1865 by Charles E. Young & The Story of a Pioneer by V. Devinny, two Accounts of Early Emigrants to Colorado.

CROSSING THE PLAINS *by William Audley Maxwell*—A First Hand Narrative of the Early Pioneer Trail to California in 1857.

CHIEF OF SCOUTS *by William F. Drannan*—A Pilot to Emigrant and Government Trains, Across the Plains of the Western Frontier.

THIRTY-ONE YEARS ON THE PLAINS AND IN THE MOUNTAINS *by William F. Drannan*—William Drannan was born to be a pioneer, hunter, trapper and wagon train guide during the momentous days of the Great American West.

THE INDIAN WARS VOLUNTEER *by William Thompson*—Recollections of the Conflict Against the Snakes, Shoshone, Bannocks, Modocs and Other Native Tribes of the American North West.

THE 4TH TENNESSEE CAVALRY *by George B. Guild*—The Services of Smith's Regiment of Confederate Cavalry by One of its Officers.

COLONEL WORTHINGTON'S SHILOH *by T. Worthington*—The Tennessee Campaign, 1862, by an Officer of the Ohio Volunteers.

FOUR YEARS IN THE SADDLE *by W. L. Curry*—The History of the First Regiment Ohio Volunteer Cavalry in the American Civil War.

AVAILABLE ONLINE AT **www.leonaur.com**
AND FROM ALL GOOD BOOK STORES

ALSO FROM LEONAUR
AVAILABLE IN SOFTCOVER OR HARDCOVER WITH DUST JACKET

LIFE IN THE ARMY OF NORTHERN VIRGINIA *by Carlton McCarthy*—The Observations of a Confederate Artilleryman of Cutshaw's Battalion During the American Civil War 1861-1865.

HISTORY OF THE CAVALRY OF THE ARMY OF THE POTOMAC *by Charles D. Rhodes*—Including Pope's Army of Virginia and the Cavalry Operations in West Virginia During the American Civil War.

CAMP-FIRE AND COTTON-FIELD *by Thomas W. Knox*—A New York Herald Correspondent's View of the American Civil War.

SERGEANT STILLWELL *by Leander Stillwell*—The Experiences of a Union Army Soldier of the 61st Illinois Infantry During the American Civil War.

STONEWALL'S CANNONEER *by Edward A. Moore*—Experiences with the Rockbridge Artillery, Confederate Army of Northern Virginia, During the American Civil War.

THE SIXTH CORPS *by George Stevens*—The Army of the Potomac, Union Army, During the American Civil War.

THE RAILROAD RAIDERS *by William Pittenger*—An Ohio Volunteers Recollections of the Andrews Raid to Disrupt the Confederate Railroad in Georgia During the American Civil War.

CITIZEN SOLDIER *by John Beatty*—An Account of the American Civil War by a Union Infantry Officer of Ohio Volunteers Who Became a Brigadier General.

COX: PERSONAL RECOLLECTIONS OF THE CIVIL WAR--VOLUME 1 *by Jacob Dolson Cox*—West Virginia, Kanawha Valley, Gauley Bridge, Cotton Mountain, South Mountain, Antietam, the Morgan Raid & the East Tennessee Campaign.

COX: PERSONAL RECOLLECTIONS OF THE CIVIL WAR--VOLUME 2 *by Jacob Dolson Cox*—Siege of Knoxville, East Tennessee, Atlanta Campaign, the Nashville Campaign & the North Carolina Campaign.

KERSHAW'S BRIGADE VOLUME 1 *by D. Augustus Dickert*—Manassas, Seven Pines, Sharpsburg (Antietam), Fredricksburg, Chancellorsville, Gettysburg, Chickamauga, Chattanooga, Fort Sanders & Bean Station.

KERSHAW'S BRIGADE VOLUME 2 *by D. Augustus Dickert*—At the wilderness, Cold Harbour, Petersburg, The Shenandoah Valley and Cedar Creek..

AVAILABLE ONLINE AT **www.leonaur.com**
AND FROM ALL GOOD BOOK STORES

ALSO FROM LEONAUR
AVAILABLE IN SOFTCOVER OR HARDCOVER WITH DUST JACKET

THE RELUCTANT REBEL *by William G. Stevenson*—A young Kentuckian's experiences in the Confederate Infantry & Cavalry during the American Civil War..

BOOTS AND SADDLES *by Elizabeth B. Custer*—The experiences of General Custer's Wife on the Western Plains.

FANNIE BEERS' CIVIL WAR *by Fannie A. Beers*—A Confederate Lady's Experiences of Nursing During the Campaigns & Battles of the American Civil War.

LADY SALE'S AFGHANISTAN *by Florentia Sale*—An Indomitable Victorian Lady's Account of the Retreat from Kabul During the First Afghan War.

THE TWO WARS OF MRS DUBERLY *by Frances Isabella Duberly*—An Intrepid Victorian Lady's Experience of the Crimea and Indian Mutiny.

THE REBELLIOUS DUCHESS *by Paul F. S. Dermoncourt*—The Adventures of the Duchess of Berri and Her Attempt to Overthrow French Monarchy.

LADIES OF WATERLOO *by Charlotte A. Eaton, Magdalene de Lancey & Juana Smith*—The Experiences of Three Women During the Campaign of 1815: Waterloo Days by Charlotte A. Eaton, A Week at Waterloo by Magdalene de Lancey & Juana's Story by Juana Smith.

TWO YEARS BEFORE THE MAST *by Richard Henry Dana. Jr.*—The account of one young man's experiences serving on board a sailing brig—the Penelope—bound for California, between the years 1834-36.

A SAILOR OF KING GEORGE *by Frederick Hoffman*—From Midshipman to Captain—Recollections of War at Sea in the Napoleonic Age 1793-1815.

LORDS OF THE SEA *by A. T. Mahan*—Great Captains of the Royal Navy During the Age of Sail.

COGGESHALL'S VOYAGES: VOLUME 1 *by George Coggeshall*—The Recollections of an American Schooner Captain.

COGGESHALL'S VOYAGES: VOLUME 2 *by George Coggeshall*—The Recollections of an American Schooner Captain.

TWILIGHT OF EMPIRE *by Sir Thomas Ussher & Sir George Cockburn*—Two accounts of Napoleon's Journeys in Exile to Elba and St. Helena: Narrative of Events by Sir Thomas Ussher & Napoleon's Last Voyage: Extract of a diary by Sir George Cockburn.

AVAILABLE ONLINE AT **www.leonaur.com**
AND FROM ALL GOOD BOOK STORES

ALSO FROM LEONAUR
AVAILABLE IN SOFTCOVER OR HARDCOVER WITH DUST JACKET

ESCAPE FROM THE FRENCH *by Edward Boys*—A Young Royal Navy Midshipman's Adventures During the Napoleonic War.

THE VOYAGE OF H.M.S. PANDORA *by Edward Edwards R. N. & George Hamilton, edited by Basil Thomson*—In Pursuit of the Mutineers of the Bounty in the South Seas—1790-1791.

MEDUSA *by J. B. Henry Savigny and Alexander Correard and Charlotte-Adélaïde Dard* —Narrative of a Voyage to Senegal in 1816 & The Sufferings of the Picard Family After the Shipwreck of the Medusa.

THE SEA WAR OF 1812 VOLUME 1 *by A. T. Mahan*—A History of the Maritime Conflict.

THE SEA WAR OF 1812 VOLUME 2 *by A. T. Mahan*—A History of the Maritime Conflict.

WETHERELL OF H. M. S. HUSSAR *by John Wetherell*—The Recollections of an Ordinary Seaman of the Royal Navy During the Napoleonic Wars.

THE NAVAL BRIGADE IN NATAL *by C. R. N. Burne*—With the Guns of H. M. S. Terrible & H. M. S. Tartar during the Boer War 1899-1900.

THE VOYAGE OF H. M. S. BOUNTY *by William Bligh*—The True Story of an 18th Century Voyage of Exploration and Mutiny.

SHIPWRECK! *by William Gilly*—The Royal Navy's Disasters at Sea 1793-1849.

KING'S CUTTERS AND SMUGGLERS: 1700-1855 *by E. Keble Chatterton*—A unique period of maritime history-from the beginning of the eighteenth to the middle of the nineteenth century when British seamen risked all to smuggle valuable goods from wool to tea and spirits from and to the Continent.

CONFEDERATE BLOCKADE RUNNER *by John Wilkinson*—The Personal Recollections of an Officer of the Confederate Navy.

NAVAL BATTLES OF THE NAPOLEONIC WARS *by W. H. Fitchett*—Cape St. Vincent, the Nile, Cadiz, Copenhagen, Trafalgar & Others.

PRISONERS OF THE RED DESERT *by R. S. Gwatkin-Williams*—The Adventures of the Crew of the Tara During the First World War.

U-BOAT WAR 1914-1918 *by James B. Connolly/Karl von Schenk*—Two Contrasting Accounts from Both Sides of the Conflict at Sea During the Great War.

AVAILABLE ONLINE AT **www.leonaur.com**
AND FROM ALL GOOD BOOK STORES

ALSO FROM LEONAUR
AVAILABLE IN SOFTCOVER OR HARDCOVER WITH DUST JACKET

IRON TIMES WITH THE GUARDS *by An O. E. (G. P. A. Fildes)*—The Experiences of an Officer of the Coldstream Guards on the Western Front During the First World War.

THE GREAT WAR IN THE MIDDLE EAST: 1 *by W. T. Massey*—The Desert Campaigns & How Jerusalem Was Won---two classic accounts in one volume.

THE GREAT WAR IN THE MIDDLE EAST: 2 *by W. T. Massey*—Allenby's Final Triumph.

SMITH-DORRIEN *by Horace Smith-Dorrien*—Isandlwhana to the Great War.

1914 *by Sir John French*—The Early Campaigns of the Great War by the British Commander.

GRENADIER *by E. R. M. Fryer*—The Recollections of an Officer of the Grenadier Guards throughout the Great War on the Western Front.

BATTLE, CAPTURE & ESCAPE *by George Pearson*—The Experiences of a Canadian Light Infantryman During the Great War.

DIGGERS AT WAR *by R. Hugh Knyvett & G. P. Cuttriss*—"Over There" With the Australians by R. Hugh Knyvett and Over the Top With the Third Australian Division by G. P. Cuttriss. Accounts of Australians During the Great War in the Middle East, at Gallipoli and on the Western Front.

HEAVY FIGHTING BEFORE US *by George Brenton Laurie*—The Letters of an Officer of the Royal Irish Rifles on the Western Front During the Great War.

THE CAMELIERS *by Oliver Hogue*—A Classic Account of the Australians of the Imperial Camel Corps During the First World War in the Middle East.

RED DUST *by Donald Black*—A Classic Account of Australian Light Horsemen in Palestine During the First World War.

THE LEAN, BROWN MEN *by Angus Buchanan*—Experiences in East Africa During the Great War with the 25th Royal Fusiliers—the Legion of Frontiersmen.

THE NIGERIAN REGIMENT IN EAST AFRICA *by W. D. Downes*—On Campaign During the Great War 1916-1918.

THE 'DIE-HARDS' IN SIBERIA *by John Ward*—With the Middlesex Regiment Against the Bolsheviks 1918-19.

AVAILABLE ONLINE AT **www.leonaur.com**
AND FROM ALL GOOD BOOK STORES

ALSO FROM LEONAUR
AVAILABLE IN SOFTCOVER OR HARDCOVER WITH DUST JACKET

FARAWAY CAMPAIGN by F. James—Experiences of an Indian Army Cavalry Officer in Persia & Russia During the Great War.

REVOLT IN THE DESERT by T. E. Lawrence—An account of the experiences of one remarkable British officer's war from his own perspective.

MACHINE-GUN SQUADRON by A. M. G.—The 20th Machine Gunners from British Yeomanry Regiments in the Middle East Campaign of the First World War.

A GUNNER'S CRUSADE by Antony Bluett—The Campaign in the Desert, Palestine & Syria as Experienced by the Honourable Artillery Company During the Great War.

DESPATCH RIDER by W. H. L. Watson—The Experiences of a British Army Motorcycle Despatch Rider During the Opening Battles of the Great War in Europe.

TIGERS ALONG THE TIGRIS by E. J. Thompson—The Leicestershire Regiment in Mesopotamia During the First World War.

HEARTS & DRAGONS by Charles R. M. F. Crutwell—The 4th Royal Berkshire Regiment in France and Italy During the Great War, 1914-1918.

INFANTRY BRIGADE: 1914 by John Ward—The Diary of a Commander of the 15th Infantry Brigade, 5th Division, British Army, During the Retreat from Mons.

DOING OUR 'BIT' by Ian Hay—Two Classic Accounts of the Men of Kitchener's 'New Army' During the Great War including *The First 100,000* & *All In It*.

AN EYE IN THE STORM by Arthur Ruhl—An American War Correspondent's Experiences of the First World War from the Western Front to Gallipoli-and Beyond.

STAND & FALL by Joe Cassells—With the Middlesex Regiment Against the Bolsheviks 1918-19.

RIFLEMAN MACGILL'S WAR by Patrick MacGill—A Soldier of the London Irish During the Great War in Europe including *The Amateur Army*, *The Red Horizon* & *The Great Push*.

WITH THE GUNS by C. A. Rose & Hugh Dalton—Two First Hand Accounts of British Gunners at War in Europe During World War 1- Three Years in France with the Guns and With the British Guns in Italy.

THE BUSH WAR DOCTOR by Robert V. Dolbey—The Experiences of a British Army Doctor During the East African Campaign of the First World War.

AVAILABLE ONLINE AT **www.leonaur.com**
AND FROM ALL GOOD BOOK STORES

ALSO FROM LEONAUR
AVAILABLE IN SOFTCOVER OR HARDCOVER WITH DUST JACKET

THE 9TH—THE KING'S (LIVERPOOL REGIMENT) IN THE GREAT WAR 1914 - 1918 *by Enos H. G. Roberts*—Mersey to mud—war and Liverpool men.

THE GAMBARDIER *by Mark Severn*—The experiences of a battery of Heavy artillery on the Western Front during the First World War.

FROM MESSINES TO THIRD YPRES *by Thomas Floyd*—A personal account of the First World War on the Western front by a 2/5th Lancashire Fusilier.

THE IRISH GUARDS IN THE GREAT WAR - VOLUME 1 *by Rudyard Kipling*—Edited and Compiled from Their Diaries and Papers—The First Battalion.

THE IRISH GUARDS IN THE GREAT WAR - VOLUME 1 *by Rudyard Kipling*—Edited and Compiled from Their Diaries and Papers—The Second Battalion.

ARMOURED CARS IN EDEN *by K. Roosevelt*—An American President's son serving in Rolls Royce armoured cars with the British in Mesopotamia & with the American Artillery in France during the First World War.

CHASSEUR OF 1914 *by Marcel Dupont*—Experiences of the twilight of the French Light Cavalry by a young officer during the early battles of the great war in Europe.

TROOP HORSE & TRENCH *by R.A. Lloyd*—The experiences of a British Lifeguardsman of the household cavalry fighting on the western front during the First World War 1914-18.

THE EAST AFRICAN MOUNTED RIFLES *by C.J. Wilson*—Experiences of the campaign in the East African bush during the First World War.

THE LONG PATROL *by George Berrie*—A Novel of Light Horsemen from Gallipoli to the Palestine campaign of the First World War.

THE FIGHTING CAMELIERS *by Frank Reid*—The exploits of the Imperial Camel Corps in the desert and Palestine campaigns of the First World War.

STEEL CHARIOTS IN THE DESERT *by S. C. Rolls*—The first world war experiences of a Rolls Royce armoured car driver with the Duke of Westminster in Libya and in Arabia with T.E. Lawrence.

WITH THE IMPERIAL CAMEL CORPS IN THE GREAT WAR *by Geoffrey Inchbald*—The story of a serving officer with the British 2nd battalion against the Senussi and during the Palestine campaign.

AVAILABLE ONLINE AT **www.leonaur.com**
AND FROM ALL GOOD BOOK STORES

www.ingramcontent.com/pod-product-compliance
Lightning Source LLC
Chambersburg PA
CBHW031619160426
43196CB00006B/204